P9-DFK-744

GROWTH
and
STRUCTURE
of the
ENGLISH
LANGUAGE

by Otto Jespersen

NINTH EDITION

Doubleday Anchor Books

DOUBLEDAY & COMPANY, INC., GARDEN CITY, N.Y.

OTTO JESPERSEN (1860–1943), born and educated in Denmark, was professor of English language and literature at the University of Copenhagen, and one of the world's greatest philologists. His central work was *A Modern English Grammar on Historical Principles* in four volumes, the first of which was published in 1909 and the last in 1931. Some of his best-known books are *Language: Its Nature, Development and Origin* (1922), *The Philosophy of Grammar* (1924), *Mankind, Nation and Individual from a Linguistic Point of View* (1925), and *Analytic Syntax* (1937).

GROWTH AND STRUCTURE OF THE ENGLISH LANGUAGE, awarded the Volney Prize of the Institut de France, was first published in 1905, and is here reprinted in its ninth edition.

Reprinted by arrangement with
The Macmillan Company
TYPOGRAPHY: *Joseph P. Ascherl*

Printed in the United States

Preface

The scope and plan of this volume have been set forth in the introductory paragraph. I have endeavoured to write at once popularly and so as to be of some profit to the expert philologist. In some cases I have advanced new views without having space enough to give all my reasons for deviating from commonly accepted theories, but I hope to find an opportunity in future works of a more learned character to argue out the most debatable points.

I owe more than I can say to numerous predecessors in the fields of my investigations, most of all to the authors of the *New English Dictionary*. The dates given for the first and last appearance of a word are nearly always taken from that splendid monument of English scholarship, and it is hardly necessary to warn the reader not to take these dates too literally. When I say, for instance, that *fenester* was in use from 1290 to 1548, I do not mean to say that the word was actually heard for the first and for the last time in those two years, but only that no earlier or later quotations have been discovered by the painstaking authors of that dictionary.

I have departed from a common practice in retaining the spelling of all authors quoted. I see no reason why in so many English editions of Shakespeare the spelling is modernized while in quotations from other Elizabethan authors the old spelling is followed. Quotations from Shakespeare are here regularly given in the spelling of the First Folio (1623). The only point where, for the convenience of modern readers, I regulate the old usage, is with regard to capital letters and *u, v, i, j,* printing, for instance, *us* and *love* instead of *vs* and *loue.* To avoid misunderstandings, I must here expressly state that by Old English (OE.) I always understand the language before 1150, still often termed Anglo-Saxon.

As for the philosophy of speech underlying this book I may refer the reader to three recent books, *Language, Its Nature, Development and Origin* (London, G. Allen & Unwin, 1922; German translation, "Die Sprache, ihre Natur, Entwickelung und Entstehung," Heidelberg, C. Winter, 1925), *The Philosophy of Grammar* (London, G. Allen & Unwin, 1924), and *Mankind, Nation and Individual* (Oslo, H. Aschehoug & Co., 1925). I have dealt with English grammar in the four volumes of *Modern English Grammar* (MEG., Heidelberg) and in the shorter *Essentials of English Grammar* (London).

The ninth edition has been carefully revised and brought up to date. The changes concern chiefly chapters VII (which has been made into two, VII and VIII) and VIII (which is now IX).

For some valuable suggestions I am much obliged to Professor R. Hittmair, of Vienna.

O. J.

Lundehave, Helsingør (Elsinore)
    July 1938

Contents

CHAPTER I

Preliminary Sketch

1. It will be my endeavour in this volume to characterize the chief peculiarities of the English language, and to explain the growth and significance of those features in its structure which have been of permanent importance. The older stages of the language, interesting as their study is, will be considered only in so far as they throw light either directly or by way of contrast on the main characteristics of present-day English, and an attempt will be made to connect the teachings of linguistic history with the chief events in the general history of the English people so as to show their mutual bearings on each other, and the relation of language to national character. The knowledge that the latter conception is a very difficult one to deal with scientifically, as it may easily tempt one into hasty generalizations, should make us wary, but not deter us from grappling with problems which are really both interesting and important. My plan will be, first to give a rapid sketch of the language of our own days, so as to show how it strikes a foreigner—a foreigner who has devoted much time to the study of English, but who feels that in spite of all his efforts he is only able to look at it as a foreigner does, and not exactly as a native would—and then in the following chapters to enter more deeply into the history of the language in order to describe its first

shape, to trace the various foreign influences it has undergone, and to give an account of its own inner growth.

2. It is, of course, impossible to characterize a
language in one formula; languages, like men, are too
composite to have their whole essence summed up in
one short expression. Nevertheless, there is one expression that continually comes to my mind whenever I
think of the English language and compare it with
others: it seems to me positively and expressly *masculine,* it is the language of a grown-up man and has very
little childish or feminine about it. A great many things
go together to produce and to confirm that impression,
things phonetical, grammatical, and lexical, words and
turns that are found, and words and turns that are not
found, in the language. In dealing with the English
language one is often reminded of the characteristic
English handwriting; just as an English lady will nearly
always write in a manner that in any other country
would only be found in a man's hand, in the same manner the language is more manly than any other language
I know.

3. First I shall mention the sound system. The
English consonants are well defined; voiced and voiceless consonants stand over against each other in neat
symmetry, and they are, as a rule, clearly and precisely
pronounced. You have none of those indistinct or half-
slurred consonants that abound in Danish, for instance
(such as those in ha*d*e, ha*g*e, li*v*lig), where you hardly
know whether it is a consonant or a vowel-glide that
meets the ear. The only thing that might be compared
to this in English is the *r* when not followed by a vowel,
but then this has really given up definitely all pretensions to the rank of a consonant, and is (in the pronunciation of the South of England) either frankly a

vowel (as in *here*) or else nothing at all (in *hart,* etc.).
Each English consonant belongs distinctly to its own
type, a *t* is a *t,* and a *k* is a *k,* and there an end. There
is much less modification of a consonant by the sur-
rounding vowels than in some other languages, thus
none of that palatalization of consonants which gives an
insinuating grace to such languages as Russian. The
vowel sounds, too, are comparatively independent of
their surroundings, and in this respect the language now
has deviated widely from the character of Old English
and has become more clear-cut and distinct in its phonetic structure, although, to be sure, the diphthongiza-
tion of most long vowels (in *ale, whole, eel, who,* phonetically eil, houl, ijl, huw) counteracts in some degree
this impression of neatness and evenness.

4. Besides these characteristics, the full nature of
which cannot, perhaps, be made intelligible to any but
those familiar with phonetic research, but which are
still felt more or less instinctively by everybody hearing
the language spoken, there are other traits whose importance can with greater ease be made evident to anybody possessed of a normal ear.

5. To bring out clearly one of these points I select
at random, by way of contrast, a passage from the language of Hawaii: 'I kona hiki ana aku ilaila ua hookipa
ia mai la oia me ke aloha pumehana loa.' Thus it goes on,
no single word ends in a consonant, and a group of two
or more consonants is never found. Can any one be in
doubt that even if such a language sound pleasantly and
be full of music and harmony the total impression is
childlike and effeminate? You do not expect much vigour
or energy in a people speaking such a language; it seems
adapted only to inhabitants of sunny regions where the
soil requires scarcely any labour on the part of man to

yield him everything he wants, and where life therefore does not bear the stamp of a hard struggle against nature and against fellow-creatures. In a lesser degree we find the same phonetic structure in such languages as Italian and Spanish; but how different are our Northern tongues. English has no lack of words ending in two or more consonants—I am speaking, of course, of the pronunciation, not of the spelling—*age, hence, wealth, tent, tempt, tempts, months, helped, feasts,* etc., etc., and thus requires, as well as presupposes, no little energy on the part of the speakers. That many suchlike consonant groups do not tend to render the language beautiful, one is bound readily to concede; however, it cannot be pretended that their number in English is great enough to make the language harsh or rough. While the fifteenth century greatly increased the number of consonant groups by making the *e* mute in *monthes, helped,* etc., the following centuries, on the contrary, lightened such groups as *-ght* in *night, thought* (where the 'back-open' consonant as German *ch* is still spoken in Scotch) and the initial *kn-, gn-* in *know, gnaw,* etc. Note also the disappearance of *l* in *alms, folk,* etc., and of *r* in *hard, court,* etc.; the final consonant groups have also been simplified in *comb* and the other words in *-mb* (whereas *b* has been retained in *timber*) and in the exactly parallel group *-ng,* for instance in *strong,* where now only one consonant is heard after the vowel, a consonant partaking of the nature of *n* and of *g,* but identical with neither of them; formerly it was followed by a real *g,* which has been retained in *stronger.*

6. In the first ten stanzas of Tennyson's *Locksley Hall,* three hundred syllables, we have only thirty-three words ending in two consonants, and two ending in three, certainly no excessive number, especially if we

take into account the nature of the groups, which are
nearly all of the easiest kind (-dz: comrades, Pleiads;
-mz: gleams, comes; -nz: robin's, man's, turns; -ns:
distance, science; -ks: overlooks; -ts: gets, thoughts;
-kts: tracts, cataracts; -zd: reposed, closed; -st: rest,
West, breast, crest; -ʃt: burnish'd; -nd: sound, around,
moorland, behind, land; -nt: want, casement, went,
present; -ld: old, world; -lt: result; -lf: himself; -pt:
dipt). Thus we may perhaps characterize English, phonetically speaking, as possessing male energy, but not
brutal force. The accentual system points in the same
direction, as will be seen below (26–28).

7. The Italians have a pointed proverb: 'Le parole
son femmine e i fatti son maschi.' If briefness, concise-
ness and terseness are characteristic of the style of men,
while women as a rule are not such economizers of
speech, English is more masculine than most languages.
We see this in a great many ways. In grammar it has
got rid of a great many superfluities found in earlier
English as well as in most cognate languages, reducing
endings, etc., to the shortest forms possible and often
doing away with endings altogether. Where German has,
for instance, *alle diejenigen wilden tiere, die dort leben,*
so that the plural idea is expressed in each word separately (apart, of course, from the adverb), English has
all the wild animals that live there, where *all,* the article,
the adjective, and the relative pronoun are alike incapable of receiving any mark of the plural number; the
sense is expressed with the greatest clearness imaginable, and all the unstressed endings *-e* and *-en,* which
make most German sentences so drawling, are avoided.

8. Rimes based on correspondence in the last syllable only of each line (as bet, set; laid, shade) are
termed male rimes, as opposed to feminine rimes, where

each line has two corresponding syllables, one strong and one weak (as better, setter; lady, shady). It is true that these names, which originated in France, were not at first meant to express any parallelism with the characteristics of the two sexes, but arose merely from the grammatical fact that the weak -e was the ending of the feminine gender (grande, etc.). But the designations are not entirely devoid of symbolic significance; there is really more of abrupt force in a word that ends with a strongly stressed syllable, than in a word where the maximum of force is followed by a weak ending. 'Thanks' is harsher and less polite than the two-syllabled 'thank you.' English has undoubtedly gained in force what it has possibly lost in elegance, by reducing so many words of two syllables to monosyllables. If it had not been for the great number of long foreign, especially Latin, words, English would have approached the state of such monosyllabic languages as Chinese. Now one of the best Chinese scholars, G. v. d. Gabelentz, somewhere remarks that an idea of the condensed power of the monosyllabism found in old Chinese may be gathered from Luther's advice to a preacher, 'Geh rasch 'nauf, tu's Maul auf, hör bald auf.' He might with equal justice have reminded us of many English sentences. 'First come, first served' is much more vigorous than the French 'premier venu, premier moulu' or 'le premier venu engrène,' the German 'wer zuerst kommt, mahlt zuerst' and especially than the Danish 'den der kommer først til mølle, får først malet.' Compare also 'no cure, no pay,' 'haste makes waste,' and 'waste makes want,' 'live and learn,' 'Love no man: trust no man: speak ill of no man to his face; nor well of any man behind his back' (Ben Jonson), 'to meet, to know, to love, and then to part' (Coleridge), 'Then none were for the party;

Then all were for the state; Then the great man help'd the poor, And the poor man loved the great' (Macaulay).

9. It will be noticed, however—and the quotations just given serve to exemplify this, too—that it is not every collocation of words of one syllable that produces an effect of strength, for a great many of the short words most frequently employed are not stressed at all and therefore impress the ear in nearly the same way as prefixes and suffixes do. There is nothing particularly vigorous in the following passage from a modern novel: 'It was as if one had met part of one's self one had lost for a long time,' and in fact most people hearing it read aloud would fail to notice that it consisted of nothing but one-syllable words. Such sentences are not at all rare in colloquial prose, and even in poetry they are found oftener than in most languages, for instance:

And there a while it bode; and if a man
Could touch or see it, he was heal'd at once,
By faith, of all his ills.
Tennyson, *The Holy Grail*

But then, the weakness resulting from many small connecting words is to some extent compensated in English by the absence of the definite article in a good many cases where other languages think it indispensable, e.g. 'Merry Old England'; 'Heaven and Earth'; 'life is short'; 'dinner is ready'; 'school is over'; 'I saw him at church,' and this peculiarity delivers the language from a number of those short 'empty words' which when accumulated cannot fail to make the style somewhat weak and prolix.

10. Business-like shortness is also seen in such convenient abbreviations of sentences as abound in

English, for instance, 'While fighting in Germany he was
taken prisoner' (= while he was fighting). 'He would
not answer when spoken to.' 'To be left till called for.'
'Once at home, he forgot his fears.' 'We had no idea
what to do.' 'Did they run? Yes, I made them' (= made
them run). 'Shall you play tennis today? Yes, we are
going to. I should like to, but I can't.' 'Dinner over, he
left the house.' Such expressions remind one of the abbreviations used in telegrams; they are syntactical cor-
respondencies to the morphological shortenings that are
also of such frequent occurrence in English: *cab* for
cabriolet, bus for *omnibus, photo* for *photograph, phone*
for *telephone,* and innumerable others.

11. This cannot be separated from a certain sobriety in expression. As an Englishman does not like to
use more words or more syllables than are strictly necessary, so he does not like to say more than he can stand
to. He dislikes strong or hyperbolical expressions of
approval or admiration; 'that isn't half bad' or 'she is
rather good-looking' are often the highest praises you
can draw out of him, and they not seldom express the
same warmth of feeling that makes a Frenchman ejacu-
late his 'charmant' or 'ravissante' or 'adorable.' German
kolossal or *fabelhaft* can often be correctly rendered by
English *great* or *biggish,* and where a Frenchman uses
his adverbs *extrêmement* or *infiniment,* an Englishman
says only *very* or *rather* or *pretty.* 'Quelle horreur!' is
'That's rather a nuisance.' 'Je suis ravi de vous voir' is
'Glad to see you,' etc. An Englishman does not like to
commit himself by being too enthusiastic or too dis-
tressed, and his language accordingly grows sober, too
sober perhaps, and even barren when the object is to
express emotions. There is in this trait a curious mixture
of something praiseworthy, the desire to be strictly true

without exaggerating anything or promising more than you can perform, and on the other hand of something blameworthy, the idea that it is affected, or childish and effeminate, to give vent to one's feelings, and the fear of appearing ridiculous by showing strong emotions. But this trait is certainly found more frequently in men than in women, so I may be allowed to add this feature of the English language to the signs of masculinity I have collected.

12. Those who use many strong words to express their likes or dislikes will generally also make an extensive use of another linguistic appliance, namely, violent changes in intonation. Their voices will now suddenly rise to a very high pitch and then as suddenly fall to low tones. An excessive use of this emotional tonic accent is characteristic of many savage nations; in Europe it is found much more in Italy than in the North. In each nation it seems as if it were more employed by women than by men. Now, it has often been observed that the English speak in a more monotonous way than most other nations, so that an extremely slight rising or lowering of the tone indicates what in other languages would require a much greater interval. 'Les Anglais parlent extrêmement bas,' say H. Taine (*Notes sur l'Angleterre,* p. 66). 'Une société italienne, dans laquelle je me suis fourvoyé par hasard, m'a positivement étourdi; je m'étais habitué à ce ton modéré des voix anglaises.' Even English ladies are in this respect more restrained than many men belonging to other nations:

She had the low voice of your English dames,
Unused, it seems, to need rise half a note
To catch attention.

Elizabeth Browning, *Aurora Leigh,* p. 99[1]

[1] Cf. my *Lehrbuch der Phonetik,* 15, 34.

13. If we turn to other provinces of the language we shall find our impression strengthened and deepened.

It is worth observing, for instance, how few diminutives the language has and how sparingly it uses them. English in this respect forms a strong contrast to Italian with its *-ino* (ragazzino, fratellino, originally a double diminutive), *-ina* (donnina), *-etto* (giovinetto), *-etta* (oretta), *-ello, -ella* (asinello, storiella) and other endings, German with its *-chen* and *-lein,* especially South German with its *-le, -el, -erl,* Dutch with its *-je,* Russian, Magyar, and Basque, with their various endings. Too frequent a recurrence of these endings without any apparent necessity tends to produce the impression that the speakers are innocent, childish, genial beings, with no great business capacities or seriousness in life. But in English there are very few of these fondling-endings; *-let* is in the first place a comparatively modern ending, very few of the words in which it is used go back more than a hundred years; and then its extensive use in modern times is chiefly due to the naturalists who want it to express in a short and precise manner certain small organs (*budlet,* Darwin; *bladelet,* Todd; *conelet,* Dana; *bulblet,* Gray; *leaflet, fruitlet, featherlet,* etc.)—an employment of the diminutive which is as far removed as possible from the terms of endearment found in other languages. The endings *-kin* and *-ling* (princekin, princeling) are not very frequently used and generally express contempt or derision. Then, of course, there is *-y, -ie* (Billy, Dicky, auntie, birdie, etc.), which corresponds exactly to the fondling-suffixes of other languages; but its application in English is restricted to the nursery and it is hardly ever used by grown-up people except in speaking to children. Besides, this ending is more Scotch than English.

14. The business-like, virile qualities of the English language also manifest themselves in such things as word-order. Words in English do not play at hide-and-seek, as they often do in Latin, for instance, or in German, where ideas that by right belong together are widely sundered in obedience to caprice, or more often to a rigorous grammatical rule. In English an auxiliary verb does not stand far from its main verb, and a negative will be found in the immediate neighbourhood of the word it negatives, generally the verb (auxiliary). An adjective nearly always stands before its noun; the only really important exception is when there are qualifications added to it which draw it after the noun so that the whole complex serves the purpose of a relative clause: 'a man every way prosperous and talented' (Tennyson), 'an interruption too brief and isolated to attract more notice' (Stevenson). And the same regularity is found in modern English word-order in other respects as well. A few years ago I made my pupils calculate statistically various points in regard to word-order in different languages. I give here only the percentage in some modern authors of sentences in which the subject preceded the verb, and the latter in its turn preceded its object (as in 'I saw him' as against 'Him I saw, but not her' or 'Whom did you see?'):

Shelley, prose 89, poetry 85.
Byron, prose 93, poetry 81.
Macaulay, prose 82.
Carlyle, prose 87.
Tennyson, poetry 88.
Dickens, prose 91.
Swinburne, poetry 83.
Pinero, prose 97.

For the sake of comparison I mention that one
Danish prose-writer (J. P. Jacobsen) had 82, a Danish
poet (Drachmann) 61, Goethe (poetry) 30, a modern
German prose-writer (Tovote) 31, Anatole France 66,
Gabriele d'Annunzio 49 per cent of the same word-
order. That English has not always had the same regularity is shown by the figure for Beowulf being 16, and
for King Alfred's prose 40. Even if I concede that our
statistics did not embrace a sufficient number of extracts
to give fully reliable results,[2] still it is indisputable that
English shows more regularity and less caprice in this
respect than most or probably all cognate languages,
without however, attaining the rigidity found in Chinese,
where the percentage in question would be 100 (or very
near it). English has not deprived itself of the expedient
of inverting the ordinary order of the members of a sentence when emphasis requires it, but it makes a more
sparing use of it than German and the Scandinavian
languages, and in most cases it will be found that these
languages emphasize without any real necessity, especially in a great many every-day phrases: 'dær har jeg
ikke været,' 'dort bin ich nicht gewesen,' 'I haven't been
there'; 'det kan jeg ikke,' 'das kann ich nicht,' 'I can't do
that.' In the usual phrase, 'det veed jeg ikke,' 'das weiss
ich nicht,' *det* or *das* is often superfluously stressed,
where the Englishman does not even find it necessary to
state the object at all: 'I don't know.' Note also that in
English the subject precedes the verb after most introductory adverbs: 'now he comes'; 'there she goes,' while
German and Danish have, and English had till a few
centuries ago, the inverted order: 'jetzt kommt er,' 'da
geht sie'; 'nu kommer han,' 'dær går hun'; 'now comes

[2] Supplemental statistics are given by Curtis, Anglia Beiblatt,
1908, p. 137.

he,' 'there goes she.' Thus order and consistency signalize the modern stage of the English language.

15. No language is logical in every respect, and we must not expect usage to be guided always by strictly logical principles. It was a frequent error with the older grammarians that whenever the actual grammar of a language did not seem conformable to the rules of abstract logic they blamed the language and wanted to correct it. Without falling into that error we may, nevertheless, compare different languages and judge them by the standard of logic, and here again I think that, apart from Chinese, which has been described as pure applied logic, there is perhaps no language in the civilized world that stands so high as English. Look at the use of the tenses; the difference between the past *he saw* and the composite perfect *he has seen* is maintained with great consistency as compared with the similarly formed tenses in Danish, not to speak of German, so that one of the most constant faults committed by English-speaking Germans is the wrong use of these forms ('Were you in Berlin?' for 'Have you been in (or to) Berlin?' 'In 1815 Napoleon has been defeated at Waterloo' for 'was defeated'). And then the comparatively recent development of the expanded (or 'progressive') tenses has furnished the language with the wonderfully precise and logically valuable distinction between 'I write' and 'I am writing,' 'I wrote,' and 'I was writing.' French has something similar in the distinction between *le passé défini* (*j'écrivis*) and *l'imparfait* (*j'écrivais*), but on the one hand the former tends to disappear, or rather has already disappeared in the spoken language, at any rate in Paris and in the northern part of the country, so that *j'ai écrit* takes its place and the distinction between 'I wrote' and 'I have written' is abandoned; on the other hand the distinction applies only to the past while in English it is carried through all tenses. Furthermore, the distinction as made in English is superior to the similar one found in the Slavic languages, in that it is made uniformly in all verbs and in all tenses by means of the same device (*am -ing*), while the Slavic languages employ a much more complicated system of prepositions and derivative endings, which has almost to be learned separately for each new verb or group of verbs.

16. In praising the logic of the English language we must not lose sight of the fact that in most cases where, so to speak, the logic of facts or of the exterior world is at war with the logic of grammar, English is free from the narrow-minded pedantry which in most languages sacrifices the former to the latter or makes people shy of saying or writing things which are not 'strictly grammatical.' This is particularly clear with regard to number. *Family* and *clergy* are, grammatically speaking, of the singular number; but in reality they indicate a plurality. Most languages can treat such words only as singulars, but in English one is free to add a verb in the singular if the idea of unity is essential, and then to refer to this unit as *it,* or else to put the verb in the plural and use the pronoun *they,* if the idea of plurality is predominant. It is clear that this liberty of choice is often greatly advantageous. Thus we find sentences like these: 'As the clergy are or are not what they ought to be, so are the rest of the nation' (Jane Austen), or 'the whole race of man (sing.) proclaim it lawful to drink wine' (De Quincey), or 'the club all know that he is a disappointed man' (the same). In 'there are no end of people here that I don't know' (George Eliot) *no end* takes the verb in the plural because it is equivalent to 'many,' and when Shelley writes in one of his letters, 'the

Quarterly are going to review me,' he is thinking of the Quarterly (Review) as a whole staff of writers. Inversely, there is in English a freedom paralleled nowhere else of expressing grammatically a unity consisting of several parts, of saying, for instance, 'I do not think I ever spent a more delightful three weeks' (Darwin), 'for a quiet twenty minutes,' 'another United States,' cf. also 'a fortnight' (originally a fourteen-night); 'three years is but short' (Shakespeare), 'sixpence was offered him' (Darwin), 'ten minutes is heaps of time' (E. F. Benson), etc., etc.

17. A great many other phenomena in English show the same freedom from pedantry, as when passive constructions such as 'he was taken no notice of' are allowed, or when adverbs or prepositional complexes may be used attributively as in 'his then residence,' 'an almost reconciliation' (Thackeray), 'men invite their out-College friends' (Steadman), 'smoking his before-breakfast pipe' (Conan Doyle), 'in his threadbare, out-at-elbow shooting-jacket' (G. du Maurier), or when even whole phrases or sentences may be turned into a kind of adjective, as in 'with a quite at home kind of air' (Smedley), 'in the pretty diamond-cut-diamond scene between Pallas and Ulysses' (Ruskin), 'a little man with a puffy Say-nothing-to-me-or-I'll-contradict-you sort of countenance' (Dickens), 'with an I-turn-the-crank-of-the-Universe air' (Lowell), 'Rose is simply self-willed; a "she will" or "she won't" sort of little person' (Meredith). Although such combinations as the last-mentioned are only found in more or less jocular style, they show the possibilities of the language, and some expressions of a similar order belong permanently to the language, for instance, 'a would-be artist,' 'a stay-at-home man,' 'a turn-up collar.' Such things—and they might be easily

multiplied—are inconceivable in such a language as
French, where everything is condemned that does not
conform to a definite set of rules laid down by grammarians. The French language is like the stiff French
garden of Louis XIV, while the English is like an English park, which is laid out seemingly without any definite plan, and in which you are allowed to walk everywhere according to your own fancy without having to
fear a stern keeper enforcing rigorous regulations. The
English language would not have been what it is if the
English had not been for centuries great respecters of
the liberties of each individual and if everybody had not
been free to strike out new paths for himself.

18. This is seen, too, in the vocabulary. In spite of
the efforts of several authors of high standing, the English have never suffered an Academy to be instituted
among them like the French or Italian Academies, which
had as one of their chief tasks the regulation of the
vocabulary so that every word not found in their Dictionaries was blamed as unworthy of literary use or
distinction. In England every writer is, and has always
been, free to take his words where he chooses, whether
from the ordinary stock of everyday words, from native
dialects, from old authors, or from other languages,
dead or living. The consequence has been that English
dictionaries comprise a larger number of words than
those of any other nation, and that they present a varie-
gated picture of terms from the four quarters of the
globe. Now, it seems to be characteristic of the two sexes
in their relation to language that women move in narrower circles of the vocabulary, in which they attain to
perfect mastery so that the flow of words is always
natural and, above all, never needs to stop, while men
know more words and always want to be more precise

in choosing the exact word with which to render their idea, the consequence being often less fluency and more hesitation. It has been statistically shown that a comparatively greater number of stammerers and stutterers are found among men (boys) than among women (girls). Teachers of foreign languages have many occasions to admire the ease with which female students express themselves in another language after so short a time of study that most men would be able to say only few words hesitatingly and falteringly, but if they are put to the test of translating a difficult piece either from or into the foreign language, the men will generally prove superior to the women. With regard to their native language the same difference is found, though it is perhaps not so easy to observe. At any rate our assertion is corroborated by the fact observed by every student of languages that novels written by ladies are much easier to read and contain much fewer difficult words than those written by men. All this seems to justify us in setting down the enormous richness of the English vocabulary to the same masculinity of the English nation which we have now encountered in so many various fields.

19. To sum up: The English language is a methodical, energetic, business-like and sober language, that does not care much for finery and elegance, but does care for logical consistency and is opposed to any attempt to narrow-in life by police regulations and strict rules either of grammar or of lexicon. As the language is, so also is the nation,

> For words, like Nature, half reveal
> And half conceal the Soul within.
> Tennyson

CHAPTER II

The Beginnings

20. The existence of the English language as a separate idiom began when Germanic tribes had occupied all the lowlands of Great Britain and when accordingly the invasions from the continent were discontinued, so that the settlers in their new homes were cut off from that steady intercourse with their continental relations which always is an imperative condition of linguistic unity. The historical records of English do not go so far back as this, for the oldest written texts in the English language (in 'Anglo-Saxon') date from about 700 and are thus removed by about three centuries from the beginnings of the language. And yet comparative philology is able to tell us something about the manner in which the ancestors of these settlers spoke centuries before that period, and to sketch the prehistoric development of what was to become the language of King Alfred, of Chaucer, and of Shakespeare.

21. The dialects spoken by the settlers in England belonged to the great Germanic[1] (or Teutonic) branch

[1] I retain the usual term *Germanic* for the whole branch of languages, though it is not very felicitous as it is liable to be mistaken for German by English-speaking people or to produce the impression that German is more important than, or even the source of, the other languages—a mistake which will not so easily happen on the continent, where other words are used for German (*deutsch, duitsch, tysk, tedesco, allemand, niemiecki,*

of the most important of all linguistic families, termed
by many philologists the Indo-European (or Indo-
Germanic) and by others, and to my mind more appro-
priately, Aryan (Arian).[2] The Aryan family comprises
a great variety of languages, including, besides some
languages of less importance, Sanskrit with Prakrit and
many living languages of India; Iranian with modern
Persian; Greek; Latin, with the modern Romanic languages (Italian, Spanish, French, etc.); Keltic, two divisions of which still survive, one in Welsh and Armorican
or Breton, the other in the closely connected Irish and
Scotch-Gaelic, besides the now probably extinct Manx;
Baltic (Lithuanian and Lettic) and Slavonic (Russian,
Czech, Polish, etc.). Among the extinct Germanic languages Wulfila's Gothic was the most important; the
living are High German, Dutch, Low German, Frisian,
English, Danish, Swedish, Norwegian, and Icelandic.
The first five are often grouped together as West-
Germanic, but Frisian and English seem more naturally
to be considered a separate group intermediate between
the first three and the Scandinavian languages.

22. The Aryan language, which was in course of
time differentiated into all these languages, or as the
same fact is generally expressed in a metaphor of dubious value, was the parent-language from which all these
languages have descended, must by no means be imagined as a language characterized by a simple and regular structure. On the contrary it must have been, grammatically and lexically, extremely complicated and full

---

etc.). Personally I prefer the term *Gothonic* and have used it
in my book *Language;* cf. especially G. Schütte's great work
Our Forefathers (Cambridge, I, 1929; II, 1933).

[2] Aryan is here taken in its purely linguistic sense and has
nothing to do with 'race.'

of irregularities. Its grammar was highly inflexional, the
relations between the ideas being expressed by means
of endings more intimately fused with the chief element
of the word than is the case in such agglutinative languages as Hungarian (Magyar). Nouns and verbs were
kept distinct, and where the same sense-modifications
were expressed in both, such as plurality, it was by
means of totally different endings. In fact, the indication
of number—the threefold division into singular, dual,
and plural—was inseparable from the case-endings in
the nouns and from the person-endings as well as signs
of mood and tense in the verbs: one cannot point to distinct parts of such a Latin form as *est* (*cantat*) or *sunt*
(*cantant*) or *fuissem* (*cantavissem*) and say this element
means singular (or plural), this one means indicative
(or subjunctive) and that one indicates what tense the
whole form belongs to. There were eight cases, but they
did not, for the greater part, indicate such clear, concrete outward relations as the Finnic (local) cases do;
the consequence was a comparatively great number of
clashings and overlappings, in form as well as in function. Each noun belonged to one of three genders,
masculine, feminine, and neuter; but this division by
no means corresponded with logical consistency to the
natural division into (1) living beings of one sex, (2)
living beings of the other sex, and (3) everything else.
Nor did the moods and tenses of the verb agree very
closely with any definite logical categories, the idea of
time, for instance, being mixed up with that of 'tense-
aspect' (in German 'Aktionsart'), i.e. distinctions according as an action was viewed as momentary or pro-
tracted or iterated, etc. In the nominal as well as in the
verbal inflexions the endings varied with the character
of the stem they were added to, and very often the accent

was shifted from one syllable to another according to seemingly arbitrary rules, just as in modern Russian. In a great many cases, too, one form was taken from one word and another from a totally different one, a phenomenon (called by Osthoff 'Suppletivwesen') which we have in a few instances in modern English (*good, better; go, went,* etc.). An idea of the phonetic system of the old Aryan language may best be gathered from Greek, which has preserved the old system with great fidelity on the whole, especially the vowels. But of course, no one of the historically transmitted languages, not even one of the oldest, can give more than an approximate idea of the common Aryan language distant from us by so many thousand years, and scholars have now learnt more prudence than was shown when Schleicher was bold enough to print a fable in what he believed to be a fairly accurate representation of primitive Aryan.

23. In historical times we find Aryan split up into a variety of languages, each with its own peculiarities in sounds, in grammar, and in vocabulary. So different were these languages that the Greeks had no idea of any similarity or relationship between their own tongue and that of their Persian enemies; nor did the Romans suspect that the Gauls and Germans they fought spoke languages of the same stock as their own. Whenever the Germanic languages are alluded to, it is always in expressions like these, 'a Roman tongue can hardly pronounce such names' or (after giving the names of some Germanic tribes) 'the names sound like a noisy wartrumpet, and the ferocity of these barbarians adds horror even to the words themselves.' Julian the Apostate compares the singing of Germanic popular ballads to the croaking and shrill screeching of birds.[3] Much of this,

[3] Kluge, Paul's *Grundriss,* I, 354.

of course, must be put down to the ordinary Greek and Roman contempt for foreigners generally; nor can it be wondered at that they did not recognize in these languages congeners of their own, for the similarities had been considerably blurred by a great many important changes in sound and in structure, so that it is only the patient research of the nineteenth century that has enabled us to identify words in separate languages which are now so dissimilar as not to strike the casual observer as in any way related. What contributed, perhaps, more than anything else to make Germanic words look strange were two great phonetic changes affecting large parts of the vocabulary, the *consonant-shift*[4] and the *stress-shift*.

24. The consonant-shift must not be imagined as having taken place at one moment; on the contrary it must have taken centuries, and modern research has begun to point out the various stages in this development. This is not the proper place to deal with detailed explanations of this important change, as we must hurry on to more modern times; suffice it then to give a few examples to show how it affected the whole look of the language. Any *p* was changed to *f*—thus we have *father* corresponding to *pater* and similar forms in the cognate languages; any *t* was made into *th* [þ], as in *three*— compare Latin *tres;* any *k* became *h*—as *cornu = horn*.[5] And as any *b* or *d* or *g*, any *bh, dh, gh* was similarly shifted, you will understand that there were compara-

---

[4] In English books this change ('die erste Lautverschiebung') is often, though not quite correctly, called Grimm's law. On Rask's and Grimm's merits in this discovery, see *Language*, p. 43 ff.

[5] Latin words are here chosen for convenience only as representing these old consonants with great fidelity; but of course it must not be supposed that the English words named come from the Latin. *P, t, k* were not shifted after *s*.

tively few words that were not altered past recognition; still such there were, for instance, *mus,* now *mouse,* which contained none of the consonants susceptible of the shifting in question.

25. The second change affected the general character of the language even more thoroughly. Where previously the stress was sometimes on the first syllable of the word, sometimes on the second, or on the third, etc., without any seeming reason and without any regard to the intrinsic importance of that syllable, a complete revolution simplified matters so that the stress rules may be stated in a couple of lines: nearly all words were stressed on the first syllable; the chief exceptions occurred only where the word was a verb beginning with one out of a definite number of prefixes, such as those we have in modern English *beget, forget, overthrow, abide,* etc. Verner has shown that this shifting of the place of the accent took place later than the Germanic consonant-shift, and we shall now inquire into the relative importance of the two.

26. The consonant-shift is important to the modern philologist, in so far as it is to him the clearest and least ambiguous criterion of the Germanic languages: a word with a shifted consonant is Germanic, and a word with an unshifted consonant in any of the Germanic languages must be a loan-word; whereas the shifted stress is no such certain criterion, chiefly because many words had always had the stress on the first syllable. But if we ask about the intrinsic importance of the two changes, that is, if we try to look at matters from the point of view of the language itself, or rather the speakers, we shall see that the second change is really the more important one. It does not matter much whether a certain number of words begin with *p* or with *f,* but it does matter, or at any rate, it *may* matter, very much, whether the language has a rational system of accentuation or not; and I have no hesitation in saying that the old stress-shift has left its indelible mark on the structure of the language and has influenced it more than any other phonetic change.[6] The significance of the stress-shift will, perhaps, appear most clearly if we compare two sets of words in modern English. Something like the Aryan stress system is found in numerous words taken in recent times from the classical languages, thus 'family, fa'miliar, famili'arity or 'photograph, pho'tographer, photo'graphic.[7] The shifted Germanic system is shown in such groups as 'love, 'lover, 'loving, 'lovingly, 'lovely, 'loveliness, 'loveless, 'lovelessness, or 'king, 'kingdom, 'kingship, 'kingly, 'kingless, etc. As it is characteristic of all Aryan languages that suffixes play a much greater role than prefixes, word formation being generally by endings, it follows that where the Germanic stress system has come into force, the syllable that is most important has also the strongest stress, and that the relatively insignificant modifications of the chief idea which are indicated by formative syllables are also accentually subordinate. This is, accordingly, a perfectly logical system, corresponding to the principal rule observed in sentence stress, viz. that the stressed words are generally the most important ones. As, moreover, want of stress tends everywhere to obscure vowel-sounds, languages with movable accent are exposed to the danger that related words, or different forms of the same word, are made more different than they would else have been,

[6] Except perhaps the disappearance of so many weak *e*'s about 1400.

[7] I indicate stress by means of a short vertical stroke ǀ immediately *before* the beginning of the strong syllable.

and their connexion is more obscured than is strictly necessary; compare, for instance, the two sounds in the first syllable of *family* [æ][8] and *familiar* [ə], or the different treatment of the vowels in *photograph, photographer* and *photographic* [ˈfoutograf, foˈtɔɡrəfə, foutoˈgræfik]. The phonetic clearness inherent in the consistent stress system is certainly a linguistic advantage, and the obscuration of the connexion between related words is generally to be considered a drawback. The language of our forefathers seems therefore to have gained considerably by replacing the movable stress by a fixed one.

27. The question naturally arises: why was the accent shifted in this way? Two possible answers present themselves. The change may have been either a purely mechanical process, by which the first syllable was stressed without any regard to signification, or else it may have been a psychological process, by which the root syllable became stressed because it was the most important part of the word. As in the vast majority of cases the root syllable is the first, the question must be decided from those cases where the two things are not identical. Kluge[9] infers from the treatment of reduplicated forms of the perfect corresponding to Latin *cecidi, peperci,* etc., that the shifting was a purely mechanical process; for it was not the most important syllable that was stressed in Gothic *haihait* 'called,' *rairop* 'reflected,' *lailot* 'let' (read *ai* as short *e*), while in the Old English forms of these words *heht, reord, leort* the vowel of the root syllable actually disappears. But it may be objected to this view that the reduplicated syllable was in some measure the bearer of the root signification, as it had

---

[8] A list of the phonetic symbols used in this book will be found on the last page.

[9] Paul's *Grundriss,* I, 2, 389.

enough left of the root to remind the hearer of it, and in pronouncing it the speaker had before him part at least of the significant elements. The first syllable of a reduplicated perfect must to him have been of a far greater importance than one of those prefixes which served only to modify to a small extent the principal idea expressed in the root syllable. The fact that the reduplicated syllable attracted the accent therefore speaks less strongly in favour of the mechanical explanation than does the want of stress on the verbal prefixes in the opposite direction, so that the case seems to me stronger for the psychological theory. In other words, we have here a case of *value-stressing;*[10] that part of the word which is of greatest value to the speaker and which therefore he especially wants the hearer to notice, is pronounced with the strongest stress.

28. We find the same principle of value-stressing everywhere, even in those languages whose traditional stress rests or may rest on other syllables than the root —this word is here used not in the sense of the etymologically original part of the word, but in the sense of what is to the actual instinct of the speaker intrinsically the most significant element—but in these languages it only plays the part of causing a deviation from the traditional stress now and then whereas in Germanic it became *habitual* to stress the root syllable, and this led to other consequences of some interest. In those languages where the stress syllable is not always the most significant one, the difference between stressed and unstressed syllables is generally less than in the Germanic languages; there is a nicer and subtler play of accent, which we may observe in French, perhaps, better than elsewhere. In *nous chantons* the last syllable

[10] See my *Lehrbuch der Phonetik,* ch. 14, 3.

is stressed, but *chan-* is stronger than *for-* in Eng. *we forget,* because its psychological value is greater. Where a contrast is to be expressed it will most often be associated with one of the traditionally unstressed syllables, and the result is that the contrast is brought vividly before the mind with much less force than is necessary in English; in *nous chantons, et nous ne dansons pas* you need not even make *chan* and *dan* stronger, at any rate not much stronger than the endings, while in English *we sing, but we don't dance,* the syllables *sing* and *dance* must be spoken with an enormous force, because they are in themselves strongly stressed even when no contrast is to be pointed out. A still better example is French *c'est un acteur et non pas un auteur* and English *he is an actor, but not an author;* the Frenchman produces the intended effect by a slight tap, so to speak, on the two initial syllables of the contrasted words, while an Englishman hammers or knocks the corresponding syllables into the head of the hearer. The French system is more elegant, more artistic; the Germanic system is heavier or more clumsy, perhaps, in such cases as those just mentioned, but on the whole it must be said to be more rational, more logical, as an exact correspondence between the inner and the outer world is established if the most significant element receives the strongest phonetic expression. This Germanic stress-principle has been instrumental in bringing about important changes in other respects than those considered here. But what has been said here seems to me to indicate a certain connexion between language and national character; for has it not always been considered characteristic of the Germanic peoples (English, Scandinavians, Germans) that they say their say bluntly without much considering the artistic effect, and that they emphasize what is essential without always having due regard to nuances or accessory notions? and does not the stress system we have been considering present the very same aspect?

29. We do not know in what century the stress was shifted,[11] but the shifting certainly took place centuries before the immigration of the English into Great Britain. To a similar remote period we must refer several other great changes affecting equally all the Germanic languages. One of the most important is the simplification of the tense system in the verb, no Germanic language having more than two tenses, a present and a past. As many of the old endings gradually wore off, they were not in themselves a sufficiently clear indication of the difference of tense, and the apophony or gradation (ablaut) of the root vowel, which had at first been only an incidental consequence of differences of accentuation, was felt more and more as the real indicator of tense. But neither apophony nor the remaining endings were fit to make patterns for the formation of tenses in new verbs; consequently, we see very few additions to the old stock of 'strong' verbs, and a new type of verbs, 'weak verbs,' is constantly gaining ground. Whatever may have been the origin of the dental ending used in the past tense of these verbs, it is very extensively used in all Germanic languages and is, indeed, one of the

[11] Nothing can be concluded from the existence at the time of Tacitus of such series of alliterating names for members of the same family as *Segestes Segimerus Segimundus,* etc. (Kluge, Paul's *Grundriss* [2]357, 388), for alliteration does not necessarily imply that the syllable has the chief stress of the word; cf. the French formulas *messe et matines, Florient et Florette, Basans et Basilie, monts et merveilles, qui vivra verra, à tort et à travers* (Nyrop, *Grammaire historique,* I, [3]453).

characteristic features of their inflexional system. It
has become the 'regular' mode of forming the preterit,
that is, the one resorted to whenever new verbs are
called into existence.

30. To this early period, while the English were
still living on the Continent with their Germanic brethren, belong the first class of loan-words. No language is
entirely pure; we meet with no nation that has not
adopted some loan-words, so we must suppose that the
forefathers of the old Germanic tribes adopted words
from a great many other nations with whom they came
into contact; and scholars have attempted to point out
words borrowed very early from various sources. Some
of these, however, are doubtful, and none of them are
important enough to arrest our attention before we arrive at the period when Latin influence began to be felt
in the Germanic world, that is, about the beginning of
our Christian era. But before we look at these borrowings in detail, let us first consider for a moment the
general lesson that may be derived from the study of
words taken over from one language into another.

31. Loan-words have been called the milestones of
philology, because in a great many instances they permit us to fix approximately the dates of linguistic
changes. But they might with just as much right be
termed some of the milestones of general history, because they show us the course of civilization and the
wanderings of inventions and institutions, and in many
cases give us valuable information as to the inner life
of nations when dry annals tell us nothing but the dates
of the deaths of kings and bishops. When in two languages we find no trace of the exchange of loan-words
one way or the other, we are safe to infer that the two
nations have had nothing to do with each other. But if

they have been in contact, the number of the loan-words
and still more the quality of the loan-words, if rightly
interpreted, will inform us of their reciprocal relations,
they will show us which of them has been the more
fertile in ideas and on what domains of human activity
each has been superior to the other. If all other sources
of information were closed to us except such loan-words
in our modern North-European languages as *piano,
soprano, opera, libretto, tempo, adagio,* etc., we should
still have no hesitation in drawing the conclusion that
Italian music has played a great role all over Europe.
Similar instances might easily be multiplied, and in many
ways the study of language brings home to us the fact
that when a nation produces something that its neighbours think worthy of imitation these will take over not
only the thing but also the name. This will be the general
rule, though exceptions may occur, especially when a
language possesses a native word that will lend itself
without any special effort to the new thing imported
from abroad. But if a native word is not ready to hand
it is easier to adopt the ready-made word used in the
other country; nay, this foreign word is very often imported even in cases where it would seem to offer no
great difficulty to coin an adequate expression by means
of native word-material. As, on the other hand, there
is generally nothing to induce one to use words from
foreign languages for things one has just as well at home,
loan-words are nearly always *technical* words belonging
to one special branch of knowledge or industry, and may
be grouped so as to show what each nation has learnt
from each of the others. It will be my object to go
through the different strata of loans in English with
special regard to their significance in relation to the
history of civilization.

32. What, then, were the principal words that the barbarians learnt from Rome in this period which may be called the pagan or pre-Christian period?[12] One of the earliest, no doubt, was *wine* (Lat. *vinum*), and a few other words connected with the cultivation of the vine and the drinking of wine such as Lat. *calicem,* OE. *calic* (Germ. *kelch*), 'a cup.' It is worth noting, too, that the chief type of Roman merchants that the Germanic people dealt with were the *caupones,* 'wine-dealers, keepers of wine-shops or taverns'; for the word German *kaufen,* OE. *ceapian,* 'to buy,' is derived from it, as is also *cheap,* the old meaning of which was 'bargain, price.' (Cf. Cheapside.) Another word of commercial significance is *monger* (fishmonger, ironmonger, costermonger), OE. *mangere,* from an extinct verb *mangian,* derived from Lat. *mango,* 'retailer.' Lat. *moneta, pondo,* and *uncia* were also adopted as commercial terms: OE. *mynet,* 'coin, coinage,' now *mint;* OE. *pund,* now *pound;* OE. *ynce,* now *inch;* the sound-changes point to very early borrowing. Other words from the Latin connected with commerce and travel are: *mile, anchor, punt* (OE. *punt* from Lat. *ponto*); a great many names for vessels or receptacles of various kinds; the following are still living: *cist* (chest), *omber* or *amber* (amber, from amphora), *disc* (dish), *cytel* (kettle), *mortere* (mortar), *earc* (ark), but many are extinct, e.g. *byden* (barrel), *bytt* (leathern flask), *cylle* (id.), *scutel* (dish), *orc* (pitcher), etc.[13] This makes us suspect a complete revolution in the art of cooking food, an impression which is strengthened by such Latin

[12] See especially Kluge, Paul's *Grundriss,* p. 327 ff.; Pogatscher, *Lautlehre der griech., lat. u. roman. Lehnworte im Altenglischen* (Strassb., 1888). I give the words in their modern English forms, wherever possible.

[13] Pogatscher, p. 122. Cf. also Kluge, p. 331.

loan-words as *cook* (OE. *coc* from *coquus*), *kitchen*
(OE. *cycene* from *coquina*) and *mill* (OE. *mylen* from
molina), as well as names for a great many plants and
fruits which had not previously been cultivated in the
north of Europe, such as *pear* (OE. *cirs,* 'cherry'),
persoc, 'peach' (the modern forms are later adoptions
from the French), *plum* (OE. *plume* from *prunus*), *pea*
(OE. *pise* from *pisum*), *cole* (*caul, kale,* Scotch *kail,*
from Lat. *caulis*), OE. *næp,* found in the second syllable of mod. *turnip,* from *napus, beet*(root), *mint,*
pepper, etc. As military words, though not wanting, were
not taken over in such great numbers as one might expect, we have now gone through the principal categories
of early loans from the Latin language, from which
conclusions as to the state of civilization may be drawn.
In comparing them with later loan-words from the same
source we are struck by their concrete character. It was
not Roman philosophy or the higher mental culture that
impressed our Germanic forefathers; they were not yet
ripe for that influence, but in their barbaric simplicity
they needed and adopted a great many purely practical
and material things, especially such as might sweeten
everyday life. It is hardly necessary to say that the words
for such things were learnt in a purely oral manner, as
shown in many cases by their forms; and this, too, is a
distinctive feature of the oldest Latin loans as opposed
to later strata of loan-words. They were also short
words, mostly of one or two syllables, so that it would
seem that the Germanic tongues and minds could not
yet manage such big words as form the bulk of later
loans. These early words were easy to pronounce and to
remember, being of the same general type as most of the
indigenous words, and therefore they very soon came to
be regarded as part and parcel of the native language,

indispensable as the things themselves which they sym-
bolized.[14]

[14] Loan-words from later periods will take up much space in
the following chapters. There is now a very full treatment of the
subject in *A History of Foreign Words in English,* by Mary S.
Serjeantson (London, 1935). As the author's points of view
differ very considerably from mine, being concerned chiefly
with details and chronology, whereas I try to bring out the
broad lines and great principles, I have found occasion to alter
very little in my former exposition.

CHAPTER III

Old English

33. We now come to the first of those important historical events which have materially influenced the English language, namely, the settlement of Britain by Germanic tribes. The other events of paramount importance, which we shall have to deal with in succession, are the Scandinavian invasion, the Norman conquest, and the revival of learning. A future historian will certainly add the spreading of the English language in America, Australia, and South Africa. But none of these can compare in significance with the first conquest of England by the English, an event which was, perhaps, fraught with greater consequences for the future of the world in general than anything else in history. The more is the pity that we know so very little either of the people who came over or of the state of things they found in the country they invaded. We do not know exactly *when* the invasion began; the date usually given is 449, but Bede, on whose authority this date rests, wrote about three hundred years later, and much may have been forgotten in so long a period. Many considerations seem to make it more advisable to give a much earlier date;[1] however, as we must imagine that the invaders did not come all at once, but that the settlement took up a com-

[1] R. Thurneysen, *Wann sind die Germanen nach England gekommen?* in Eng. Studien, 22, 163.

paratively long period during which new hordes were
continually arriving, the question of date is of no great
consequence, and we are probably on the safe side if we
say that after a long series of Germanic invasions the
greater part of the country was in their power in the
latter half of the fifth century.

34. *Who* were the invaders, and where did they
come from? This, too, has been a point of controversy.[2]
According to Bede, the invaders belonged to the three
tribes of Angles, Saxons, and Jutes; and linguistic history corroborates his statement in so far as we have
really three dialects, or groups of dialects: the Anglian
dialects in the North with two subdivisions, Northumbrian and Mercian, the Saxon dialects in the greater part
of the South, the most important of which was the
dialect of Wessex (West-Saxon), and the Kentish dialect, Kent having been, according to tradition, settled
by the Jutes. These were closely connected linguistically
with the Angles and Saxons, thus did not, like those
inhabitants of Jutland whom we meet with in historical

[2] The complicated and often contradictory evidence, from
old chroniclers, archæology, place-names and personal names,
has been ably dealt with by G. Schütte in *Our Forefathers*
(Cambridge, 1933), II, 218–326, where also a full bibliography
is found for each special question. See also A. Erdmann, *Über
die Heimat und den Namen der Angeln*, Uppsala, 1890.—H.
Möller, Anzeiger für deutsches Altertum, XXII, 129 ff.—O.
Bremer in Paul's *Grundriss* I, 2, 115 ff., where other references
will be found.—Chambers, *Widsith*, 1912, pp. 237, 241.—J.
Hoops, 'Angelsachsen' in *Reallexikon der germanischen Alter-
tumskunde* (Strassburg, 1911).—A. Brandl, *Zur Geographie
der altenglischen Dialekte* (Berlin, Akademie, 1915).—Luick,
Histor. Grammatik, 1921, p. 10–11.—J. Hoops, *Englische
Sprachkunde* (Stuttgart, 1923), p. 5 ff.—E. Wadstein, *On the
Origin of the English* (Uppsala, 1927).—On the question of
'Standard Old English' (the language of Alfred or of Ælfric),
see C. L. Wrenn, *Transact. of the Philological Soc.* 1933, p.
65 ff.

times, speak a Danish dialect. Though the Saxons were numerically superior to the Angles, the latter were influential enough to impose their name on the whole: the country is called England (OE. Englaland), the nation English (OE. Englisc, Engliscmon, cf. also Angelcynn, Angelþeod), and the language English (OE. Englisc, Englisc gereord). The continental language that shows the greatest similarity to English is Frisian, and it is interesting to note that Frisian has some points in common with Kentish and some with Anglian, some even with the northernmost divisions of the Anglian dialect, points in which these OE. dialects differ from literary West-Saxon. Kentish resembles more particularly West Frisian, and Anglian East Frisian,[3] facts which justify us in looking upon the Frisians as the neighbours and relatives of the English before their emigration from the continent.

35. What language or what languages did the settlers find on their arrival in Britain? The original population was Keltic; but what about the Roman conquest? The Romans had been masters of the country for centuries; had they not succeeded in making the native population learn Latin as they had succeeded in Spain and Gaul? Some years ago Pogatscher[4] took up the view that they had succeeded, and that the Angles and Saxons found a Brito-Roman dialect in full vigour; he endorsed Wright's view that if the Angles and Saxons had never come, we should have been now a people talking a Neo-Latin tongue, closely resembling French. But this view was very strongly attacked by Loth[5] and

[3] W. Heuser, *Altfriesisches Lesebuch*, 1903, pp. 1–5, and Indogermanische Forschungen, Anzeiger XIV, 29.

[4] *Zur Lautlehre der . . . Lehnworte im Altenglischen*, 1888.

[5] *Les mots latins dans les langues brittoniques*. Paris, 1892.

Pogatscher, in a subsequent article,[6] had to withdraw
his previous theory, if not completely, yet to a great
extent, so that he no longer maintains that Latin ever
was the *national* language of Britain, though he does not
go the length of saying with Loth that the Latin language disappeared from Britain when the Roman troops
were withdrawn. The possibility is left that while people
in the country spoke Keltic, the inhabitants of the towns
spoke Latin, or that some of them did. However this
may be, the fact remains that the English found on their
arrival a population speaking a different language from
their own. Did that, then, affect their own language,
and in what manner and to what extent?

36. In his *Student's History of England,* p. 31,
Gardiner, who here follows Freeman, says: 'So far as
British words have entered into the English language
at all, they have been words such as *gown* or *curd,*
which are likely to have been used by women, or words
such as *cart* or *pony,* which are likely to have been used
by agricultural labourers, and the evidence of language
may therefore be adduced in favour of the view that
many women and many agricultural labourers were
spared by the conquerors.' Here, then, we seem to have
a Keltic influence from which an important historical
inference can be drawn. Unfortunately, however, not a
single word of those adduced can prove anything of the
kind. For *gown* is not an old Keltic word, but was taken
over from French in the 14th century (medieval Latin
gunna); *curd,* too, dates only from the 14th century,
whereas if it had been introduced from Keltic in the
old period we should certainly find it in older texts; 'it

[6] *Angelsachsen und Romanen.* Engl. Studien, XIX, 329–352
(1894). See now R. E. Zachrisson, *Romans, Kelts and Saxons
in Ancient Britain* (Uppsala, 1927).

is not certain what relation, if any, the Keltic words hold to the English' (NED.). *Cart* is probably a native English word; it is found in Keltic languages, but is there 'palpably a foreign word' (NED.) introduced from English; and *pony*,[7] finally, is Lowland Scotch *powney* from Old French *poulenet*, 'a little colt,' a diminutive of *poulain*, 'a colt.' Similarly, most of the other words of alleged Keltic origin are either Germanic or French words which the Kelts have borrowed from English, or else they have not been used in England more than a century or two; in neither of these cases do they teach us anything with regard to the relations between the two nationalities fifteen hundred years ago.[8] The net result of modern investigation seems to be that (apart from numerous place-names) only about a dozen words did pass over into English from the British aborigines (among them are *ass, bannock, binn, brock*). How may we account for this very small number of loans? Are we to account for it, as some writers would, from the unscrupulous character of the conquest, the English having killed all those Britons who did not run away into

[7] Skeat, *Notes on English Etymology*, 224.

[8] *Dry* 'magician,' *cross*, and probably *curse* belong to a somewhat later stratum of words taken from Irish. See the able treatment of these questions in M. Förster, *Keltisches Wortgut im Englischen*, Halle, 1921. *Cradle*, OE. *cradol*, seems to be a diminutive of an old Germanic word meaning 'basket' (OHG. *chratto*). See also *bog* in NED. Windisch, in the article quoted below, note 1, thinks that the Germanic *tun* in English took over the meaning of Keltic *dunum* (Latin *arx*) on account of the numerous old Keltic names of places in *-dunum;* but in OE. *tun* had more frequently the meaning of 'enclosure, yard' (cf. Dutch *tuin*), 'enclosed land round a dwelling,' 'a single dwelling house or farm' (cf. Old Norse *tún;* still in Devonshire and Scotland); it was only gradually that the word acquired its modern meaning of village or town, long after the influence of the Kelts must have disappeared.—*Slogan, pibroch, clan*, etc., are modern loans from Keltic.

the mountainous districts? The supposition of wholesale
slaughter seems, however, to have been disproved by
Zachrisson from the distribution of Keltic elements in
place-names and the frequent occurrence of Keltic personal names among the Anglo-Saxons. The Britons were
not exterminated, but absorbed by their Saxon conquerors. Their civilization and language vanished but
the race remained. On the other hand, a thorough consideration of the general conditions under which borrowings from one language by another take place will
give us a clue to the mystery.[9] And as the whole history
of the English language may be described from one
point of view as one chain of borrowings, it will be as
well at the outset to give a little thought to this general
question.

37. The whole theory of Windisch about mixed
languages turns upon this formula: it is not the foreign
language a nation learns that it turns into a mixed
language, but its own native language becomes mixed
under the influence of the foreign language. When we
try to learn and talk a foreign language we do not inter-
mix it with words taken from our own language; our
endeavour will always be to speak the other language as
purely as possible, and generally we are painfully con-
scious of every native word that we use in the middle
of phrases framed in the other tongue. But what we thus
avoid in speaking a foreign language we very often do
in our own. One of Windisch's illustrations is taken

[9] See especially Windisch, *Zur Theorie der Mischsprachen und
Lehnwörter.* Berichte über die Verhandl. d. sächs. Gesellsch. d.
Wissensch. XLIX, 1897, p. 101 ff.—G. Hempl, *Language-
Rivalry and Speech Differentiation in the Case of Race-Mixture,*
Trans. of the Amer. Philol. Association XXIX, 1898, p. 30 ff.—
A full treatment of the question of mixed languages and loan-
words is found in my own book, *Language,* ch. XI.

from Germany in the eighteenth century. It was then
the height of fashion to imitate everything French, and
Frederick the Great prided himself on speaking and
writing good French. In his French writings one finds
not a single German word, but whenever he wrote German, French words and phrases in the middle of German
sentences abounded, for French was considered more
refined, more *distingué*. Similarly, in the last remains of
Cornish, the extinct Keltic language of Cornwall, numerous English loan-words occur, but the English did
not mix any Cornish words with their own language,
and the inhabitants of Cornwall themselves, whose
native language was Cornish, would naturally avoid
Cornish words when talking English, because in the
first place English was considered the superior tongue,
the language of culture and civilization, and second,
the English would not understand Cornish words.
Similarly in the Brittany of to-day, people will interlard
their Breton talk with French words, while their French
is pure, without any Breton words. We now see why
so few Keltic words were taken over into English.[10]
There was nothing to induce the ruling classes to learn
the language of the inferior natives; it could never be
fashionable for them to show an acquaintance with that
despised tongue by using now and then a Keltic word.
On the other hand the Kelt would have to learn the
language of his masters, and learn it well; he could not
think of addressing his superiors in his own unintelligible
gibberish, and if the first generation did not learn good
English, the second or third would, while the influence
they themselves exercised on English would be infinitesi-
mal. There can be no doubt that this theory of Windisch's is in the main correct, though we shall, perhaps,

[10] And so few Gallic words into French.

later on see instances where it holds good only with some qualification. At any rate we need look for no other explanation of the fewness of Keltic words in English.

38. About 600 A.D. England was Christianized, and the conversion had far-reaching linguistic consequences. We have no literary remains of the pre-Christian period, but in the great epic of Beowulf we see a strange mixture of pagan and Christian elements. It took a long time thoroughly to assimilate the new doctrine, and, in fact, much of the old heathendom survives to this day in the shape of numerous superstitions. On the other hand we must not suppose that people were wholly unacquainted with Christianity before they were actually converted, and linguistic evidence points to their knowing, and having had names for, the most striking Christian phenomena centuries before they became Christians themselves. One of the earliest loan-words belonging to this sphere is *church,* OE. *cirice, cyrice,* ultimately from Greek *kuriakón* '(house) of the Lord' or rather the plural *kuriaká.* It has been well remarked that 'it is by no means necessary that there should have been a single *kirikā* in Germany itself; from 313 onwards, Christian churches with their sacred vessels and ornaments were well-known objects of pillage to the German invaders of the Empire: if the first with which these made acquaintance, wherever situated, were called *kuriaká,* it would be quite sufficient to account for their familiarity with the word.'[11] They knew this word so well that when they became Christians they did not adopt the word universally used in the Latin church and in the

[11] See the full and able article *church* in the NED. We need not suppose, as is often done, that the word passed through Gothic, where the word is not found in the literature that has come down to us.

Romanic languages (*ecclesia, église, chiesa,* etc.), and
the English even extended the signification of the word
church from the building to the congregation, the whole
body of Christians. *Minster,* OE. *mynster* from *mo-
nasterium,* belongs also to the earliest period. Other
words of very early adoption were *devil* from *diabolus,*
Greek *diábolos,* and *angel,* OE. *engel*[12] from *angelus,*
Greek *ággelos.* But the great bulk of specifically Christian terms did not enter the language till after the conversion.

39. The number of new ideas and things introduced with Christianity was very considerable, and it
is interesting to note how the English managed to express them in their language.[13] In the first place they
adopted a great many foreign words together with the
ideas. Such words are *apostle,* OE. *apostol, disciple,*
OF. *discipul,* which has been more of an ecclesiastical
word in English than in other languages, where it has
the wider Latin sense of 'pupil' or 'scholar,' while in
English it is more or less limited to the twelve Disciples
of Jesus or to similar applications. Further, the names
of the whole scale of dignitaries of the church, from
the *Pope,* OE. *papa,* downwards through *archbishop,*
OE. *ercebiscop, bishop,* OE. *biscop,* to *priest,* OE.
preost; so also *monk,* OE. *munuc, nun,* OE. *nunna,*
with *provost,* OE. *prafost* (præpositus) and *profost*
(propositus) *abbot, OE. abbod* (*d* from Romanic form)

---

[12] See below, § 86, on the relation between the OE. and the
modern forms.

[13] See especially H. S. MacGillivray, *The Influence of Christianity on the Vocabulary of Old English* (Halle, 1902). I arrange
his material from other points of view and must often pass the
limits of his book, of which only one half has appeared. Cf. also
A. Keiser, *The Influence of Christianity on the Vocabulary of
OE. Poetry* (Univ. of Illinois, 1919).

and the feminine OE. *abbudisse*. Here belong also such obsolete words as *sacerd* 'priest,' *canonic* 'canon,' *decan* 'dean,' *ancor* or *ancra* 'hermit' (Latin anachoreta). To these names of persons must be added not a few names of things, such as *shrine,* OE. *scrin* (scrinium), *cowl,* OE. *cugele* (cuculla), *pall,* OE. *pæll* or *pell* (pallium); *regol* or *reogol* '(monastic) rule,' *capitul* 'chapter,' *mæsse* 'mass,' and *offrian,* in Old English used only in the sense of 'sacrificing, bringing an offering'; the modern usage in 'he offered his friend a seat and a cigar' is later and from the French.

40. It is worth noting that most of these loans were short words that tallied perfectly well with the native words and were easily inflected and treated in every respect like these; the composition of the longest of them, *ercebishop,* was felt quite naturally as a native one. Such long words as *discipul* or *capitul,* or as *exorcista* and *acolitus,* which are also found, never became popular words; and *anachoreta* only became popular when it had been shortened to the convenient *ancor.*

41. The chief interest in this chapter of linguistic history does not, however, to my mind concern those words that were adopted, but those that were not. It is not astonishing that the English should have learnt some Latin words connected with the new faith, but it is astonishing, especially in the light of what later generations did, that they should have utilized the resources of their own language to so great an extent as was actually the case. This was done in three ways: by forming new words from the foreign loans by means of native affixes, by modifying the sense of existing English words, and finally by framing new words from native stems.

At that period the English were not shy of affixing native endings to foreign words; thus we have a great many words in *-had* (mod. *-hood*): *preosthad* 'priest-hood,' *clerichad, sacerdhad, biscophad* 'episcopate,' etc.; also such compounds as *biscopsetl* 'episcopal see,' *biscopscir* 'diocese,' and with the same ending *profostscir* 'provostship' and the interesting *scriftscir* 'parish confessor's district' from *scrift* 'confession,' a derivative of *scrifan* (*shrive*) from Lat. *scribere* in the sense 'impose penance, hear confession.' Note also such words as *cristendom* 'Christendom, Christianity' (also *cristnes*), and *cristnian* 'christen' or rather 'prepare a candidate for baptism'[14] and *biscopian* 'confirm' with the noun *biscepung* 'confirmation.'

42. Existing native words were largely turned to account to express Christian ideas, the sense only being more or less modified. Foremost among these must be mentioned the word *God*. Other words belonging to the same class and surviving to this day are *sin*, OE. *synn*, *tithe*, OE. *teoða*, the old ordinal for 'tenth'; *easter*, OE. *eastron*, was the name of an old pagan spring festival, called after Austro, a goddess of spring.[15] Most of the native words adapted to Christian usage have since been superseded by terms taken from Latin or French. Where we now say *saint* from the French, the old word was *halig* (mod. holy), preserved in *All-hallows-day* and *Allhallow-e'en;* the Latin *sanct* was very rarely used. *Scaru,* from the verb *scieran,* 'shear, cut,' has been supplanted by *tonsure, had* by *order, hadian* by *consecrate* and *ordain, gesomnung* by *congregation, þegnung* by

---

[14] '*Cristnian* signifies primarily the "prima signatio" of the catechumens as distinguished from the baptism proper.' Mac-Gillivray, p. 21. Cf. *fulwian* § 44.

[15] Connected with Sanscrit *usra* and Latin *aurora* and, therefore, originally a dawn-goddess.

service, witega by *prophet, þrowere* (from *þrowian,* 'to suffer') by *martyr, þrowerhad* or *þrowung* by *martyrdom, niwcumen mann* ('newcome man') by *novice, hrycghrægel* (from *hrycg,* 'back,' and *hrægel,* 'dress') by *dossal,* and *ealdor* by *prior.* Compounds of the last-mentioned Old English word were also applied to things connected with the new religion, thus *teoðing-ealdor* 'dean' (chief of ten monks). *Ealdormann,* the native term for a sort of viceroy or lord-lieutenant, was used to denote the Jewish High-Priests as well as the Pharisees. OE. *husl,* mod. *housel,* 'the Eucharist,'[16] was an old pagan word for sacrifice or offering; an older form is seen in Gothic *hunsl.* The OE. word for 'altar,' *weofod,* is an interesting heathen survival, for it goes back to a compound *wigbeod,* 'idol-table,' and it was probably only because phonetic development had obscured its connexion with *wig,* 'idol' that it was allowed to remain in use as a Christian technical term.

43. This second class is not always easily distinguished from the third, or those words that had not previously existed but were now framed out of existing native speech-material to express ideas foreign to the pagan world. Word-composition and other formative processes were resorted to, and in some instances the new terms were simply fitted together from translations of the component parts of the Greek or Latin word they were intended to render, as when Greek *euaggélion* was rendered *god-spell* (good spell, afterwards with shortening of the first vowel *godspell,* which was often taken to be the 'spell' or message of God), mod. *gospel;* thence *godspellere,* where now the foreign word *evangelist* is used. *Heathen,* OE. *hæðen,* according to the generally

---

[16] Still used in the nineteenth century, e.g. by Tennyson, as an archaism.

accepted theory, is derived from *hæþ* 'heath' in close imitation of Latin *paganus* from *pagus* 'a country district.' Cf. also *þrynnes* or *þrines* ('three-ness') for *trinity*.

44. But in most cases we have no such literal rendering of a foreign term, but excellent words devised exactly as if the framers of them had never heard of any foreign expression for the same conception—as, perhaps, indeed, in some instances they had not. Some of these display not a little ingenuity. The Scribes and Pharisees of the New Testament were called *boceras* (from *boc* 'book') and *sunder-halgan* (from *sundor* 'apart, asunder, separate'); in the north the latter were also called *ælarwas* 'teachers of the Law' or *ældo* 'elders.' A patriarch was called *heahfæder* 'high-father' or *ealdfæder* 'old-father'; the three Magi were called *tungolwitegan* from *tungol* 'star,' and *witega* 'wise man.' For 'chaplain' we have *handpreost* or *hiredpreost* ('family-priest'); for 'acolyte' different words expressive of his several functions: *huslþegn* ('Eucharist-servant'), *taporberend* ('taper-bearer') and *wæxberend* ('wax-bearer'); instead of *ercebiscop* 'archbishop' we sometimes find *heahbiscop* and *ealdorbiscop*. For 'hermit' *ansetla* and *westensetla* ('sole-settler,' 'desert-settler') were used. 'Magic art' was called *scincræft* ('phantom-art'); 'magician' *scincræftiga* or *scinlæca, scinnere,* 'phantom' or 'superstition,' *scinlac*. For the disciples of Christ we find, beside *discipul* mentioned above, no less than ten different English renderings (*cniht, folgere, gingra, hieremon, læringman, leornere, leorning-cniht, leorning-man, underþeodda, þegn*).[17] To 'baptize' was expressed by *dyppan* 'dip' (cf. German *taufen*, Dan. *døbe*) or more often by *fulwian* (from *ful-wihan* 'to consecrate completely'); 'baptism' by *fulwiht* or, the last

[17] MacGillivray, p. 44.

syllable being phonetically obscured, *fulluht,* and John
the Baptist was called *Johannes se fulluhtere.*

45. The power and boldness of these numerous
native formations can, perhaps, be best appreciated if
we go through the principal compounds of *God: godbot*
'atonement made to the church,' *godcund* 'divine, religious, sacred,' *godcundnes* 'divinity, sacred office,' *god-
ferht* 'pious,' *godgield* 'idol,' *godgimm* 'divine gem,' *god-
had* 'divine nature,' *godmægen* 'divinity,' *godscyld* 'impiety,' *godscyldig* 'impious,' *godsibb* 'sponsor,' *godsib-
bræden* 'sponsorial obligations,' *godspell* (cf. however,
§ 43), *godspelbodung* 'gospel-preaching,' *godspellere*
'evangelist,' *godspellian* 'preach the gospel,' *godspellisc*
'evangelical,' *godspeltraht* 'gospel-commentary,' *god-
spræce* 'oracle,' *godsunu* 'godson,' *godþrymm* 'divine
majesty,' *godwræc* 'impious,' *godwræcnes* 'impiety.'
Such a list as this, with the modern translations, shows
the gulf between the old system of nomenclature, where
everything was native and, therefore, easily understood
by even the most uneducated, and the modern system,
where with few exceptions classical roots serve to express even simple ideas; observe that although *gospel*
has been retained, the easy secondary words derived
from it have given way to learned formations. Nor was
it only religious terms that were devised in this way;
for Christianity brought with it also some acquaintance
with the higher intellectual achievements in other domains, and we find such scientific terms as *læce-cræft*
'leech-craft' for medicine, *tungol-æ* 'star-law' for astronomy, *efnniht* for equinox, *sunn-stede* and *sunn-gihte* for
solstice, *sunnfolgend* (sunfollower) for heliotrope, *tid*
'tide' and *gemet* 'measure' for tense and mood in grammar, *foresetnes* for preposition, etc., in short a number
of scientific expressions of native origin, such as is

48   GROWTH AND STRUCTURE

equalled among the Germanic languages in Icelandic
only.[18]

46. If now we ask, why did not the Anglo-Saxons
adopt more of the ready-made Latin or Greek words,
it is easy to see that the conditions here are quite different from those mentioned above when we asked a similar
question with regard to Keltic. There we had a real race-
mixture, where people speaking two different languages
were living in actual contact in the same country. Here
we have no Latin-speaking nation or community in
actual intercourse with the English; and though we must
suppose that there was a certain mouth-to-mouth influence from missionaries which might familiarize part
of the English nation with some of the specifically
Christian words, these were certainly at first introduced
in far greater number through the medium of writing,
exactly as is the case with Latin and Greek importations
in recent times. Why, then, do we see such a difference
between the practice of that remote period and our own
time? One of the reasons seems obviously to be that
people then did not know so much Latin as they learnt
later, so that these learned words, if introduced, would
not have been understood. We have it on King Alfred's
authority that in the time immediately preceding his own
reign 'there were very few on this side of the Humber
who could understand their [Latin] rituals in English,
or translate a letter from Latin into English, and I believe that there were not many beyond the Humber.
There were so few of them that I cannot remember a
single one south of the Thames when I came to the
throne . . . and there was also a great multitude of

[18] On later Old English loans from Latin see especially O.
Funke, *Die gelehrten lateinischen Lehn- und Fremdwörter in der
altengl. Lit.* (Halle, 1914).

God's servants, but they had very little knowledge of the books, for they could not understand anything of them, because they were not written in their language.'[19] And even in the previous period which Alfred regrets, when 'the sacred orders were zealous in teaching and learning,' and when, as we know from Bede and other sources,[20] Latin and Greek studies were pursued successfully in England, we may be sure that the percentage of those who would have understood the learned words, had they been adopted into English, was not large. There was, therefore, good reason for devising as many popular words as possible. However, the manner in which our question was put was not, perhaps, quite fair, for we seemed to presuppose that it would be natural for a nation to adopt as many foreign terms as its linguistic digestion would admit, and that it would be matter for surprise if a language had fewer foreign elements than Modern English. But on the contrary, it is rather the natural thing for a language to utilize its own resources before drawing on other languages. The Anglo-Saxon principle of adopting only such words as were easily assimilated with the native vocabulary, for the most part names of concrete things, and of turning to the greatest possible account native words and roots, especially for abstract notions—that principle may be taken as a symptom of a healthful condition of a language and a nation: witness Greek, where we have the most flourishing and vigorous growth of abstract and other scientifically serviceable terms on a native basis that the world has ever seen, and where the highest development

[19] King Alfred's West-Saxon Version of Gregory's Pastoral Care, Preface (Sweet's translation).

[20] See T. N. Toller, *Outlines of the History of the English Language,* Cambridge, 1900, p. 68 ff.

of intellectual and artistic activity went hand in hand
with the most extensive creation of indigenous words
and an extremely limited importation of words from
abroad. It is not, then, the Old English system of utilizing the vernacular stock of words, but the modern
system of neglecting the native and borrowing from a
foreign vocabulary that has to be accounted for as
something out of the natural state of things. A particular
case in point will illustrate this better than long explanations.

47. To express the idea of a small book that is
always ready at hand, the Greeks had devised the word
egkheirídion from *en* 'in,' *kheír* 'hand' and the suffix
-idion denoting smallness; the Romans similarly employed their adjective *manualis* 'pertaining to *manus,*
the hand' with *liber* 'book' understood. What could be
more natural then, than for the Anglo-Saxons to frame
according to the genius of their own language the compound *handboc?* This naturally would be especially
applied to the one kind of handy books that the clergy
were in particular need of, the book containing the occasional and minor public offices of the Roman church.
Similar compounds were used, and are used, as a matter
of course, in the other cognate languages—German
handbuch, Danish *håndbog,* etc. But in the Middle
English period, *handboc* was disused, the French
(Latin) *manual* taking its place, and in the sixteenth
century the Greek word (*enchiridion*) too was introduced into the English language. And so accustomed had
the nation grown to preferring strange and exotic words
that when in the nineteenth century *handbook* made its
reappearance, it was treated as an unwelcome intruder.
The oldest example of the new use in the NED. is from
1814, when an anonymous book was published with the

title *A Handbook for modelling wax flowers.* In 1833
Nicolas in the preface to a historical work wrote, 'What
the Germans would term and which, if our language admitted of the expression, would have been the fittest title
for it, *The Handbook of History*'—but he dared not use
that title himself. Three years later Murray the publisher
ventured to call his guide-book *A Hand-Book for
Travellers on the Continent,* but reviewers as late as
1843 apologized for copying this coined word. In 1838
Rogers speaks of the word as a tasteless innovation, and
Trench in his *English Past and Present* (1854; 3rd ed.,
1856, p. 71) says, 'we might have been satisfied with
"manual" and not put together that very ugly and very
unnecessary word "handbook," which is scarcely, I
should suppose, ten or fifteen years old.' Of late years,
the word seems to have found more favour, but I cannot
help thinking that state of language a very unnatural one
where such a very simple, intelligible and expressive
word has to fight its way instead of being at once admitted to the very best society.

48. The Old English language, then, was rich in
possibilities, and its speakers were fortunate enough to
possess a language that might with very little exertion
on their part be made to express everything that human
speech can be called upon to express. There can be no
doubt that if the language had been left to itself, it would
easily have remedied the defects that it certainly had, for
its resources were abundantly sufficient to provide natural and expressive terms even for such a new world of
concrete things and abstract ideas as Christianity meant
to the Anglo-Saxons. It is true that we often find Old
English prose clumsy and unwieldy, but that is more
the fault of the literature than of the language itself. A
good prose style is everywhere a late acquirement, and

the work of whole generations of good authors is needed
to bring about the easy flow of written prose. Neither,
perhaps, were the subjects treated of in the extant Old
English prose literature those most suitable for the development of the highest literary qualities. But if we
look at such a closely connected language as Old Norse,
we find in that language a rapid progress to a narrative
prose style which is even now justly admired in its
numerous sagas; and I do not see so great a difference
between the two languages as would justify a scepticism
with regard to the perfectibility of Old English in the
same direction. And, indeed, we have positive proof in
a few passages that the language had no mean power as
a literary medium; I am thinking of Alfred's report of
the two great Scandinavian explorers, Ohthere and Wulfstan, who visited him, of a few passages in the Saxon
Chronicle, and especially of some pages of the homilies
of Wulfstan, where we find an impassioned prose of real
merit.

49. If Old English prose is undeveloped, we have a
very rich and characteristic poetic literature, ranging
from powerful pictures of battles and of fights with
mythical monsters to religious poems, idyllic descriptions
of an ideal country and sad ones of moods of melan-
choly. It is not here the place to dwell upon the literary
merit of these poems, as we are only concerned with the
language. But to anyone who has taken the trouble—
and it is a trouble—to familiarize himself with that
poetry, there is a singular charm in the language it is
clothed in, so strangely different from modern poetic
style. The movement is slow and leisurely; the measure
of the verse does not invite us to hurry on rapidly, but
to linger deliberately on each line and pause before we
go on to the next. Nor are the poet's thoughts too light-

footed; he likes to tell us the same thing two or three times. Where a single *he* would suffice he prefers to give a couple of such descriptions as 'the brave prince, the bright hero, noble in war, eager and spirited' etc., descriptions which add no new trait to the mental picture, but which, nevertheless, impress us artistically and work upon our emotions, very much like repetitions and variations in music. These effects are chiefly produced by heaping synonym on synonym, and the wealth of synonymous terms found in Old English poetry is really astonishing, especially in certain domains, which had for centuries been the stock subjects of poetry. For 'hero' or 'prince' we find in Beowulf alone at least thirty-six words (*æðeling, æscwiga, aglæca, beadorinc, beaggyfa, bealdor, beorn, brego, brytta, byrnwiga, ceorl, cniht, cyning, dryhten, ealdor, eorl, eðelweard, fengel, frea, freca, fruma, hæleð, hlaford, hyse, leod, mecg, nið, oretta, ræswa, rinc, secg, þegn, þengel, þeoden, wer, wiga*). For 'battle' or 'fight' we have in Beowulf at least twelve synonyms (*beadu, guð, heaðo, hild, lindplega, nið, orleg, ræs, sacu, geslyht, gewinn, wig*). Beowulf has seventeen expressions for the 'sea' (*brim, flod, garsecg, hæf, heaðu, holm, holmwylm, hronrad, lagu, mere, merestræt, sæ, seglrad, stream, wæd, wæg, yþ*), to which should be added thirteen more from other poems (*flodweg, flodwielm, flot, flotweg, holmweg, hronmere, mereflod, merestream, sæflod, sæholm, sæstream, sæweg, yþmere*). For 'ship' or 'boat' we have in Beowulf eleven words (*bat, brenting, ceol, fær, flota, naca, sæbat, sægenga, sæwudu, scip, sundwudu*), and in other poems at least sixteen more words (*brimhengest, brimþisa, brimwudu, cnearr, flodwudu, flotscip, holmærn, merebat, merehengest, mereþyssa, sæflota, sæhengest, sæmearh, yþbord, yþhengest, yþhof, yþlid, yþlida*).

50. How are we to account for this wealth of synonyms? We may subtract, if we like, such compound words as are only variations of the same comparison, as when a ship is called a sea-horse, and then different words for sea (*sæ, mere, yþ*) are combined with the words *hengest* 'stallion' and *mearh* 'mare'; but even if this class is not counted, the number of synonyms is great enough to call for an explanation. A language has always many terms for those things that interest the speakers in their daily doings; thus Sweet says: 'If we open an Arabic dictionary at random, we may expect to find something about a camel: "a young camel," "an old camel," "a strong camel," "to feed a camel on the fifth day," "to feel a camel's hump to ascertain its fatness," all these being not only simple words, but root-words.'[21] And when we read that the Araucanians (in Chile) distinguished nicely in their languages between a great many shades of hunger, our compassion is excited, as Gabelentz remarks.[22] In the case of the Anglo-Saxons, however, the conclusion we are justified in drawing from their possessing such a great number of words connected with the sea is not, perhaps, that they were a seafaring nation, but rather, as these words are chiefly poetical and not used in prose, that the nation *had been* seafaring, but had given up that life while reminiscences of it were still lingering in their imagination.

51. In many cases we are now unable to see any difference in signification between two or more words, but in the majority of these instances we may assume that even if, perhaps, the Anglo-Saxons in historical times felt no difference, their ancestors did not use them indiscriminately. It is characteristic of primitive peoples

[21] Sweet, *The Practical Study of Language*, 1899, p. 163.
[22] Gabelentz, *Sprachwissenschaft*, 1891, p. 463.

that their languages are highly specialized, so that where
we are contented with one generic word they have several specific terms. The aborigines of Tasmania had a
name for each variety of gum-tree and wattle-tree, etc.,
but they had no equivalent for the expression 'a tree.'
The Mohicans have words for cutting various objects,
but none to convey *cutting* simply. The Zulus have such
words as 'red cow,' 'white cow,' 'brown cow,' etc., but
none for 'cow' generally. In Cherokee, instead of one
word for 'washing' we find different words, according to
what is washed. 'I wash myself,—my head,—the head
of somebody else,—my face,—the face of somebody
else,—my hands or feet,—my clothes,—dishes,—a
child,' etc.[23]

52. Very little has been done hitherto to investi-
gate the exact shades of meaning in Old English words,[24]
but I have little doubt that when we now render a
number of words indiscriminately by 'sword,' they meant
originally distinct kinds of swords, and so in other cases
as well. With regard to washing, we find something
corresponding, though in a lesser degree, to the exuberance of Cherokee, for we have two words, *wacsan*
(*wascan*) and *þwean,* and if we go through all the
examples given in Bosworth and Toller's Dictionary, we
find that the latter word is always applied to the washing of persons (hands, feet, etc.), never to inanimate
objects, while *wascan* is used especially of the washing
of clothes, but also of sheep, of 'the inwards' (of the
victim, Leviticus I, 9 and 13).[25] Observe also that

[23] Jespersen, *Language,* London, 1922, p. 430 ff.

[24] A notable contribution towards this study is L. Schücking,
Untersuchungen zur Bedeutungslehre der angels. Dichtersprache,
Heidelberg, 1915.

[25] In a late text (R. Ben. 59, 7), we find the contrast *agðer ge
fata þwean, ge wæterclaðas wascan,* which does not agree

wascan was originally used in the present tense only (as Kluge infers from *-sk-*)—a clear instance of that restriction in the use of words which is so common in the old stages of the language, but which so often appears unnatural to us.

53. The old poetic language on the whole showed a great many divergences from everyday prose in the choice of words, in the word-forms, and also in the construction of the sentences. King Alfred in his prose always uses the form *het* as the preterit of *hatan*, but when he breaks out occasionally into a few lines of poetry he says *heht* instead. This should not surprise us, for we find the same thing everywhere, and the difference between the dictions of poetry and of prose is perhaps greater in old or more primitive languages than in those most highly developed. In English, certainly, the distance between poetical and prose language was much greater in this first period than it has ever been since. The language of poetry seems to have been to a certain extent identical all over England, a kind of more or less artificial dialect, absorbing forms and words from the different parts of the country where poetry was composed at all, in much the same way as Homer's language had originated in Greece. This hypothesis seems to me to offer a better explanation of the facts than the current theory, according to which the bulk of Old English poetry was written at first in Northumbrian dialect and later translated into West-Saxon with some of the old Anglian forms kept inadvertently—and translated to such an extent that no trace of the originals should

---

exactly with the distinction made above. Curiously enough, in Old Norse, *vaska* is in the Sagas used only of washing the head with some kind of soap. In Danish, as well as in English, *vaske, wash,* is now the only word in actual use.

have been preserved. The very few and short pieces extant in old Northumbrian dialect are easily accounted for, even if we accept the theory of a poetical *koinē* or standard language prevailing in the time when Old English poetry flourished. But the whole question should be taken up by a more competent hand than mine.

54. The external form of Old English poetry was in the main the same as that of Old Norse, Old Saxon, and Old High German poetry; besides definite rules of stress and quantity, which were more regular than might at first appear, but which were not so strict as those of classical poetry, the chief words of each line were tied together by alliteration, that is, they began with the same sound, or, in the case of *sp, st, sc,* with the same sound group. The effect is peculiar, and may be appreciated in such a passage as this (I italicize the alliterative letters):

*Str*æt wæs *st*anfah, *st*ig wisode
*g*umum ætgædere. *G*uðbyrne scan
*h*eard *h*ondlocen, *h*ringiren scir
*s*ong in *s*earwum, þa hie to *s*ele furðum
in hyra *g*ryregeatwum *g*angan swomon.
*S*etton *s*æmeoðe *s*ide scyldas,
*r*ondas *r*egnhearde wiþ þæs *r*ecedes weal;
*b*ugon þa to *b*ence,—*b*yrnan hringdon,
*g*uþsearo *g*umena; *g*aras stodon,
*s*æmanna *s*earo *s*amod ætgædere,
*æ*scholt *u*fan græg; wæs se *i*renbreat
*w*æpnum gewurðad. þa þær *w*lonc hæleþ
*o*retmecgas, æfter *æ*ðelum frægn:
'Hwanon *f*erigeaþ ge *f*ætte scyldas,
*g*ræge syrcan, ond *g*rimhelmas,
*h*eresceafta *h*eap? Ic eom *H*roðgares
*a*r ond *o*mbiht. Ne seah ic *e*lþeodige
þus *m*anige *m*en *m*odiglicran.

*W*en ic þæt ge for *w*lenco,   nalles for *w*ræcsiðum,
ac for *h*igeþrymmum   *H*roðgar sohton.'[26]

55. Very rarely, combined with alliteration, we
find a sort of rime or assonance. In the prose of the
last period of Old English the same artistic means were
often resorted to to heighten the effect, and we find in
Wulfstan's homilies such passages as the following,
where all tricks of phonetic harmony are brought into
play: 'in mordre and on mane, in susle and on sare, in
wean and on wyrmslitum, betweonan deadum and deo-
flum, in bryne and on biternesse, in bealewe and on
bradum ligge, in yrmþum, and on earfeðum, on swylt-
cwale and sarum sorgum, in fyrenum bryne and on
fulnesse, in toða gristbitum and in tintegrum' or again
'þær is êce ece and þær is sorgung and sargung, and a
singal heof; þær is benda bite and dynta dyne, þær is

---

[26] Beowulf, 320 ff.; in W. E. Leonard's rendering:

The street was laid with bright stones;	the road led on the band;
The battle-byrnies shimmered,	the hard, the linked-by-hand
The iron-rings, the gleaming,	amid their armor sang,
Whilst thither, in dread war-gear,	to hall they marched alang;
The ocean-weary warriors	set down their bucklers wide,
Their shields, so hard and hardy,	
They stacked points up, these seamen,	against that House's side;
	their ash-wood, gray-tipped spears;
And bent to bench, as clankéd	their byrnies, battle-gears—
An iron-troop well-weaponed!	Then proud a Dane forthwith
Did of these men-at-arms there	enquire the kin and kith:
'Ye bear these plated bucklers	hither from what realms;
These piléd shafts of onset,	gray sarks, and visored helms?
The Henchman and the Herald	of Hrothgar, lo, am I!
Never so many strangers	I've seen of mood more high.
I ween that it is for prowess,	and not for exile far,
That 't is indeed for glory,	that ye have sought Hrothgar.'

wyrma slite and ealra wædla gripe, þær is wanung and granung, þær is yrmða gehwylc and ealra deofla geþring.'[27]

56. Nor has this love of alliterative word-combinations ever left the language; we find it very often in modern poetry, where however it is always subordinate to end-rime, and we find it in such stock phrases as: 'it can neither *m*ake nor *m*ar me,' '*b*usy as *b*ees' (Chaucer, E 2422), '*p*art and *p*arcel,' '*f*aint and *f*eeble,' '*d*ucks and *d*rakes' (sometimes: 'play dick-duck-drake'; Stevenson, Merry Men, 277), 'what ain't *m*issed ain't *m*ourned' (Pinero, Magistrate, 5), 'as *b*old as *b*rass,' '*f*ree and *f*ranke' (Caxton, Reynard 41), '*b*arnes are *b*lessings' (Shakesp. All's I, 3, 28), 'as *c*ool as a *c*ucumber,' 'as *s*till as (a) *s*tone' (Chaucer, E 121, 'as any stoon,' E 171, 'he stode stone style,' Malory 145), 'over *s*tile and *s*tone' (Chaucer, B 1988), 'from *t*op to *t*oe' ('from the top to toe,' Shakesp. R 3, III, 1, 155), '*m*ight and *m*ain,' '*f*uss and *f*ume,' '*m*anners *m*akyth *m*an,' '*c*are *k*illed a *c*at,' '*r*ack and *r*uin,' '*n*ature and *n*urture' (Shakesp. Tp. IV, 1, 189; English Men of Science, their Nature and Nurture, the title of a book by Galton), etc., etc., even to Thackeray's 'faint fashionable fiddle-faddle and feeble court slipslop.' Alliteration sometimes modifies the meaning of a word, as when we apply *chick*

---

[27] 'In murder and in crime, in torment and grief, in pangs and in snakebites, between dead men and devils, in flames and in torture, in harm and in extensive fire, in misery and labour, in agony and serious sorrows, in blazing flames and in filth, in tooth-gnashing and in torments,' and 'There is eternal ache and sorrow and lamentation, and never-ending grief; there is gnawing of chains and noise of blows; there snakes will bite and all miseries attack; there are groanings and moanings, troubles of every kind and a crowding together of all devils.' Wulfstan, Homilies, ed. by Napier, p. 187, 209. It is worthy of note that these poetical flights occur in descriptions of hell.

to human offspring in 'no chick or child,' or when we
say 'a *labour* of *love*,' without giving to *labour* the shade
of meaning which it generally has as different from
work. The word *foe*, too, which is generally used in
poetry or archaic prose only, is often used in ordinary
prose for the sake of alliteration in connexion with
friend ('Was it an irruption of a friend or a foe?' Meredith, *Egoist*, 439; 'The Danes of Ireland had changed
from foes to friends,' Green, *Short Hist*. 107). Indeed
alliteration comes so natural to English people, that
Tennyson says that 'when I spout my lines first, they
come out so alliteratively that I have sometimes no end
of trouble to get rid of the alliteration.'[28] I take up the
thread of my narrative after this short digression.

[28] *Life*, by his son, Tauchn. ed. II, 285; cf. R. L. Stevenson,
The Art of Writing, p. 31, and what the Danish poet and
metricist, E. v. d. Recke, says to the same effect, *Principerne for
den danske verskunst*, 1881, p. 112; see also the amusing note
by De Quincey, *Opium Eater*, p. 96 (Macmillan's Library of
Engl. Classics): 'Some people are irritated, or even fancy themselves insulted, by overt acts of alliteration, as many people are
by puns. On their account let me say, that although there are
here [in the passage to which the note is appended] eight separate f's in less than half a sentence, this is to be held as pure
accident. In fact, at one time there were nine f's in the original
cast of the sentence, until I, in pity of the affronted people,
substituted *female agent* for *female friend*.' The reader need
not be reminded of the excessive use of alliteration in Euphuism
and of Shakespeare's satire in *Love's Labour's Lost* and *Midsummer Night's Dream*.

CHAPTER IV

The Scandinavians

57. The Old English language, as we have seen, was essentially self-sufficing; its foreign elements were few and did not modify the character of the language as a whole. But we shall now consider three very important factors in the development of the language, three superstructures, as it were, that came to be erected on the Anglo-Saxon foundation, each of them modifying the character of the language, and each preparing the ground for its successor. A Scandinavian element, a French element, and a Latin element now enter largely into the texture of the English language, and as each element is characteristically different from the others, we shall treat them separately. First, then, the Scandinavian element.[1]

[1] The chief works on these loan-words, most of them treating nearly exclusively phonetic questions, are: Erik Björkman, *Scandinavian Loan-Words in Middle English* (Halle, I, 1900, II, 1902), an excellent book; Erik Brate, *Nordische Lehnwörter im Orrmulum* (Beiträge zur Gesch. d. deutschen Sprache X, Halle, 1884); Arnold Wall, *A Contribution towards the Study of the Scandinavian Element in the English Dialects* (Anglia XX, Halle, 1898); G. T. Flom, *Scandinavian Influence on Southern Lowland Scotch* (New York, 1900). The dialectal material of the two last-mentioned treatises is necessarily to a great extent of a doubtful character. See also Kluge in Paul's *Grundriss d. germ. Philol.*, 2nd ed., p. 931 ff. (Strassburg, 1899), Skeat, *Principles of English Etymology*, p. 453 ff. (Oxford, 1887), P. Thorson,

58. The English had resided for about four centuries in the country called after them, and during that time they had had no enemies from abroad. The only wars they had been engaged in were internal struggles between kingdoms belonging to, but not yet feeling themselves as one and the same nation. The Danes were to them not deadly enemies but a brave nation from over the sea, that they felt to be of a kindred race with themselves. The peaceful relations between the two nations may have been more intimate than is now generally supposed. An attempt has been made to show that an interesting but hitherto mysterious Old English poem which is generally ascribed to the eighth century is a translation of a lost Scandinavian poem dealing with an incident in what was later to become the Volsunga Saga.[2] If this were not rather doubtful it would establish a literary intercourse between England and Scandinavia previous to the Viking ages, and therefore accord with the fact that the old Danish legends about King Hrothgar and his beautiful hall Heorot were preserved in England, even more faithfully than by the Danes themselves. Had the poet of *Beowulf* been able to foresee all that his countrymen were destined to suffer at the hands of the Danes, he would have chosen another subject for his great epic, and we should have missed the earliest noble outcome of the sympathy so often displayed by Englishmen for the fortunes of Denmark. But as it is,

---

Anglo-Norse Studies (Amsterdam, 1936), and some other works mentioned below. I have excluded doubtful material; but a few of the words I give as Scandinavian have been considered as native by other writers. In most cases I have been convinced by the reasons given by Björkman.

[2] W. W. Lawrence, *The First Riddle of Cynewulf;* W. H. Schofield, *Signy's Lament.* (Publications of the Modern Language Association of America, vol. XVII, Baltimore, 1902.)

in *Beowulf* no coming events cast their shadow before,[3] and the English nation seems to have been taken entirely by surprise when about 790 the long series of inroads began, in which 'Danes' and 'heathens' became synonyms for murderers and plunderers. At first the strangers came in small troops and disappeared as soon as they had filled their boats with gold and other valuables; but from the middle of the ninth century, 'the character of the attack wholly changed. The petty squadrons which had till now harassed the coast of Britain made way for larger hosts than had as yet fallen on any country in the west; while raid and foray were replaced by the regular campaign of armies who marched to conquer, and whose aim was to settle on the land they won.'[4] Battles were fought with various success, but on the whole the Scandinavians proved the stronger race and made good their footing in their new country. In the peace of Wedmore (878), King Alfred, the noblest and staunchest defender of his native soil, was fain to leave them more than half of what we now call England; all Northumbria, all East Anglia, and one half of Central England made out the district called the Danelaw.

59. Still, the relations between the two races were not altogether hostile. King Alfred not only effected the repulse of the Danes; he also gave us the first geographical description of the countries that the fierce invaders came from, in the passage already referred to

[3] This was written before Schücking (*Beiträge*, 43, 347) had called in question the date usually assigned to *Beowulf* (ab. 700). Schücking thinks it was written ab. 900 at a Scandinavian court in England. See against this R. W. Chambers, *Beowulf*, 2nd ed. (Cambridge, 1932), pp. 322, 397, 487. On different strata in *Beowulf*, see especially W. A. Berendsohn, *Zur Vorgeschichte des Beowulf* (Copenhagen, 1935).

[4] J. R. Green, *A Short History of the English People*, Illustr. ed., p. 87.

(§ 48). Under the year 959, one of the chroniclers says of the Northumbrian king that he was widely revered on account of his piety, but in one respect he was blamed: 'he loved foreign vices too much and gave heathen (i.e., Danish) customs a firm footing in this country, alluring mischievous foreigners to come to this land.' And in the only extant private letter in Old English[5] the unknown correspondent tells his brother Edward that 'it is a shame for all of you to give up the English customs of your fathers and to prefer the customs of heathen men, who grudge you your very life; you show thereby that you despise your race and your forefathers with these bad habits, when you dress shamefully in Danish wise with bared neck and blinded eyes' (with hair falling over the eyes?). We see, then, that the English were ready to learn from, as well as to fight with, the Danes. It is a small but significant fact that in the glorious patriotic war-poem written shortly after the battle of Maldon (993) which it celebrates, we find for the first time one of the most important Scandinavian loan-words, *to call;* this shows how early the linguistic influence of the Danes began to be felt.

60. A great number of Scandinavian families settled in England never to return, especially in Norfolk, Suffolk and Lincolnshire, but also in Yorkshire, Northumberland, Cumberland, Westmorland, etc. Numerous names of places, ending in *-by, -thorp (-torp), -beck, -dale, -thwaite,* etc., bear witness to the preponderance of the invaders in great parts of England, as do also many names of persons found in English from about 1000 A.D.[6] But these foreigners were not felt by the

[5] Edited by Kluge, Engl. Studien VIII, 62.

[6] Björkman, *Nordische Personennamen in England* (Halle, 1910), H. Lindkvist, *Middle-English Place-Names of Scandi-*

natives to be foreigners in the same manner as the English themselves had been looked upon as foreigners by the Kelts. As Green has it, 'when the wild burst of the storm was over, land, people, government, reappeared unchanged. England still remained England; the conquerors sank quietly into the mass of those around them; and Woden yielded without a struggle to Christ. The secret of this difference between the two invasions was that the battle was no longer between men of different races. It was no longer a fight between Briton and German, between Englishman and Welshman. The life of these northern folk was in the main the life of the earlier Englishmen. Their customs, their religion, their social order were the same; they were in fact kinsmen bringing back to an England that had forgotten its origins the barbaric England of its pirate forefathers. Nowhere over Europe was the fight so fierce, because nowhere else were the combatants men of one blood and one speech. But just for this reason the fusion of the northmen with their foes was nowhere so peaceful and so complete.[7] It should be remembered, too, that it was a Dane, King Knut, who achieved what every English ruler had failed to achieve, the union of the whole of England into one peaceful realm.

61. King Knut was a Dane, and in the Saxon Chronicle the invaders were always called Danes, but from other sources we know that there were Norwegians too among the settlers. Attempts have been made to

---

navian Origin (Uppsala, 1912), E. Ekwall, *Scandinavians and Celts in the North-West of England* (Lund, 1918), and in *Introduction to the Survey of Engl. Place-Names,* I (Cambridge, 1924). According to Ekwall, the Scandinavians in the North-West did not come direct from Norway, but through Ireland.

[7] J. R. Green, *A Short History of the English People,* Illustr. ed., p. 87.

decide by linguistic tests which of the two nations had the greater influence in England,[8] a question beset with considerable difficulties and which need not detain us here. Suffice it to say that some words, such as ME. *boun,* Mod. *bound* 'ready' (to go to), *busk, boon, addle,* point rather to a Norwegian origin, while others such as *-by* in place names, *drown,* ME. *sum* 'as,' agree better with Danish forms. In the great majority of cases, however, the Danish and Norwegian forms were at that time either completely or nearly identical, so that no decision as to the special homeland of the English loans is warranted. In the present work I therefore leave the question open, quoting Danish or ON. (Old Norse, practically = Old Icelandic) forms according as it is most convenient in each case, meaning simply Scandinavian.[9]

62. In order rightly to estimate the Scandinavian influence it is very important to remember how great the similarity was between Old English and Old Norse. To those who know only modern English and modern Danish, this resemblance is greatly obscured, first on account of the dissimilarities that are unavoidable when two nations live for nearly one thousand years with very

[8] Brate thought the loan-words exclusively Danish; Kluge, Wall, and Björkman consider some of them Danish, others Norwegian, though in details they arrive at different results. See Björkman, *Zur dialektischen Provenienz der nordischen Lehnwörter im Englischen,* Språkvetensk. sällskapets förhandlingar, 1898–1901, Uppsala, and his *Scand. Loan-Words,* p. 281 ff. Cf. also Ekwall as quoted on p. 58, and J. Hoops, *Englische Sprachkunde* (Stuttgart, 1923), p. 26 f.

[9] Björkman's final words are: 'These facts would seem to point to the conclusion that a considerable number of Danes were found everywhere in the Scandinavian settlements, while the existence in great numbers of Norwegians was confined to certain definite districts.'

little intercommunication, and when there is, accordingly, nothing to counterbalance the natural tendency towards differentiation, and secondly on account of a powerful foreign influence to which each nation has in the meantime been subjected, English from French, and Danish from Low German. But even now we can see the essential conformity between the two languages, which in those times was so much greater as each stood so much nearer to the common source. An enormous number of words were then identical in the two languages, so that we should now have been utterly unable to tell which language they had come from if we had had no English literature before the invasion; nouns such as *man, wife, father, folk, mother, house, thing, life, sorrow, winter, summer,* verbs like *will, can, meet, come, bring, hear, see, think, smile, ride, stand, sit, set, spin,* adjectives and adverbs like *full, wise, well, better, best, mine* and *thine, over* and *under,* etc. etc. The consequence was that an Englishman would have no great difficulty in understanding a viking—nay, we have positive evidence that Norse people looked upon the English language as one with their own. On the other hand, Wulfstan speaks of the invaders as 'people who do not know your language' (ed. Napier, p. 295), and in many cases indeed the words were already so dissimilar that they were easily distinguished, for instance, when they contained an original *ai,* which in OE. had become long *a* (OE. *swan* = ON. *sveinn*), or *au,* which in OE. had become *ea* (OE. *leas* = ON. *lauss, louss*), or *sk,* which in English became *sh* (OE. *scyrte,* now *shirt* = ON. *skyrta*).

63. But there are, of course, many words to which no such reliable criteria apply, and the difficulty in deciding the origin of words is further complicated by the

fact that the English would often modify a word, when
adopting it, according to some more or less vague feeling of the English sound that corresponded generally
to this or that Scandinavian sound. Just as the name of
the English king Æðelred Eadgares sunu is mentioned
in the Norse saga of Gunnlaugr Ormstunga as Aðalráðr
Játgeirsson, in the same manner *shift* is an Anglicized
form of Norse *skipta*;[10] ON. *brúðlaup* 'wedding' was
modified into *brydlop* (cf. OE. *bryd* 'bride'; a consistent
Anglicizing would be *brydhleap*); *tiðende* is unchanged
in Orrms *tiþennde,* but was generally changed into
tiding(s), cf. OE. *tid* and the common English ending
-ing; ON. *þjónusta* 'service' appears as *þeonest, þenest,*
and *þegnest;* ON. words with the negative prefix *ú* are
made into English *un-,* e.g. *untime* 'unseasonableness,'
unbain (ON. *úbeinn*) 'not ready,' *unrad* or *unræd* 'bad
counsel';[11] cf. also *wæpnagetæc* below, and others.

64. Sometimes the Scandinavians gave a fresh
lease of life to obsolescent or obsolete native words.
The preposition *till,* for instance, is found only once or
twice in OE. texts belonging to the pre-Scandinavian
period, but after that time it begins to be exceedingly
common in the North, from whence it spreads southward; it was used as in Danish with regard to both time
and space and it is still so used in Scotch. Similarly
dale (OE. *dæl*) 'appears to have been reinforced from
Norse (*dal*), for it is in the North that the word is a
living geographical name' (NED.), and *barn,* Scotch
bairn (OE. *bearn*) would probably have disappeared in
the North, as it did in the South, if it had not been
strengthened by the Scandinavian word. The verb *blend,*

---

[10] In ME. forms with *sk* are also found; Björkman, p. 126.

[11] Though the Scand. form is also found in a few instances:
oulist 'listless,' *oumautin* 'swoon.'

too, seems to owe its vitality (as well as its vowel) to Old Norse, for *blandan* was very rare in Old English.

65. We also see in England a phenomenon which, I think, is paralleled nowhere else to such an extent, namely, the existence side by side for a long time, sometimes for centuries, of two slightly differing forms for the same word, one the original English form and the other Scandinavian. In the following the first form is the native one, the form after the dash the imported one.

66. In some cases both forms survive in standard speech, though, as a rule, they have developed slightly different meanings: *whole* (formerly *hool*)—*hale;* both were united in the old phrase 'hail and hool' | *no—nay;* the latter is now used only to add an amplifying remark ('it is enough, nay too much'), but formerly it was used to answer a question, though it was not so strong a negative as *no* ('Is it true? Nay.' 'Is it not true? No') | *rear—raise* | *from—fro,* now used only in 'to and fro' | *shirt—skirt* | *shot—scot* | *shriek—screak, screech* | *true —trigg,* 'faithful, neat, tidy' | *edge—egg* vb. ('to egg on,' 'to incite'). OE. *leas* survives only in the suffix *-less* (nameless, etc.), while the Scand. *loose* has entirely supplanted it as an independent word.

67. In other cases, the Scandinavian form survives in dialects only, while the other belongs to the literary language: *dew—dag,* 'dew, thin rain'; vb. 'to drizzle' | *leap—loup* | *neat—nowt,* 'cattle' | *church—kirk* | *churn —kirn* | *chest—kist* | *mouth—mun* | *yard—garth,* 'a small piece of enclosed ground.' All these dialectal forms belong to Scotland or the North of England.

68. As a rule, however, one of the forms has in course of time been completely crowded out by the other. The surviving form is often the native form, as in the following instances: *goat—gayte* | *heathen—*

heythen, haithen | *loath—laith* | *grey—gra, gro* | *few*
—fa, fo | *ash(es)—ask* | *fish—fisk* | *naked—naken* |
yarn—garn | *bench—bennk* | *star—sterne* | *worse—*
werre. Similarly the Scand. *thethen, hethen, hwethen* are
generally supposed to have been discarded in favour of
the native forms, OE. *þanon, heonan, hwanon,* to which
was added an adverbial *s: thence, hence, whence;* but
in reality these modern forms may just as well be due to
the Scandinavian ones; for the loss of *th,* cf. *since* from
sithence (*sithens,* OE. *siþþan + s*).

69. This then leads us on to those instances in
which the intruder succeeded in ousting the legitimate
heir. Caxton, in a well-known passage, gives us a graphic
description of the struggle between the native *ey* and the
Scandinavian *egg:*

And certaynly our langage now used varyeth ferre
from that whiche was used and spoken when I was
borne. For we englysshe men ben borne under the
domynacyon of the mone, whiche is never stedfaste, but
ever waverynge, wexynge one season, and waneth &
dyscreaseth another season. And that comyn englysshe
that is spoken in one shyre varyeth from a nother. In so
moche that in my dayes happened that certayn mar-
chauntes were in a shippe in tamyse, for to have sayled
over the see into zelande. And for lacke of wynde, thei
taryed atte forlond, and wente to lande for to refreshe
them. And one of theym named sheffelde,[12] a mercer,
cam in-to an hows and axed for mete; and specyally he
axyd after eggys. And the goode wyf answerde, that she
coude speke no frenshe. And the marchaunt was angry,
for he also coude speke no frenshe, but wolde have
hadde egges, and she understode hym not. And thenne
at laste a nother sayd that he wolde have eyren. Then
the good wyf sayd that she understod hym wel. Loo,

---

[12] Probably a north-country man.

what sholde a man in thyse dayes now wryte, egges or
eyren. Certaynly it is harde to playse every man, by
cause of dyversite & chaunge of langage.[13]

Very soon after this was written, the Old English
forms *ey, eyren* finally went out of use.

70. Among other word-pairs similarly fated may
be mentioned: OE. *a,* ME. *o,* 'ever'—*ay* (both were
found together in the frequent phrase 'for ay and oo'
| *tho* (cf. *those*)—*they* | *theigh, thah, theh* and other
forms—*though* | *swon*—*swain* (boatswain, etc.) | *ibirde*
—*birth* | *eie*—*awe* | *þunresdæi*—*Thursday* | *in* (on) *þe
lifte*—*on lofte,* now *aloft* | *swuster*—*sister* | *chetel*—
kettle; and finally not a few words with English *y* over
against Scand. *g: yete*—*get* | *yeme,* 'care, heed'—
gom(e), dialectal *gaum,* 'sense, wit, tact' | *yelde*—*guild,*
'fraternity, association' | *yive* or *yeve*—*give* | *yift*—*gift.*
In this last-mentioned word *gift,* not only is the initial
sound due to Scandinavian, but also the modern meaning, for the Old English word meant 'the price paid by
a suitor in consideration of receiving a woman to wife'
and in the plural 'marriage, wedding.' No subtler linguistic influence can be imagined than this, where a
word has been modified both with regard to pronunciation and meaning, and curiously enough has by that
process been brought nearer to the verb from which it
was originally derived (*give*).

71. In some words the old native form has survived, but has adopted the signification attached in
Scandinavian to the corresponding word; thus *dream*
in OE. meant 'joy,' but in ME. the modern meaning of
'dream' was taken over from ON., *draumr,* Dan., *dröm;*

analogous cases are *bread* (OE. *bread,* 'fragment'), *bloom* (OE. *bloma,* 'mass of metal'?). In one word, this same process of sense-shifting has historical significance; the OE. *eorl* meant vaguely a 'nobleman' or more loosely 'a brave warrior' or 'man' generally; but under Knut it took over the meaning of the Norse *jarl,* 'an under-king' or governor of one of the great divisions of the realm, thus paving the way for the present significance of *earl* as one of the grades in the (French) scale of rank. OE. *freond* meant only 'friend,' whereas ON. *frœndi,* Dan. *frœnde* means 'kinsman,' but in Orrm and other ME. texts the word sometimes has the Scand. meaning[14] and so it has to this day in Scotch and American dialects (see many instances in J. Wright's Dialect Dictionary, e.g. 'We are near friends, but we don't speak'); the Scotch proverb, 'Friends agree best at a distance' corresponds to the Danish 'Frænde er frænde værst.' OE. *dwellan* or *dwelian* meant only 'to lead astray, lead into error, thwart' or intr. 'to go astray';[15] the intransitive meanings, 'to tarry, abide, remain in a place,' which correspond with the Scandinavian meanings, are not found till the beginning of the 13th century. OE. *ploh* is found only with the meaning of 'a measure of land' (still in Scotch *pleuch*), but in ME. it came to mean the implement *plough* (OE. *sulh*) as in ON. *plógr.* OE. *holm* meant 'ocean,' but the modern word owes its signification of 'islet, flat ground by a river' to Scandinavian *holmr.*

72. These were cases of native words conforming

[14] Saxon Chron., 1135, which is given in the NED. as an instance of this meaning, appears to me to be doubtful.

[15] *Dwelode,* in Ælfric, *Homilies,* 1, 384, is wrongly translated by Thorpe 'continued,' so that Kluge is wrong in giving this passage as the earliest instance of the modern meaning; it means 'wandered, went astray.'

to foreign speech habits; in other instances the Scandinavians were able to place words at the disposal of the English which agreed so well with other native words as to be readily associated with them, nay which were felt to be fitter expressions for the ideas than the Old English words and therefore survived. *Death* (deaþ) and *dead* are OE. words, but the corresponding verbs were *steorfan* and *sweltan;* now it is obvious that Danish *deya* (now dø) was more easily associated with the noun and the adjective than the old verbs, and accordingly it was soon adopted (*deyen,* now *die*), while *sweltan* was discarded and the other verb acquired the more special signification of *starving. Sæte* (Mod.E. *seat*) was adopted because it was at once associated with the verbs *to sit* and *to set.* The most important importation of this kind was that of the pronominal forms *they, them* and *their,* which entered readily into the system of English pronouns beginning with the same sound (*the, that, this*) and were felt to be more distinct than the old native forms which they supplanted. Indeed these were liable to constant confusion with some forms of the singular number (*he, him, her*) after the vowels had become obscured, so that *he* and *hie, him* and *heom, her* (*hire*) and *heora* could no longer be kept easily apart. We thus find the obscured form, which was written *a* (or *'a*), in use for 'he' till the beginning of the 16th century (compare the dialectal use, for instance, in Tennyson's 'But Parson a cooms an' a goäs'), and in use for 'she' and for 'they' till the end of the 14th century. Such a state of things would naturally cause a great number of ambiguities; but although the *th*-forms must consequently be reckoned a great advantage to the language, it took a long time before the old forms were finally displaced, nay, the dative *hem* still

survives in the form *'em* ('take 'em'), which is now by
people ignorant of the history of the language taken
to be a shortened *them; her* 'their' is the only form for
the possessive of the plural found in Chaucer (who says
they in the nominative) and there are two or three instances in Shakespeare. One more Scandinavian pronoun is *same,* which was speedily associated with the
native adverb *same* (*swa, same,* 'similarly'). Other
words similarly connected with the native stock are
want (adj. and vb.), which reminded the English of
their own *wan* 'wanting,' *wanna* 'want' and *wanian*
'wane, lessen,' and *ill,* which must have appeared like
a stunted form of *evil,* especially to a Scotchman who
had made his own *devil* into *deil* and *even* into *ein.*

73. If now we try to find out by means of the loan-
word test (see above, § 31) what were the spheres of
human knowledge or activity in which the Scandinavians
were able to teach the English, the first thing that strikes
us is that the very earliest stratum of loan-words,[16]
words which by the way were soon to disappear again
from the language,[17] relate to war and more particularly
to the navy: *orrest* 'battle,' *fylcian* 'to collect, marshal,'
liþ 'fleet,' *barda, cnear, scegþ* different sorts of warships,
ha 'rowlock.' This agrees perfectly well with what the
Saxon Chronicle relates about the English being inferior
to the heathen in ship-building, until King Alfred un-
dertook to construct a new kind of warship.[18]

[16] See Björkman, p. 5.

[17] They were naturally supplanted by French words; see below.

[18] ON. *bāt* (boat) is generally supposed to be borrowed from
OE. *bāt,* but according to E. Wadstein, *Friserna och forntida
handelsvägar* (Göteborg, 1920), both were borrowed from
Frisian. The latest treatment of this phonetically difficult word
is by J. Sverdrup (*Maalogminne,* 1922), who thinks that it is a
native Scandinavian word.

74. Next, we find a great many Scandinavian law-terms; they have been examined by Professor Steenstrup in his well-known work on 'Danelag.'[19] He has there been able, in an astonishing number of cases, to show conclusively that the Vikings modified the legal ideas of the Anglo-Saxons, and that numerous new law-terms sprang up at the time of the Scandinavian settlements which had previously been utterly unknown. Most of them were simply the Danish or Norse words, others were Anglicizings, as when ON. *vapnatak* was made into *wæpnagetæc* (later *wapentake*) or when ON. *heimsokn* appears as *hamsocn* 'house-breaking or the fine for that offence,' or *saklauss* as *sacleas* 'innocent.' The most important of these juridical imports is the word *law* itself, known in England from the 10th century in the form *lagu,* which must have been the exact Scandinavian form, as it is the direct forerunner of the ON. form *lǫg,* ODan. *logh.*[20] *By-law* is now felt to be a compound of the preposition *by* and *law,* but originally *by* was the Danish *by* 'town, village' (found in Derby, Whitby, etc.), and the Danish genitive-ending is preserved in the other English form *byr-law.* Other words belonging to this class are *niðing* 'criminal, wretch,' *thriding* 'third part,' preserved in the mutilated form *riding,*[21] *carlman* 'man' as opposed to woman, *bonda* or *bunda* 'peasant,' *lysing* 'freedman,' *þræll,* Mod. *thrall,*

---

[19] Copenhagen, 1882 (= Normannerne IV).

[20] The OE. word was *æ* or *æw,* which meant 'marriage' as well and was restricted to that sense in late OE., until it was displaced by the French word.

[21] *North-thriding* being heard as *North-riding;* in the case of the two other ridings of Yorkshire, *East-thriding* and *West-thriding,* the *th*-sound was assimilated to the preceding *t,* the result in all three cases being the same misdivision of the word ('metanalysis').

mall 'suit, agreement,' *wiþermal* 'counterplea, defence,'
seht 'agreement,' *stefnan* 'summon,' *crafian* now *crave,*
landcop or Anglicized *landceap* and *lahcop* or *lahceap*
(for the signification see Steenstrup, p. 192 ff.); *ran*
'robbery'; *infangenþeof* later *infangthief* 'jurisdiction
over a thief apprehended within the manor.' It will be
seen that with the exception of *law, bylaw, thrall* and
crave—the least juridical of them all—these Danish
law-terms have disappeared from the language as a
simple consequence of the Norman conquerors taking
into their own hands the courts of justice and legal
affairs generally. Steenstrup's research, which is largely
based on linguistic facts, may be thus summarized. The
Scandinavian settlers reorganized the administration of
the realm and based it on a uniform and equable division of the country; taxes were imposed and collected
after the Scandinavian pattern; instead of the lenient
criminal law of former times, a virile and powerful law
was introduced which was better capable of intimidat-
ing fierce and violent natures. More stress was laid on
personal honour, as when a sharp line was drawn between stealthy or clandestine crimes and open crimes
attributable to obstinacy or vindictiveness. Commerce,
too, was regulated so as to secure trade.

75. Apart from these legal words it would be very
difficult to point out any single group of words belonging
to one and the same sphere from which a superiority
of any description might be concluded. *Window* is borrowed from *vindauga* ('wind-eye'); but we dare not
infer that the northern settlers taught the English anything in architecture, for the word stands quite alone;
besides, OE. had another word for 'window,' which is
also based on the eye-shape of the windows in the old
wooden houses: *eagþyrel* 'eye-hole' (cf. *nosþyrel* 'nos-

tril').[22] Nor does the borrowing of *steak,* ME. *steyke* from ON. *steik,* prove any superior cooking on the part of the Vikings. But it is possible that the Scandinavian *knives* (ME. *knif* from Scand. *knif*) were better than or at any rate different from those of other nations, for the word was introduced into French (*canif*) as well as into English.

76. If, then, we go through the lists of loan-words, looking out for words from which conclusions as to the state of culture of the two nations might be drawn, we shall be doomed to disappointment, for they all seem to denote objects and actions of the most commonplace description and certainly do not represent any new set of ideas hitherto unknown to the people adopting them. We find such everyday nouns as *husband, fellow, sky, skull, skin, wing, haven, root, skill, anger, gate,*[23] etc. Among the adjectives adopted from Scand. we find *meek, low, scant, loose, odd,*[24] *wrong, ill, ugly, rotten.* The impression produced perhaps by this list that only unpleasant adjectives came into English from Scandinavia, is easily shown to be wrong, for *happy* and *seemly* too are derived from Danish roots, not to speak of *stor,* which was common in Middle English for 'great,' and dialectal adjectives like *glegg* 'clear-sighted, clever,' *heppen,* 'neat, tidy,' *gain* 'direct, handy' (Sc.

[22] Most European languages use the Lat. *fenestra* (G. *fenster,* Dutch *venster,* Welsh *ffenester*), which was also imported from French into English as *fenester,* in use from 1290 to 1548. Slavis languages have *okno,* derived from *oko* 'eye.' (On the eye-shape of old windows, see R. Meringer, Indogerm. Forschungen, XVI, 1904, p. 125.)

[23] *Gate* 'way, road, street,' frequent in some northern towns in the names of streets, frequent also in ME. adverbial phrases *algate, anothergate*(*s*) (corrupted into *anotherguess*), etc. In the sense 'manner of going' it is now spelt *gait.*

[24] Cf. North-Jutland dialect (Vendsyssel) *oj* 'odd (number).'

and North E. the gainest way, ON. hinn gegnsta veg,
Dan., den genneste vej). The only thing common to the
adjectives, then, is seen to be their extreme commonplaceness, and the same impression is confirmed by the
verbs, as for instance, *thrive, die, cast, hit, take, call,
want, scare, scrape, scream, scrub, scowl, skulk, bask,
drown, ransack, gape, guess* (doubtful), etc. To these
must be added numerous words preserved only in dialects (north country and Scotch) such as *lathe* 'barn'
Dan. *lade, hoast* 'cough' Dan. *hoste, flit* 'move' Dan.
flytte, gar 'make, do' Dan. *göre, lait* 'search for' Dan.
lede, red up 'to tidy' Dan. *rydde op, keek in* 'peep in,'
ket 'carrion, horseflesh, tainted flesh, rubbish,' originally
'flesh, meat' as Dan. *köd*, etc., all of them words belonging to the same familiar sphere, and having nothing
about them that might be called technical or indicative
of a higher culture. The same is true of that large class
of words which have been mentioned above (§ 65–72),
where the Scandinavians did not properly bring the word
itself, but modified either the form or the signification
of a native word; among them we have seen such everyday words as *get, give, sister, loose, birth, awe, bread,
dream*, etc.[25] It is precisely the most indispensable
elements of the language that have undergone the
strongest Scandinavian influence, and this is raised into
certainty when we discover that a certain number of
those grammatical words, the small coin of language,
which Chinese grammarians term 'empty words,' and
which are nowhere else transferred from one language
to another, have been taken over from Danish into

[25] It is noticeable, too, that the native word *heaven* has been
more and more restricted to the figurative and religious accepta-
tion, while *sky* is used of the visible firmament, a meaning it
has in Jutlandish dialects: the ordinary Danish meaning is
'cloud.'

English: pronouns like *they, them, their, the same* and probably *both;* a modal verb like Scotch *maun, mun* (ON. *munu,* Dan. *mon, monne*); comparatives like *minne* 'lesser,' *min* 'less,' *helder* 'rather'; pronominal adverbs like *hethen, thethen, whethen* 'hence, thence, whence,' *samen* 'together'; conjunctions like *though, oc* 'and,' *sum,* which for a long time seemed likely to displace the native *swa* (*so*) after a comparison, until it was itself displaced by *eallswa* > *as;* prepositions like *fro* and *till* (see above, § 64).[26]

77. It is obvious that all these non-technical words can show us nothing about mental or industrial superiority; they do not bear witness to the currents of civilization; what was denoted by them cannot have been new to the English; we have here no new ideas, only new names. Does that mean, then, that the loan-word test which we are able to apply elsewhere fails in this one case, and that linguistic facts can tell us nothing about the reciprocal relations of the two races? No; on the contrary, the suggestiveness of these loans leaves nothing to be desired, they are historically significant enough. If the English loan-words in this period extend to spheres where other languages do not borrow, if the Scandinavian and the English languages were woven more intimately together, the reason must be a more intimate fusion of the two nations than is seen anywhere else. They fought like brothers and afterwards settled down peacefully, like brothers, side by side. The numbers of the Danish and Norwegian settlers must have been considerable, else they would have disappeared without leaving such traces in the language.

---

[26] Another preposition, *umbe,* was probably to a large extent due to Scandinavian, the native form being *ymbe, embe;* but perhaps in some texts *u* in *umbe* may represent the vowel [y].

78. It might at the first blush seem reasonable to
think that what was going on among Scandinavian
settlers in England was parallel to what we see going
on now in the United States. But there is really no great
similarity between the two cases. The language of Scandinavian and other settlers in America is often a curious
mixture, but it is very important to notice that it is
Danish or Norwegian, sprinkled with English words:
'han har fencet sin farm og venter en god krop' he has
fenced his farm and expects a good crop; 'lad os krosse
streeten' let us cross the street; 'tag det træ' take that
tray; 'hun suede ham i courten for 25,000 daler,' etc.
But this is *toto cœlo* different from the English language
of the Middle Ages. And if we do not take into account
those districts where Scandinavians constitute the im-
mense majority of the population and keep up their old
speech as pure as circumstances will permit, the children or at any rate the children's children of the immigrants speak English, and very pure English too,
without any Danish admixture. The English language of
America has no loan-words worth mentioning from
the languages of the thousands and thousands of Germans, Scandinavians, French, Poles and others that
have settled there. Nor are the reasons far to seek.[27]
The immigrants come in small groups and find their
predecessors half, or more than half, Americanized;
those belonging to the same country cannot, accordingly,
maintain their nationality collectively; they come in
order to gain a livelihood, generally in subordinate posi-
tions where it is important to each of them separately

---

[27] See G. Hempl's paper on *Language-Rivalry* quoted above,
p. 35. Hempl's very short mention of the Scandinavians in England is, perhaps, the least satisfactory portion of his paper; none
of his classes apply to our case.

to be as little different as possible from his new surroundings, in garb, in manners, and in language. The
faults each individual commits in talking English, therefore, can have no consequences of lasting importance,
and at any rate his children are in most respects situated
like the children of the natives and learn the same
language in essentially the same manner. In old times,
of course, many a Dane in England would speak his
mother-tongue with a large admixture of English, but
that has no significance in linguistic history, for in course
of time the descendants of the immigrants would no
longer learn Scandinavian as their mother-tongue, but
English. But that which is important is the fact of the
English themselves intermingling their own native speech
with Scandinavian elements. Now the manner in which
this is done shows us that the culture or civilization of
the Scandinavian settlers cannot have been of a higher
order than that of the English, for then we should have
seen in the loan-words special groups of technical terms
indicative of this superiority. Neither can their state
of culture have been much inferior to that of the English,
for in that case they would have adopted the language
of the natives without appreciably influencing it. This is
what happened with the Goths in Spain, with the Franks
in France and with the Danes in Normandy, in all of
which cases the Germanic tongues were absorbed into
the Romanic languages.[28] It is true that the Scandi-

[28] It is instructive to contrast the old speech-mixture in England with what has been going on for the last two centuries in
the Shetland Islands. Here the old Norwegian dialect ('Norn')
has perished as a consequence of the natives considering it more
genteel to speak English (Scotch). All common words of their
speech now are English, but they have retained a certain number of Norn words, all of them technical, denoting different
species of fish, fishing implements, small parts of the boat or of
the house and its primitive furniture, those signs in clouds, etc.,

navians were, for a short time at least, the rulers of
England, and we have found in the juridical loan-words
linguistic corroboration of this fact; but the great majority of the settlers did not belong to the ruling class.
Their social standing must have been, on the whole,
slightly superior to the average of the English, but the
difference cannot have been great, for the bulk of
Scandinavian words are of a purely democratic character. This is clearly brought out by a comparison with
the French words introduced in the following centuries,
for here language confirms what history tells us, that
the French represent the rich, the ruling, the refined,
the aristocratic element in the English nation. How different is the impression made by the Scandinavian loan-
words. They are homely expressions for things and actions of everyday importance; their character is utterly
democratic. The difference is also shown by so many
of the French words having never penetrated into the
speech of the people, so that they have been known
and used only by the 'upper ten,' while the Scandinavian
ones are used by high and low alike; their shortness too
agrees with the monosyllabic character of the native
stock of words, consequently they are far less felt as
foreign elements than many French words; in fact, in
many statistical calculations of the proportion of native
to imported words in English, Scandinavian words have
been more or less inadvertently included in the native
elements. Just as it is impossible to speak or write in
English about higher intellectual or emotional subjects

---

from which the weather was forecast at sea, technicalities of
sheep rearing, nicknames for things which appear to them ludicrous or ridiculous, etc.—all of them significant of the language
of a subjugated and poor population. (J. Jakobsen, *Det norrøne
sprog på Shetland*, Copenhagen, 1879.)

or about fashionable mundane matters without drawing largely upon the French (and Latin) elements, in the same manner Scandinavian words will crop up together with the Anglo-Saxon ones in any conversation on the thousand nothings of daily life or on the five or six things of paramount importance to high and low alike. An Englishman cannot *thrive* or be *ill* or *die* without Scandinavian words; they are to the language what *bread* and *eggs* are to the daily fare. To this element of his language an Englishman might apply what Wordsworth says of the daisy:

Thou unassuming common-place
Of Nature, with that homely face
And yet with something of a grace
    Which Love makes for thee!

79. The form in which the words were borrowed occasions very few remarks. Those nouns which in Scand. had the nominative ending -*r*, did not keep it, the kernel only of the word (= accus.) being taken over. In one instance the Norse genitive-ending appears in English; the Norse phrase *á náttar þeli* 'in the middle of the night' (*þel* means 'power, strength') was Anglicized into *on nighter tale* (Cursor Mundi), or *bi nighter tale* (Havelock, Chaucer, etc.). The -*t* in neuters of adjectives, that distinctive Scandinavian trait, is found in *scant,*[29] *want* and (*a*)*thwart*. Most Norse verbs have the weak inflexion in English, as might be expected (e.g., *die*, which in Old Scand. was a strong verb), but there are some noteworthy exceptions, *take, rive, thrive*, that are strongly inflected as in Scand. There is at least one interesting word with the Scand.

[29] Properly *skammt*, neuter of *skammr* 'short'; the derived verb *skemta*, Dan. *skemte* 'joke' is found in ME. *skemten*.

passive voice in -sk (from the reflexive pronoun sik):
busk[30] (and bask[31]?) but in English they are treated
like active forms. The shortness of the sk-forms may
have led to their being taken over as inseparable wholes,
for ON. ǫðlask and þrívask lost the reflexive ending in
English addle 'acquire, earn' and thrive.[32]

As the Scandinavians and the English could understand one another without much difficulty it was natural that many niceties of grammar should be sac-
rificed, the intelligibility of either tongue coming to
depend mainly on its mere vocabulary.[33] So when we
find that the wearing away and levelling of grammatical forms in the regions in which the Danes chiefly
settled was a couple of centuries in advance of the
same process in the more southern parts of the country,
the conclusion does not seem unwarrantable that this
acceleration of the tempo of linguistic simplification is
due to the settlers, who did not care to learn English
correctly in every minute particular and who certainly
needed no such accuracy in order to make themselves
understood.

80. With regard to syntax our want of adequate
early texts in Scandinavia as well as in North England
makes it impossible for us to state anything very definite; but the nature of those loans which we are able

[30] ON. búa-sk 'prepare oneself.'

[31] ON. baða-sk 'bathe oneself' (doubtful).

[32] On the form of Scandinavian words, see also Ekwall, *Anglia
Beiblatt*, 21, 47.

[33] Jespersen, *Chapters on English*, p. 37. Compare the explanation of the similar simplification of Dutch in South Africa
given by H. Meyer, *Die Sprache der Buren* (Göttingen, 1901),
p. 16.—E. Classen, *Mod. Language Review*, 14, 94, thinks that
the prevalence of the plural ending -s over -n is due to the
Danes, who had no pl. in -n and whose -r was similar to s.

to verify, warrants the conclusion that the intimate fusion of the two languages must certainly have influenced syntactical relations, and when we find in later times numerous striking correspondences between English and Danish, it seems probable that some at least of them date from the Viking settlements. It is true, for instance, that relative clauses without any pronoun are found in very rare cases in Old English; but they do not become common till the Middle English period, when they abound; the use of these clauses is subject to the same restrictions in both languages, so that in ninety out of a hundred instances where an Englishman leaves out the relative pronoun, a Dane would be able to do likewise, and vice versa. The rules for the omission or retention of the conjunction *that* are nearly identical. The use of *will* and *shall* in Middle English corresponds pretty nearly with Scandinavian; if in Old English an auxiliary was used to express futurity, it was generally *sceal,* just as in modern Dutch (*zal*); *wile* was rare. In Modern English the older rules have been greatly modified, but in many cases where English commentators on Shakespeare note divergences from modern usage, a Dane would have used the same verb as Shakespeare. Furness, in his note to the sentence, 'Besides it should appear' (Merch. III, 2, 289 = 275 Globe ed.), writes: 'It is not easy to define this "should." . . . The Elizabethan use of *should* is to me always difficult to analyse. Compare Stephano's question about Caliban: Where the devil should he learn our language?' Now, a Dane would say 'det skulde synes,' and 'Hvor fanden skulde han lære vort sprog?' Abbott (Shakesp. Grammar, § 319) says 'There is a difficulty in the expression "perchance I will"; but, from its constant recurrence, it would seem to be a regular idiom'; a Dane, in the three quotations given, would say *vil*. And similarly in other instances. 'He could have done it' agrees with 'han kunde have gjort det' as against 'er hätte es tun können' (and French 'il aurait pu le faire'), and the Scotch idiom 'He wad na wrang'd the vera Deil' (Burns), 'ye wad thought Sir Arthur had a pleasure in it' (Scott), where Caxton and the Elizabethans could also omit *have,* has an exact parallel in Danish 'vilde gjort,' etc.[34] Other points in syntax might perhaps be ascribed to Scandinavian influence, such as the universal position of the genitive case before its noun (where Old English like German placed it very often after it); but in these delicate matters it is not safe to assert too much, as in fact many similarities may have been independently developed in both languages.[35]

[34] Jespersen, *Mod. Engl. Grammar,* IV, 10, 9.

[35] On cultural and literary relations between Scandinavia and England see H. G. Leach. *Angevin Britain and Scandinavia* (Harvard University Press, 1921). But when it is said (p. 20) that a Danish farmer from West Jutland has no trouble in keeping up a friendly conversation with a Yorkshireman, credence is given to a popular belief without any basis in facts. F. M. Stenton's paper, *The Danes in England* (British Academy, 1927) deals in a very able way with the cultural side of the Danish settlements.

CHAPTER V

The French

81. If with regard to the Scandinavian invasion historical documents were so scarce that the linguistic evidence drawn from the number and character of the loan-words was a very important supplement to our historical knowledge of the circumstances, the same cannot be said of the Norman Conquest. The Normans, much more than the Danes, were felt as an alien race; their occupation of the country attracted much more notice and lasted much longer; they became the ruling class and as such were much more spoken of in contemporary literature and in historical records than the comparatively obscure Scandinavian element; and finally, they represented a higher culture than the natives and had a literature of their own, in which numerous direct statements and indirect hints tell us about their doings and their relations with the native population. No wonder, therefore, that historians should have given much more attention to this fuller material and to all the interesting problems connected with the Norman Conquest than to the race-mixture attending the Scandinavian immigrations. This is true in respect not only of political and social history, but also of the language, in which the Norman-French element is so conspicuous, and so easily accessible to the student that it has been discussed very often and from various points of view.

And yet there is still much work for future investigators to do. In accordance with the general plan of my work, I shall in this chapter deal chiefly with what has been of permanent importance to the future of the English language, and endeavour to characterize the influence exercised by French as contrasted with that exercised by other languages with which English has come into contact.

82. The Normans became masters of England, and they remained masters for a sufficiently long time to leave a deep impress on the language. The conquerors were numerous and powerful, but the linguistic influence would have been far less if they had not continued for centuries in actual contact and constant intercourse with the French of France, of whom many were induced by later kings to settle in England. We need only go through a list of French loan-words in English to be firmly convinced of the fact that the immigrants formed the upper classes of the English society after the conquest, so many of the words are distinctly aristocratic. It is true that they left the old words *king* and *queen* intact, but apart from these nearly all words relating to government and to the highest administration are French; see, for instance, *crown, state, government* and to *govern, reign, realm* (OFr. realme, Mod. Fr. royaume), *sovereign, country, power, minister, chancellor, council* (and *counsel*), *authority, parliament, exchequer. People* and *nation,* too, were political words; the corresponding OE. *þeod* soon went out of ordinary use. Feudalism was imported from France, and with it were introduced a number of words, such as *fief, feudal, vassal, liege,* and the names of the various steps in the scale of rank: *prince, peer, duke* with *duchess, marquis, viscount, baron.* It is, perhaps, surprising that *lord* and *lady* should have remained in esteem, and that *earl* should have been retained, *count* being chiefly used in speaking of foreigners, but the earl's wife was designated by the French word *countess,* and *court* is French, as well as the adjectives relating to court life, such as *courteous, noble, fine* and *refined. Honour* and *glory* belong to the French, and so does *heraldry,* while nearly all English expressions relating to that difficult science (*argent, gules, verdant,* etc.) are of French origin, some of them curiously distorted.

83. The upper classes, as a matter of course, took into their hands the management of military matters; and although in some cases it was a long time before the old native terms were finally displaced (*here* and *fird,* for instance, were used till the fifteenth century when *army* began to be common), we have a host of French military words, many of them of very early introduction. Such are *war* (ME. werre, Old North Fr. werre, Central French guerre) and *peace, battle, arms, armour, buckler, hauberk, mail* (chain-mail; OFr. maille 'mesh of a net'), *lance, dart, cutlass, banner, ensign, assault, siege,* etc. Further, *officer, chieftain* (*captain* and *colonel* are later), *lieutenant, sergeant, soldier, troops, dragoon, vessel, navy* and *admiral* (orig. *amiral* in English as in French, ultimately an Arabic word). Some words which are now used very extensively outside the military sphere were without any doubt at first purely military, such as *challenge, enemy, danger, escape* (scape), *espy* (spy), *aid, prison, hardy, gallant, march, force, company, guard,* etc.

84. Another natural consequence of the power of the Norman upper classes is that most of the terms pertaining to the law are of French origin, such as *justice, just, judge; jury, court* (we have seen the word already in another sense), *suit, sue, plaintiff* and *defendant,* a *plea, plead,* to *summon, cause, assize, session, attorney, fee, accuse, crime, guile, felony, traitor, damage, dower, heritage, property, real estate, tenure, penalty, demesne, injury, privilege.* Some of these are now hardly to be called technical juridical words, and there are others which belong still more to the ordinary vocabulary of everyday life, but which were undoubtedly at first introduced by lawyers at the time when procedure was conducted entirely in French;[1] for instance, *case, marry, marriage, oust, prove, false* (perhaps also *fault*), *heir,* probably also *male* and *female,* while *defend* and *prison* are common to the juridical and the military worlds. *Petty* (Fr. petit, was, I suspect, introduced by the jurists in such combinations as *petty jury, petty larceny, petty constable, petty sessions, petty averages, petty treason* (still often spelt *petit treason*), etc., before it was used commonly. The French *puis né* in its legal sense remains *puisne* in English (in law it means 'younger or inferior in rank,' but originally 'later born'), while in ordinary language it has adopted the spelling *puny,* as if the -*y* had been the usual adjective ending.

85. Besides, there are a good many words that have never become common property, but have been known to jurists only, such as *mainour* (to be taken with the mainour, to be caught in the very act of stealing, from Fr. manœuvre), *jeofail* ('an oversight,' the acknowledgment of an error in pleading, from je faille), *cestui*

---

[1] From 1362 English was established as the official language spoken in the courts of justice, yet the curious mongrel language known as 'Law French' continued in use there for centuries; Cromwell tried to break its power, but it was not finally abolished till an act of Parliament of 1731. On the position of the French language in England, see J. Vising, *Anglo-Norman Language and Literature* (London, 1923).

que trust, cestui (a) que vie and other phrases equally
shrouded in mystery to the man in the street. *Larceny*
has been almost exclusively the property of lawyers,
so that it has not ousted *theft* from general use; such
words as *thief* and *steal* were of course too popular to
be displanted by French juridical terms, though *burglar*
is probably of French origin. It is also worth observing
how many of the phrases in which the adjective is in-
variably placed after its noun are law terms, taken over
bodily from the French, e.g. *heir male, issue male, fee
simple, proof demonstrative, malice prepense* (or, Eng-
lished, *malice aforethought*),[2] *letters patent* (formerly
also with the adjective inflected, *letters patents,* Shakesp.
R2, II, 1, 202), *attorney general* (and other combinations of *general,* all of which are official, though some
of them are not juridical).

86. As ecclesiastical matters were also chiefly under the control of the higher classes, we find a great
many French words connected with the church, such as
religion, service, trinity, saviour, virgin, angel (OFr.
angele, now Fr. ange; the OE. word engel was taken
direct from Latin, see § 38), *saint, relic, abbey, cloister,
friar* (ME. frère as in French), *clergy, parish, baptism,
sacrifice, orison, homily, altar, miracle, preach, pray,
prayer, sermon, psalter* (ME. sauter), *feast* ('religious
anniversary'). Words like *rule, lesson, save, tempt,
blame, order, nature,* which now belong to the common
language and have very extensive ranges of signification,
were probably at first purely ecclesiastical words. As the
clergy were, moreover, teachers of morality as well as of
religion they introduced the whole gamut of words pertaining to moral ideas from *virtue* to *vice: duty, con-
science, grace, charity, cruel, chaste, covet, desire, lech-*

[2] Cf. also *lords spiritual* and *lords temporal;* the *body politic.*

ery, fool (one of the oldest meanings is 'sensual'),
jealousy, pity, discipline, mercy, and others.

87. To these words, taken from different domains,
may be added other words of more general meaning,
which are highly significant as to the relations between
the Normans and the English, such as *sir* and *madam,
master* and *mistress* with their contrast *servant* (and the
verb to *serve*), further, *command* and *obey, order, rich*
and *poor* with the nouns *riches* and *poverty; money,
interest, cash, rent,* etc.

88. It is a remark that was first made by John
Wallis[3] and that has been very often repeated, especially
since Sir Walter Scott made it popular in *Ivanhoe,* that
while the names of several animals in their lifetime are
English (*ox, cow, calf, sheep, swine, boar, deer*), they
appear on the table with French names (*beef, veal,
mutton, pork, bacon, brawn, venison*). This is generally
explained from the masters leaving the care of the living
animals to the lower classes, while they did not leave
much of the meat to be eaten by them. But it may with
just as much right be contended that the use of the
French words here is due to the superiority of the
French *cuisine,* which is shown by a great many other
words as well, such as *sauce, boil, fry, roast, toast, pasty,
pastry, soup, sausage, jelly, dainty;* while the humbler
breakfast is English, the more sumptuous meals, *dinner*
and *supper,* as well as *feasts* generally, are French.

89. We see on the whole that the masters knew
how to enjoy life and secure the best things to themselves; note also such words as *joy* and *pleasure, delight,
ease* and *comfort; flowers* and *fruits* may be mentioned
in the same category. And if we go through the different
objects or pastimes that make life enjoyable to people

[3] *Grammatica linguae Anglicanae,* 1653.

having plenty of leisure (this word, too, is French) we shall find an exceedingly large number of French words. The *chase*[4] of course was one of the favourite pastimes, and though the native *hunt* was never displaced, yet we find many French terms relating to the chase, such as *brace* and *couple, leash, falcon, quarry, warren, scent, track*. The general term *sport,* too, is of course a French word; it is a shortened form of *desport* (*disport*). *Cards* and *dice* are French words, and so are a great many words relating to different games (*partner, suit, trump*), some of the most interesting being the numerals used by card and dice players: *ace, deuce, trey, cater, cinque, size;* cf. Chaucer's 'Sevene is my chaunce, and thyn is cynk and treye' (C 653).

90. The French led the fashion in the Middle Ages, just as they do to some extent even now, so we expect to find a great many French words relating to dress; in fact, in going through Chaucer's Prologue to the *Canterbury Tales,* where in introducing his gallery of figures he seldom omits to mention their dress, one will see that in nearly all cases where etymologists have been able to trace the special names of particular garments to their sources these are French. And of course, such general terms as *apparel, dress, costume,* and *garment* are derived from the same language.

91. The French were the teachers of the English in most things relating to art; not only such words as *art, beauty, colour, image, design, figure, ornament, to paint,* but also the greater number of the more special words of technical significance are French; from architecture may be mentioned, by way of specimens: *arch, tower, pillar, vault, porch, column, aisle, choir, reredos, tran-*

---

[4] This is the Central French form of the word that was taken over in a North French dialect form as *catch* (Latin *captiare*).

sept, chapel, cloister (the last of which belong here as
well as to our § 86), not to mention *palace, castle,
manor, mansion,* etc. If we go through the names of the
various kinds of artisans, etc., we cannot fail to be struck
with the difference between the more homely or more
elementary occupations which have stuck to their old
native names (such as *baker, miller, smith, weaver,
saddler, shoemaker, wheelwright, fisherman, shepherd,*
and others), on the one hand, and on the other those
which brought their practitioners into more immediate
contact with the upper classes, or in which fashion perhaps played a greater part; these latter have French
names, for instance, *tailor, butcher, mason, painter,
carpenter* and *joiner* (note also such words as *furniture,
table, chair,* while the native name is reserved for the
humbler *stool,* etc.).

92. I am afraid I have tired the reader a little with
all these long lists of words. My purpose was to give
abundant linguistic evidence for the fact that the French
were the rich, the powerful, and the refined classes. It
was quite natural that the lower classes should soon
begin to imitate such of the expressions of the rich as
they could catch the meaning of. They would adopt
interjections and exclamations like *alas, certes, sure,
adieu;* and perhaps *verray* (later *very*) was at first introduced as an exclamation. Whole phrases were adopted:
in the *Ancrene Riwle* (about 1225) we find (p. 268),
Deuleset (Dieu le sait) in two manuscripts, while a third
has *Crist hit wat;* and three hundred years later we find
'As good is a becke (= a wink), as is a *dewe vow garde*'
(Bale, *Three Lawes* 1, 1470). As John of Salisbury
(Johannes Sarisberiensis) says expressly in the twelfth
century,[5] it was the fashion to interlard one's speech

[5] Quoted by D. Behrens, Paul's *Grundriss*, I², 963.

with French words; they were thought modish, and that will account for the fact that many non-technical words too were taken over, such as *air, age* (juridical?), *arrive* (military?), *beast, change, cheer, cover, cry, debt* (juridical?), *feeble, large, letter, manner, matter, nurse* and *nourish, place, point, price, reason, turn, use,* and a great many other everyday words of very extensive employment.

93. If, then, the English adopted so many French words because it was the fashion in every respect to imitate their 'betters,' we are allowed to connect this adoption of *non-technical* words with that trait of their character which in its exaggerated form has in modern times been termed snobbism or toadyism, and which has made certain sections of the English people more interested in the births, deaths and especially marriages of dukes and marquises than in anything else outside their own small personal sphere.

94. But when we trace this feature of snobbishness back to the first few centuries after the Norman Conquest, we must not forget that there were great differences, so that some people would affect many French words and others would stick as far as possible to the native stock of words. We see this difference in the literary works that have come down to us. In Layamon's *Brut,* written very early in the thirteenth century and amounting in all to more than 56,000 short lines, the number of words of Anglo-French origin is only about 150.[6] The *Orrmulum,* which was written perhaps twenty years later, contains more than 20,000 lines, yet even Kluge, who criticizes the view that this very tedious work contains no French words, has not been able to find in it

[6] Skeat, *Principles of English Etymology,* II (1891), p. 8; Morris, *Historical Outl. of Engl. Accidence* (1885), p. 338.

more than twenty-odd words of French origin.[7] But in
the contemporary prose work *Ancrene Riwle*,[8] we find
on 200 pages about 500 French words. A couple of
centuries later, it would be a much harder task to count
the French words in any author, as so many words had
already become part and parcel of the English language;
but even then one author used many more than another.
Chaucer undoubtedly employs a far greater number of
French words than most other writers of his time. Nor
would it be fair to ascribe all these borrowings to what I
have mentioned as snobbism; the greater a writer's
familiarity with French culture and literature, the greater
would be his temptation to introduce French words for
everything above the commonplaces of daily life.

95. The following table shows the strength of the
influx of French words at different periods; it comprises
one thousand words (the first hundred French words in
the New English Dictionary for each of the first nine
letters and the first 50 for *j* and *l*) and gives the half-
century to which the earliest quotation in that Dictionary
belongs.[9] After $+$ I add the corresponding numbers

[7] Kluge, *Das französische Element im Orrmulum*, Englische
Studien, XXII, p. 179.

[8] This, and not *Ancren Riwle,* is the correct title. All genitive
plurals in the work end in *-ene*. Miss A. Paues has been kind
enough at my suggestion to look up the manuscripts and confirmed my suspicion that the form *Ancren* is due to a mistake
by the editor, James Morton.

[9] I have followed the authority of the same Dictionary also in
regard to the question of the origin of the words, reckoning
thus as French some words which I should, perhaps, myself
have called Latin. Derivative words that have certainly or probably arisen in English (e.g. *daintily, damageable*) have been excluded, as also those perfectly unimportant words for which the
NED. gives less than five quotations. Most of them cannot really
be said to have ever belonged to the English language. Cf. also
R. Mettig, *Die franz. Elemente im Alt- und Mittelengl.*, Engl.
St., 41, 176 ff.

found by A. Koszal[10] for those volumes of NED. which had not appeared when I worked up my statistics. It should be remembered that many or even most of these words, at any rate the more popular ones, had probably been in use some time before these quotations. Even if, however, the average age of French words is say fifty years greater than here indicated, the table retains its value for the comparative chronology of the language:

		carried forward:	581+526
Before 1050	2+ 0	1451—1500	76+ 68
1051—1100	2+ 1	1501—1550	84+ 80
1101—1150	1+ 2	1551—1600	91+ 89
1151—1200	15+ 11	1601—1650	69+ 63
1201—1250	64+ 39	1651—1700	34+ 48
1251—1300	127+122	1701—1750	24+ 32
1301—1350	120+118	1751—1800	16+ 33
1351—1400	180+164	1801—1850	23+ 35
1401—1450	70+ 69	1851—1900	2+ 14
	581+526		1000+988

The list shows conclusively that the linguistic influence did not begin immediately after the conquest, and that it was strongest in the years 1251–1400, to which nearly half of the borrowings belong. Further, it will be seen that the common assumption that the age of Dryden was particularly apt to introduce new words from French is very far from being correct.

96. In a well-known passage, Robert of Gloucester (ab. 1300) speaks about the relation of the two languages in England: 'Thus,' he says, 'England came into Normandy's hand; and the Normans at that time (*þo;* it is important not to overlook this word) could speak

[10] *Bulletin de la Faculté des Lettres de Strasbourg* (Jan., 1937). The letters Q, U, and W did not yield a full hundred.

only their own language, and spoke French just as they
did at home, and had their children taught in the same
manner, so that people of rank in this country who came
of their blood all stick to the same language that they
received of them, for if a man knows no French people
will think little of him. But the lower classes still[11] stick
to English and to their own language. I imagine there
are in all the world no countries that do not keep their
own language except England alone. But it is well known
that it is the best thing to know both languages, for the
more a man knows the more is he worth.' This passage
raises the question: How did common people manage to
learn so many foreign words?—and how far did they
assimilate them?

97. In a few cases the process of assimilation was
facilitated by the fact that a French word happened to
resemble an old native one; this was sometimes the
natural consequence of French having in some previous
period borrowed the corresponding word from some
Germanic dialect. Thus no one can tell exactly how
much modern *rich* owes to OE. *rice* 'powerful, rich,'
and how much to French *riche;* the noun (Fr. and ME.)
richesse (now *riches*) supplanted the early ME. *riche-
dom*. The old native verb *choose* was supplemented with
the noun *choice,* from Fr. *choix.* OE. *hergian* and OFr.
herier, harier, run together in Mod. E. *harry;* OE. *hege*
and Fr. *haie* run together in *hay* 'hedge, fence.' It is difficult to separate two *main*'s, one of which is OE. *mægen*
'strength, might' and the other OFr. *maine* (Latin *mag-
nus;* the root of both words is ultimately the same), cf.
main sea and *main force.* The modern *gain* (noun and
verb) was borrowed in the 15th century from French

---

[11] *yute* '*yet*'; sometimes curiously mistranslated, hold to their
own *good* speech.

(*gain, gaain; gagner, gaaignier,* cf. It. *guadagnare,* a
Germanic loan), but it curiously coincided with an
earlier noun *gain* (also spelt *gein, geyn, gayne,* etc.,
oldest form *gaʒhenn*), which meant 'advantage, use,
avail, benefit, remedy' and a verb *gain* (*gayne, geʒʒnenn*)
'to be suitable or useful, avail, serve,' both from Old
Norse. When French *isle* (now *île*) was adopted, it
could not fail to remind the English of their old *iegland,
iland* and eventually it corrupted the spelling of the
latter into *island. Neveu* (now spelled *nephew*) recalled OE. *nefa, meneye* (*menye,* Fr. *maisnie* 'retinue,
troop') recalled *many* (OE. *menigeo*), and *lake,* the
old *lacu* 'stream, river.'[12] There is some confusion between Eng. *rest* (repose) and OFr. *rest* (remainder). In
grammar, too, there were a few correspondences, as
when nouns had the voiceless and the corresponding
verbs the voiced consonants; French *us*—*user,* now *use*
sb. pronounced [ju·s], vb. [ju·z] just as Eng. *house,* sb.
[haus], vb. [hauz]; French *grief*—*griever,* Eng. *grief*—
grieve, just as *half*—*halve.* Note also the formation of
nouns in -*er* (*baker,* etc.), which is hardly distinguish-
able from French formations in words like *carpenter*
(Fr. -*ier*), *interpreter* (ME. *interpretour,* Fr. -*eur*), etc.
But on the whole such more or less accidental similarities between the two languages were few in number and
could not materially assist the English population in
learning the new words that were flooding their language.

98. A greater assistance may perhaps have been
derived from a habit which may have been common in
conversational speech, and which was at any rate not
uncommon in writing, that of using a French word side
by side with its native synonym, the latter serving more

[12] This is still the meaning of *lake* in some dialects.

or less openly as an interpretation of the former for the
benefit of those who were not yet familiar with the more
refined expression. Thus in the *Ancrene Riwle* (ab.
1225): *cherité*, þet is *luve* (p. 8) | in *desperaunce*, þet
is in *unhope* & in *unbileave* forte beon iboruwen (p. 8)
| Understondeð þet two *manere temptaciuns*—two
kunne vondunges—beoð (p. 180) | *pacience*, þet is
þolemodnesse (ibid.) | *lecherie*, þet is *golnesse* (p. 198)
| *ignoraunce*, þet is *unwisdom* & *unwitenesse* (p. 278).
I quote from Behrens's collection of similar collocations[13] the following instances that prove conclusively
that the native word was then better known than the imported one: *bigamie* is unkinde [unnatural] þing, on
engleis tale *twiewifing* (Genesis & Exod. 449) | *twelfe
iferan*, þe Freinsce heo cleopeden *dusze pers* (Layamon,
I, 1, 69) | þat craft: *to lokie in þan lufte*, þe craft his
ihote [is called] *astronomie* in oþer kunnes speche [in a
speech of a different kind] (ib. II, 2, 598). It is well
worth observing that in all these cases the French words
are perfectly familiar to a modern reader, while he will
probably require an explanation of the native words that
served then to interpret the others. In Chaucer we find
similar double expressions, but they are now introduced
for a totally different purpose; the reader is evidently
supposed to be equally familiar with both, and the
writer uses them to heighten or strengthen the effect of
the style;[14] for instance: He coude songes *make* and wel

[13] *Franz. Studien*, V., 2, p. 8. Cf. also 'of whiche *tribe*, that is
to seye, *kynrede* Jesu Crist was born' (Maundeville, 67). R.
Hittmair, *Aus Caxtons Vorreden*, p. 21 f.

[14] Cf. F. Karpf, *Studien zur Syntax . . . Chaucers*, 1930, p.
103 ff. This use of two expressions for the same idea is extremely common in the middle ages and the beginning of the
modern period, and it is not confined to those cases where one
was a native and the other an imported word; see Kellner, *Engl.
Studien*, XX, p. 11 ff. (1895); Greenough and Kittredge, *Words*

endyte (A 95) = Therto he coude *endyte* and *make* a thing (A 325) | *faire* and *fetisly* (A 124 and 273) | *swinken* with his handes and *laboure* (A 186) | Of studie took he most *cure* and most *hede* (A 303) | *Poynaunt* and *sharp* (A 352) | At sessiouns ther was he *lord* and *sire* (A 355).[15] In Caxton this has become quite a mannerism, see, e.g.: I shal so *awreke* and *avenge* this trespace (Reynard 56, cf. p. 116, *advenge* and *wreke* it) | in *honour* and *worship* (ib. p. 56) | *olde* and *auncyent* doctours (p. 62) | *feblest* and *wekest* (p. 64) | I toke a *glasse* or a *mirrour* (p. 83) | Now ye shal here of the *mirrour;* the *glas* . . . (p. 84) | *good* ne *proffyt* (p. 86) | *fowle* and *dishonestly* (p. 94) | *prouffyt* and *fordele* (p. 103). It will be observed that with the exception of the last word, the language has preserved in all cases both the synonyms that Caxton uses side by side, so that we may consider this part of the English vocabulary as settled towards the end of the fifteenth century.

99. Many of the French words, such as *cry, claim, state, poor, change,* and, indeed, most of the words enumerated above (§ 82–92), and, one might say, nearly all the words taken over before 1350 and not a few of those of later importation, have become part and parcel of the English language, so that they appear to us all just as English as the pre-Conquest stock of native words. But a great many others have never become so popular. There are a great many gradations between words of everyday use and such as are not at all understood by the common people, and to the latter

---

and their Ways, p. 113 ff.; so also in Danish, see Vilh. Andersen in *Dania,* p. 80 ff. (1890), and *Danske Studier,* 1893, p. 7 ff.

[15] Cf. also, Curteis he was, lowly, and servisable (A 99); Curteys he was, and lowly, of servyse (A 250).

class may sometimes belong words which literary people
would think familiar to everybody. Hyde Clark relates
an anecdote of a clergyman who blamed a brother
preacher for using the word *felicity*. 'I do not think all
of your hearers understood it; I should say *happiness*.'
'I can hardly think,' said the other, 'that any one does
not know what *felicity* means, and we will ask this
ploughman near us. Come hither, my man! you may
have been at church and heard the sermon; you heard
me speak of *felicity;* do you know what it means?' 'Ees,
sir!' 'Well, what does *felicity* mean?' 'Summut in the
inside of a pig, but I can't say altogether what.'[16] Note
also the way in which Touchstone addresses the rustic in
As You Like It (V., 1, 52), 'Therefore, you Clowne,
abandon,—which is in the vulgar leave,—the societie—
which in the boorish is companie,—of this female,—
which in the common is woman; which together is,
abandon the society of this Female, or, Clowne, thou
perishest; or, to thy better understanding, dyest.'

100. From what precedes we are now in a position to understand some at least of the differences that
have developed in course of time between two synonyms when both have survived, one of them native,
the other French. The former is always nearer the
nation's heart than the latter, it has the strongest associations with everything primitive, fundamental, popular, while the French word is often more formal, more
polite, more refined and has a less strong hold on the
emotional side of life. A *cottage* is finer than a *hut,* and
fine people often live in a cottage, at any rate in summer. The word *bill* was too vulgar and familiar to be
applied to a hawk, which had only a *beak* (the French

[16] *A Grammar of the English Tongue*, 4th ed., London, 1879,
p. 61.

term, whereas *bill* is the A.S. *bile*). 'Ye shall say, this
hauke has a large *beke,* or a short *beke* and call it not
bille' (Book of St. Alban's, fol. a 6, back).[17] To *dress*
means to adorn, deck, etc., and thus generally presupposes a finer garment than the old word to *clothe,* the
wider signification of which it seems, however, to be
more and more appropriating to itself. *Amity* means
'friendly relations, especially of a public character between states or individuals,' and thus lacks the warmth
of *friendship*. The difference between *help* and *aid* is
thus indicated in the Funk-Wagnalls Dictionary: '*Help*
expresses greater dependence and deeper need than *aid*.
In extremity we say "God *help* me!" rather than "God
aid me!" In time of danger we cry *"help! help!"* rather
than *"aid! aid!"* To *aid* is to second another's own ex-
ertions. We can speak of *helping* the helpless, but not
of *aiding* them. *Help* includes *aid,* but *aid* may fall short
of the meaning of *help*.' All this amounts to the same
thing as saying that *help* is the natural expression,
belonging to the indispensable stock of words, and therefore possessing more copious and profounder associations than the more literary and accordingly colder word
aid; cf. also *assist*. *Folk* has to a great extent been
superseded by *people,* chiefly on account of the political
and social employment of the word; Shakespeare rarely
uses *folk* (four times) and *folks* (ten times), and the
word is evidently a low-class word with him; it is rare
in the Authorized Version, and Milton never uses it; but
in recent usage *folk* has been gaining ground, partly,
perhaps, from antiquarian and dialectal causes. *Hearty*
and *cordial* made their appearance in the language at
the same time (the oldest quotations 1380 and 1386,
NED.), but their force is not the same, for 'a hearty

[17] Skeat, *The Works of G. Chaucer,* vol. III, p. 261.

welcome' is warmer than 'a cordial welcome,' and *hearty*
has many applications that *cordial* has not (heartfelt,
sincere; vigorous: a hearty slap on the back; abundant:
a hearty meal), etc. *Saint* smacks of the official recognition by the Catholic Church, while *holy* refers much
more to the mind. *Matin(s)* is used only with reference
to church service, while *morning* is the ordinary word.
Compare also *darling* with *favourite, deep* with *pro-
found, lonely* with *solitary, indeed* with *in fact, to give*
or *to hand* with *to present* or *to deliver, love* with
charity, etc.

101. In some cases the chief difference between
the native word and the French synonym is that the
former is more colloquial and the latter more literary,
e.g. *begin—commence, hide—conceal, feed—nourish,
hinder—prevent, look for—search for, inner* and *outer
—interior* and *exterior,* and many others. In a few cases,
however, the native word is more literary. *Valley* is
the everyday word, and *dale* has only lately been introduced into the standard language from the dialects of
the hilly northern counties. *Action* has practically supplanted *deed* in ordinary language, so that the latter can
be reserved for more dignified speech.

102. In spite of the intimate contact between
French and English it sometimes happens that French
words which have been introduced into other Germanic
languages and belong to their everyday vocabulary are
not found in English or are there much more felt to
be foreign intruders than in German or Danish. This
is true for instance of *friseur, manchette, réplique,* of
gêne and the verb *gêner* (the NED. has no instances of
it, but a few are found in the Stanford Dict.). *Serviette*
is rarer than *napkin. Atelier* is not common; it occurs
in Thackeray's *The Newcomes,* p. 242, where imme-

diately afterwards the familiar word *studio* is used: did
English artists go more to Italy and less to Paris to
learn their craft than their Scandinavian and German
confrères? To the same class belong the following words,
which, when found in English books, are generally indicated to be foreign by italic letters: *naïve, bizarre,*
and *motif*—the last word an interesting recent doublet
of *motive*.

103. As the grammatical systems of the two languages were very different, a few remarks must be made
here about the form in which French words were
adopted. Substantives and adjectives were nearly always
taken over in the accusative case, which differed in
most words from the nominative in having no *s*. The
latter ending is, however, found in a few words, such
as *fitz* (Fitzherbert, etc.; in French, too, the nominative
fils has ousted the old acc. *fil; fitz* is an Anglo-Norman
spelling), *fierce* (OFr. nom. *fiers,* acc. *fier*), *Piers* and
James.[18] In the plural, Old French had a nominative
without any ending and an accusative in *-s,* and English popular instinct naturally associated the latter form
with the native plural ending in *-es.*[19] In course of time

[18] But from the accusative *Jame* (e.g. *Ancrene,* R. 10),
Chaucer has *by seint Jame* (riming with *name,* D 1443); hence
Jem, Jim. A similar vacillation is found in the name *Steven,
Stephen,* where now the *s*-less form has prevailed, but where
formerly the Fr. nom. was also found (seynt stevyns, Malory,
104). Where the French inflexion was irregular, owing to Latin
stress shifting, etc., the accusative was adopted, in *emperor*
(*-our,* OFr. nom. *emperere*), *companion* (OFr. nom. *compain*),
neveu, nephew (OFr. nom. *nies*) and others, but the nom. is
kept in *sire* (OFr. acc. *seignor*), *mayor* (OFr. *maire,* acc.
majeur).

[19] The prevalence of the *-s* plural in English cannot possibly
be due to French influence, see *Progress in Language,* p. 169 =
Chapters on English, p. 33.

those words which had for a long time, in English as
in French, formed their plural without any ending
(e.g. *cas*) were made to conform with the general rule
(sg. *case*, pl. *cases*).[20] French adjectives had the *s* added
to them just like French nouns, and we find a few adjectives with the plural *s*, as in the *goddes celestials*
(Chaucer); *letters patents* survived as a fixed group till
the time of Shakespeare (§ 85). But the general rule
was to treat French adjectives exactly like English ones.

104. As to the verbs, the rule is that the stem of
the French present plural served as basis for the English
form; thus (*je survis*), *nous survivons, vous survivez,
ils survivent* became *survive* (*je résous*), *résolvons*, etc.,
became *resolve*, OFr. (*je desjeun*), *nous disnons*, etc.,
became *dine;* thus is explained the frequent ending
-ish, in *punish, finish*, etc. English *bound* (to leap),
accordingly, cannot be the French *bondir*, which would
have yielded *bondish*, but is an English formation from
the noun *bound*, which is the French *bond*. I think that
levy is similarly formed on the noun *levy*, which is Fr.
levée; but in *sally* the *y* represents the *i* which made the
Fr. *ll mouillé*. Where the French infinitive was imported
it was generally in a substantival function, as in *dinner,
remainder, attainder, rejoinder*, cf. the verbs *dine, remain, attain, rejoin;* so also the law terms *merger, user*
and *misnomer*. Still we have a few verbs in which the
ending *-er* can hardly be anything else but the French
infinitive ending: *render* (which is thereby kept distinct
from *rend*), *surrender, tender* (where the doublet *tend*
also exists), and perhaps *broider* (*embroider*). There is
a curious parallel to the Norse *bask* and *busk* (79) in

[20] Note *invoice, trace* (part of a horse's harness), and *quince*,
where the French plural ending now forms part of the English
singular; cf. Fr. *envoi, trait, coign.*

saunter, where the French reflective pronoun has become fixed as an inseparable element of the word, from *s'auntrer,* another form for *s'aventurer,* 'to adventure oneself.'

105. French words have, as a matter of course, participated in all the sound changes that have taken place in English since their adoption. Thus words with the long [i] sound have had it diphthongized into [ai], e.g. *fine, price, lion.* The long [u], written *ou,* has similarly become [au], e.g. OFr. *espouse* (Mod. Fr. *épouse*), ME. *spouse,* pronounced [spu·ze], now pron. [spauz], Fr. *tour,* Mod. E. *tower.* Compare also the treatment of the vowels in *grace, change, beast* (OFr. *beste*), *ease* (Fr. *aise*), etc. Such changes of loan-words are seen everywhere: they are brought about gradually and insensibly. But there is another change which has often been supposed to have come about in a different manner. A great many words are now stressed on the first syllable which in French were stressed on the final syllable, and this is often ascribed to the inability of the English to imitate the French accentuation. All English words, it is said, had the stress on the first syllable, and this habit was unconsciously extended to foreign words on their first adoption into the language. We see this manner of treating foreign words in Icelandic at the present day. But the explanation does not hold good in our case. English had a few words with unstressed first syllable (*be–, for–,* etc., see above, § 25), and as a matter of fact French words in English were for centuries accented in the French manner, as shown conclusively by Middle English poetry. It was only gradually that more and more words had their accent shifted on to its present place. The causes of this shifting were the same as are elsewhere at work in the same direction.[21] In many words the first syllable was felt as psychologically the most important one, as in *punish, finish, matter, manner, royal, army* and other words ending with meaningless or formative syllables. The initial syllable very often received the accent of contrast. In modern speech we stress the otherwise unstressed syllables to bring out a contrast clearly, as in 'not *op*pose but *sup*pose' or 'If on the one hand speech gives *ex*pression to ideas, on the other hand it receives *im*pressions from them' (Romanes, *Mental Evolution in Man*, p. 238), and in the same manner we must imagine that in the days when *real, formal, object, subject* and a hundred similar words were normally stressed on the last syllable, they were so often contrasted with each other that the modern accentuation became gradually the habitual one. This will explain the accent of *January, February, cavalry, infantry, primary, orient,* and other words. An equally powerful principle is rhythm, which tends to avoid two consecutive strong syllables; compare modern *go down'stairs,* but *the 'downstairs room, she is fif'teen,* but *'fifteen 'years.* Chaucer stresses many words in the French manner, except when they precede a stressed syllable, in which case the accent is shifted, thus *co'syn* (cousin), but *'cosyn myn; in felici'te par'fit,* but *a 'verray 'parfit 'gentil 'knight; se'cre* (secret), but in *'secre wyse,* etc. An instructive illustration is found in such a line as this (*Cant. Tales,* D 1486):

In 'divers 'art and in di'vers fi'gures.

These principles—value-stressing, contrast, rhythm —will explain all or most of the instances in which

[21] See the detailed exposition in my *Modern English Grammar* (Heidelberg, Carl Winter), I, 1909, ch. V.

English has shifted the French stress; but it is evident
that it took a very long time before the new forms of
the words which arose at first only occasionally through
their influence were powerful enough finally to supplant
the older forms.[22]

106. Not long after the intrusion of the first French
words we begin to see the first traces of a phenomenon
which was to attain very great proportions and which
must now be termed one of the most prominent features
of the language, namely hybridism. Strictly speaking,
we have a hybrid (a composite word formed of elements
from different languages) as soon as an English inflexional ending is added to a French word, as in the
genitive *the Duke's children* or the superlative *noblest*,
etc., and from such instances we rise by insensible gradations to others, in which the fusion is more surprising.
From the very first we find verbal nouns in *-ing* or *-ung*
formed from French verbs (indeed, they are found at a
time when they could not be formed from every native
verb, § 197), e.g. *prechinge; riwlunge* (*Ancrene Riwle*);
scornunge and *servinge* (Layamon); *spusinge* (Owl and
N.). Other instances of English endings added to
French words are *faintness* (from the end of the fourteenth century), *closeness* (half a century later), *secret-
ness* (Chaucer secreenesse, B 773), *simpleness* (Shakespeare and others), *materialness* (Ruskin), *abnormal-
ness* (Benson), etc. Further, a great many adjectives in
-ly (courtly, princely, etc.) and, of course, innumerable
adverbs with the same ending (faintly, easily, nobly[23]);

[22] In many recent borrowings the accent is not shifted, cf.
machine, intrigue, where the retention of the French *i*-sound is
another sign that the words are of comparatively modern introduction.

[23] Also *naïvely,* used by Pope, Ruskin, Leslie Stephen, and
many others. But some have an unwarranted aversion to the

adjectives in -*ful* (beautiful, dutiful, powerful, artful) and -*less* (artless, colourless); nouns in -*ship* (courtship, companionship) and -*dom* (dukedom, martyrdom) and so forth.

107. While hybrid words of this kind are found in comparatively great numbers in most languages, hybrids of the other kind, i.e. composed of a native stem and a foreign ending, are in most languages much rarer than in English. Before such hybrids could be formed, there must have been already in the language so great a number of foreign words with the same ending that the formation would be felt to be perfectly transparent. Here are to be mentioned the numerous hybrids in -*ess* (shepherdess, goddess; Wycliffe has dwelleresse; in a recent volume I have found '*seeress* and prophetess'), in -*ment* (endearment and enlightenment are found from the 17th century, but bewilderment not before the 19th; wonderment, frequent in Thackeray; oddment, R. Kipling, hutment), in -*age* (mileage, acreage, leakage, shrinkage, wrappage, breakage, cleavage, roughage, shortage, etc.); in -*ance* (hindrance, used in the fifteenth century in the meaning 'injury'; in the signification now usual it is found as early as 1526, and perhaps we may infer from its occurring neither in the Bible, nor in Shakespeare, Milton and Pope, that it was felt to be a bastard, though Locke, Cowper, Wordsworth, Shelley and Tennyson admit it; forbearance, originally a legal term; furtherance); in -*ous* (murderous; thunderous; slumberous is used by Keats and Carlyle); in -*ry* (fishery, bakery, etc.; gossipry, Mrs. Browning; Irishry;

---

word. In the *New Statesman* (Dec. 19, 1914) I find: 'In Hardy's elegy on Swinburne there occurs the horrid hybrid, "naïvely"— a neologism exactly calculated, one would suppose, to make the classic author of Atalanta turn in his grave' (L. Strachey).

forgettery, jocularly formed after memory); in -ty (od-
dity, womanity, nonceword after humanity); in -fy
(fishify, Shakespeare; snuggify, Ch. Lamb; Torify, Ch.
Darwin; scarify, Fielding; tipsify, Thackeray; funkify,
speechify[24]) with the corresponding nouns in -fication:
uglification, Shelley.[25]

108. One of the most fertile English derivative
endings is -able, which has been used in a great number
of words besides those French ones which were taken
over ready made (such as *agreeable, variable, tolerable*).
In comparatively few cases it is added to substantives
(*serviceable, companionable, marriageable, peaceable,
seasonable*). Its proper sphere of usefulness is in forming adjectives from verbs, rarely in an active sense
(*suitable* = that suits, *unshrinkable*), but generally in
a passive sense (*bearable* = that can or may be borne).
Thus we have now *drinkable, eatable, steerable* (bal-
loons), *weavable, unutterable, answerable, punishable,
unmistakable*, etc., and hundreds of others, so that
everybody has a feeling that he is free to form a new
adjective of this kind as soon as there is any necessity
for, or convenience in, using it, just as he feels no
hesitation in adding -ing to any verb, new or old. And
of course, no one ever objects to these adjectives (or
the corresponding nouns in -ability) because they are
hybrids or bastards, any more than one would object
to forms like *acting* or *remembering* on the same score.

109. These adjectives have now become so indispensable that the want is even felt of forming them from
composite verbal expressions, such as *get at*. But though
get-at-able and *come-at-able* are pretty frequently heard

[24] Cf. also 'Daphne—before she was happily treeified,' Lowell,
Fable for Critics.

[25] See below on hybrids with Latin and Greek endings (§ 123).

in conversation, most people shrink from writing or printing them. Sterne has *come-at-ability,* Congreve *uncome-atable,* Smiles *get-atability,* and George Eliot in a letter, *knock-upable.* Tennyson, too, writes in a jocular letter, 'thinking of you as no longer the *come-atable, runupableto, smokeablewith* J. S. of old.' Note here the place of the preposition in the last two adjectives, and compare 'enough to make the house *un-liveable in* for a month' (*The Idler,* May 1892, 366), 'the husband being fairly good-natured and *livable-with*' (Bernard Shaw, *Ibsenism,* 41), and 'she is *unspeakable to*' (Benson, *Dodo the Second,* 121). It is obvious that these adjectives are too clumsy to be ever extensively used in serious writing. But there is another way out of the difficulty which is really much more conformable to the genius of the language, namely, to leave out the preposition in all those cases where there can be no doubt of the preposition understood. *Unaccountable* (= that cannot be accounted *for*) has long been accepted by everybody; I have found it, for instance, in Congreve, Addison, Swift, Goldsmith, De Quincey, Miss Austen, Dickens and Hawthorne. *Indispensable* has been —well, indispensable, for two centuries and a half. *Laughable* is used by Shakespeare, Dryden, Carlyle, Thackeray, etc. *Dependable, disposable, objectionable,* and *available* are in general use.[26] All this being granted, it is difficult to see why *reliable* should have been one of the most abused words. It is certainly formed in accordance with the fundamental laws of the language; it is short and unambiguous, and what more should be

[26] Jane Austen writes, 'There will be work for five summers before the place is *liveable*' (Mansf. Park, 216) = the above-mentioned *liveable-in.* Cf. below *gazee* and others in *-ee* (§ 111). The principle of formation is the same as in *waiter,* 'he who waits *on* people,' *caller,* 'he who calls *on* some one.'

THE FRENCH 113

needed? Those who measure a word by its age will be
glad to hear that Miss Mabel Peacock has found it in a
letter, bearing the date of 1624, from the pen of the
Rev. Richard Mountagu, who eventually became a
bishop. And those who do not like using a word unless
it has been accepted by great writers will find a formi-
dable array of the best names in Fitzedward Hall's list[27]
of authors who have used the word.[28] It is curious to
note that the word which is always extolled at the ex-
pense of *reliable* as an older and nobler word, namely
trustworthy, is really much younger; it has not been
traced further back than the beginning of the nineteenth
century; besides, any impartial judge will find its sound
less agreeable to the ear on account of the consonant
group—*stw*—and the heavy second syllable. But then
the synonym *trusty* avoids that fault.

110. Fitzedward Hall in speaking about the recent
word *aggressive*[29] says, 'It is not at all certain whether
the French *agressif* suggested *aggressive,* or was suggested by it. They may have appeared independently of
each other.' The same remark applies to a great many
other formations on a French or Latin basis; even if the
several components of a word are Romanic, it by no
means follows that the word was first used by a Frenchman. On the contrary, the greater facility and the greater
boldness in forming new words and turns of expression

[27] On English adjectives in *-able,* with special reference to
reliable. (London, 1877). Fitzedward Hall reverted to the subject on several other occasions.

[28] Coleridge, Sir Robert Peel, John Stuart Mill, Wilberforce,
Dickens, Charles Reade, Walter Bagehot, Anthony Trollope,
Newman, Gladstone, S. Baring-Gould, Sir Leslie Stephen, H.
Maudsley, Saintsbury, Henry Sweet, Thomas Arnold. I leave
out, rather arbitrarily I fear, more than a score of the names
given by Fitzedward Hall.

[29] *Modern English,* 314.

which characterizes English generally in contradistinction to French, would in many cases speak in favour of
the assumption that an innovation is due to an English
mind. This I take to be true with regard to *dalliance,*
which is so frequent in ME. (*dalyaunce,* etc.), while it
has not been recorded in French at all. The wide chasm
between the most typical English meaning of *sensible*
(a sensible man, a sensible proposal) and those meanings which it shares with French *sensible* and Lat.
sensibilis, probably shows that in the former meaning
the word was an independent English formation. *Dura-
tion* as used by Chaucer may be a French word; it then
went out of the language, and when it reappeared after
the time of Shakespeare it may just as well have been
reformed in England as borrowed; *duratio* does not seem
to have existed in Latin. *Intensitas* is not a Latin word,
and *intensity* is older than *intensité.*

111. In not a few cases, the English soil has proved
more fertilizing than the French soil from which words
were transplanted. In French, for instance, *mutin* has
fewer derivatives than in English, where we have *mutine*
sb., *mutine* vb. (Shakespeare), *mutinous, mutinously,
mutinousness, mutiny* sb., *mutiny* vb., *mutineer* sb.,
mutineer vb., *mutinize,* of which it is true that *mutine*
and *mutinize* are now extinct. We see the same thing in
such a recent borrowing as *clique,* which stands alone
in French while in English two centuries have provided
us with *cliquedom, cliqueless, cliquery, cliquomania,
cliquomaniac, clique* vb., *cliquish, cliquishness, cliquism,
cliquy* or *cliquey.* From *due* we have *duty,* to which no
French correspondent word has been found in France
itself, although *dueté, duity, deweté* are found in Anglo-
French writers; in English *duty* is found from the 13th
century, and we have moreover *duteous, dutiable,*

dutied, dutiful, dutifully, dutifulness, dutiless, none of
which appear to be older than the 16th century. *Aim,*
the noun as well as the verb, is now among the most
useful and indispensable words in the English vocabulary and it has some derivatives, such as *aimer, aimful,*
and *aimless,* but in French the two verbs from which it
originates, *esmer* < Lat. æstimare, and *aasmer,* < Lat.
adæstimare, have totally disappeared. Note also the
differentiations of the words *strange* and *estrange, state*
and *estate,*[30] of *entry* (< Fr. *entrée*[31]) and *entrance,*
while in French *entrance* has been given up; and the less
perfect one of *guaranty* (action) and *guarantee* (person), not to speak of *warrant* and *warranty.* The extent
to which foreign speech-material has been turned to
account is really astonishing, as is seen, perhaps, most
clearly in the extensive use of the derivative ending *-ee.*
This was originally the French participial ending *-é* used
in a very few cases such as *apelé,* E. *appelee* as opposed
to *apelor,* E. *appellor, nominee, presentee,* etc., and
then gradually extended in legal use to words in which
such a formation would be prohibited in French by
formal as well as syntactical reasons: *vendee* is the man
to whom something is sold (l'homme à qui on a vend*u*
quelque chose), cf. also *referee, lessee, trustee,* etc. Now
these formations are no longer restricted to juridical
language, and in general literature there is some disposition to turn this ending to account as a convenient manner of forming passive nouns; Goldsmith and Richardson have *lovee,* Sterne speaks of 'the mortgager and
mortgagee . . . the jester and jestee'; further the *gazee*
(De Quincey) = the one gazed *at, staree* (Edgeworth),

[30] Compare also the juridical *estray* and the ordinary *stray.*
[31] This word has recently been re-adopted: *entrée,* 'made-dish
served between the chief courses.'

cursee and *laughee* (Carlyle), *flirtee, floggee, wishee, bargainee, beatee, examinee, callee* (our callee = the man we call on), etc. Such a word as *trusteeship* is eminently characteristic of the composite character of the language: Scandinavian *trust* + a French ending used in a manner unparalleled in French + an old English ending.

112. French influence has not been restricted to one particular period (see § 95), and it is interesting to compare the forms of old loan-words with those of recent ones, in which we can recognize traces of the changes the French language has undergone since medieval times. Where a *ch* in an originally French word is pronounced as in *change, chaunt,* etc. (with the sound-group tʃ), the loan is an old one; where it is sounded as in *champagne* (with simple ʃ), we have a recent loan. *Chief* is thus shown to belong to the first period, while its doublet *chef* (= chef de cuisine) is much more modern. It is curious that two pet-names should now be spelled in the same way, *Charlie,* although they are distinct in pronunciation: the masculine is derived from the old loan *Charles* and has, therefore, the sound [tʃ], the feminine is from the recent loan *Charlotte* with [ʃ]. Similarly *g* as in *age, siege, judge,* pronounced [dʒ], is indicative of old loans, while the pronunciation [ʒ] is only found in modern adoptions, such as *rouge.* Initially, however, [ʒ] is not found in English without a preposed [d]; thus *gentle, genteel* and *jaunty* represent three layers of borrowing from the same word, but they have all of them the same initial sound. Other instances of the same French word appearing in more than one shape according to its age in English are *saloon* and *salon, suit* and *suite, liquor* and *liqueur, rout* 'big party, retreat' and *route* (the diph-

thong in the former word is an English development of
the long [u] § 105), *quart,* pronounced [kwɔ·t], and
quart, pronounced [ka·t], 'a sequence of four cards in
piquet,' cf. also *quarte* or *carte* in fencing.

113. In some cases, we witness a curious reshap-
ing of an early French loan-word, by which it is made
more like the form into which the French has mean-
while developed. This, of course, can only be explained
by the uninterrupted contact between the two nations.
Chaucer had *viage* just as Old French, but now the
word is *voyage; leal* has given way to *loyal,*[32] *marchis*
to *marquis;* the noun *flaute* and the verb *floyten* are now
made into *flute* like Mod. Fr. *flûte.*[33] Similarly the signification of ME. *douten* like that of OFr. *douter* was
'to fear' (cf. *redoubt*), but now in both languages this
signification has disappeared. *Danger* was at first
adopted in the Old French sense of 'dominion, power,'
but the present meaning was developed in France before
it came to England. The many parallelisms in the employment of *cheer* and Fr. *chère* could not very well
have arisen independently in both languages at once.
This continued contact constitutes a well-marked contrast between the French and the Scandinavian influence,
which seems to have been broken off somewhat abruptly
after the Norman Conquest.

[32] Both forms are used together in Dickens, *Our Mutual
Friend,* 49.
[33] Cf. below the Latinizing of many French words (§ 116).

CHAPTER VI

Latin and Greek

114. Although Latin has been read and written in England from the Old English period till our own days, so that there has been an uninterrupted possibility of Latin influence on the English language, yet we may with comparative ease separate the latest stratum of loans from the two strata already considered (in § 32, 39). It embodies especially abstract or scientific words, adopted exclusively through the medium of writing and never attaining to the same degree of popularity as words belonging to the older strata. The words adopted are not all of Latin origin, there are perhaps more Greek than Latin elements in them, if we count the words in a big dictionary. Still the more important words are Latin and most of the Greek words have entered into English through Latin, or have, at any rate, been Latinized in spelling and endings before being used in English, so that we have no occasion here to deal separately with the two stocks. The great historical event, without which this influence would never have assumed such gigantic dimensions, was the revival of learning. Through Italy and France the Renaissance came to be felt in England as early as the fourteenth century, and since then the invasion of classical terms has never stopped, although the multitude of new words introduced was greater, perhaps, in the fourteenth, the

sixteenth and the nineteenth than in the intervening
centuries. The same influence is conspicuous in all European languages, but in English it has been stronger than
in any other language, French perhaps excepted. This
fact cannot, I think, be principally due to any greater
zeal for classical learning on the part of the English than
of other nations. The reason seems rather to be that
the natural power of resistance possessed by a Germanic
tongue against these alien intruders had been already
broken in the case of the English language by the wholesale importation of French words. They paved the way
for the Latin words which resembled them in so many
respects, and they had already created in English minds
that predilection for foreign words which made them
shrink from consciously coining new words out of native
material. If French words were more *distingués* than
English ones, Latin words were still more so, for did
not the French themselves go to Latin to enrich their
own vocabulary? The first thing noticeable about this
class of Latin importation is, therefore, that it cannot be
definitely separated from the French loans.

115. A great many words may with equal right be
ascribed to French and to Latin, since their English
form would be the same in both cases and the first users
would probably know both languages.[1] This is especially
the case with those words which in French are not
popular survivals of spoken Latin words, but later borrowings from literary Latin, *mots savants,* as Brachet
termed them in contradistinction to *mots populaires.*
As examples of words that may have been taken from
either language, I shall mention only *grave, gravity, con-
solation, solid, infidel, infernal, position.*

116. A curious consequence of the Latin influence

[1] Cf. Luick, *Histor. Grammatik,* p. 70 f.

during and after the Renaissance was that quite a number of French words were remodelled into closer resemblance with their Latin originals. Chaucer uses
descrive (riming with *on lyve* 'alive,' H 121; still in
Scotch), but in the 16th century the form *describe*
makes its appearance. *Perfet* and *parfet* (Fr. *perfait,
parfait*) were the normal English forms for centuries.
Milton writes *perfeted* (*Areop.,* 10); but the *c* was introduced from the Latin, at first in spelling only, but
afterwards in pronunciation as well.[2] Similarly *verdit*
has given way to *verdict*. Where Chaucer had *peynture*
as in French (peinture), *picture* is now the established
form. The Latin prefix *ad* is now seen in *advice* and
adventure, while Middle English had *avis* (*avys*) and
aventure. The latter form is still retained in the phrase
at aventure, where, however, *a* has been apprehended
as the indefinite article (at a venture), and another
remnant of the old form is disguised in *saunter* (Fr.
s'aventurer 'to adventure oneself'). *Avril* (avrille) has
been Latinized into *April;* and a modern reader does
not easily recognize his *February* in ME. *feouerele* or
feouerrere[3] (u = v, cf. *février*). In *debt* and *doubt,*
which used to be *dette* and *doute* as in French, the
spelling only has been affected; compare also *victuals*
for *vittles* (Fr. *vitailles,* cf. *battle* from *bataille*). Similarly *bankerota* (cf. Italian), *banqueroute, bankrout*
(Shakesp.) had to give way to *bankrupt;* the oldest
example of the *p*-form in the NED. dates from 1533.
The form *langage* was used for centuries, before it became *language* by a curious crossing of French and

---

[2] Bacon writes (*New Atlantis,* 15): all nations have *enter-
knowledge* one of another. In recent similar words, *inter-* is
always used.

[3] Juliana, p. 78, 79.

Latin forms. *Egal* was for more than two centuries the
commoner form; *equal,* now the only recognized form,
was apparently a more learned form and was used for
instance in Chaucer's *Astrolabe,* while in his poems he
writes *egal;* Shakespeare generally has *equal,* but *egal* is
found a few times in some of the old editions of his
plays. Tennyson tries to re-introduce *egality* by the side
of *equality,* not as an ordinary word, however, but as
applied to France specially ('That cursed France with
her egalities!' *Aylmer's Field*). French and Latin forms
coexist, more or less differentiated, in *complaisance* and
complacence (*complacency*), *genie* (rare) and *genius,*
base and *basis* (Greek). *Certainty* (Fr.) and *certitude*
(Lat.) are often used indiscriminately, but there is now
a tendency to restrict the latter to merely subjective
certainty, as in Cardinal Newman's 'my argument is:
that *certitude* was a habit of mind, that *certainty* was a
quality of propositions; that probabilities which did not
reach to logical *certainty,* might suffice for a mental
certitude,' etc.[4] Note also the curious difference made
between *critic* with stress on the first syllable, adjective[5]
and agent noun (from Lat. or Greek direct? or through
French?) and *critique* with stress on the second syllable,
action noun (late borrowing from Fr.); Pope uses
critick'd as a participle (stress on the first), while a verb
critique with stress on the last syllable is found in recent
use; *criticize,* which since Milton has been the usual
verb, is a pseudo-Greek formation.

117. Intricate relations between French and Latin
are sometimes shown in derivatives: *colour* is from
French, as is evident from the vowel in the first syllable
[ʌ]; but in *discoloration* the second syllable is sometimes

[4] *Apologia pro Vita Sua* (London, 1900), p. 20.
[5] With the by-form *critical.*

made [kɔl] as from Latin, and sometimes [kʌl] as from
French. Compare also *example* from French, *exemplary*
from Latin. *Machine* with *machinist* and *machinery* are
from the French, witness the pronunciation [mə'ʃiˑn];
but *machinate* and *machination* are taken direct from
Latin and accordingly pronounced [mækineit, mækiˡ-
neiʃən]; so these two groups which ought by nature to
belong together are kept apart, and no one knows
whether the obsolete *machinal* should go with one or
the other group, some dictionaries pronouncing [mə'-
ʃiˑnəl] and other [ˡmækinəl]—a suggestive symptom of
the highly artificial state of the language!

118. It would be idle to attempt to indicate the
number of Latin and Greek words in the English language, as each new treatise on a scientific subject adds
to their number. But it is interesting to see what proportion of the Latin vocabularly has passed into English.
Professors J. B. Greenough and G. L. Kittredge have
counted the words beginning with A in Harper's Latin
Dictionary, excluding proper names, doublets, parts of
verbs, and adverbs in -*e* and -*ter*. 'Of the three thousand
words there catalogued, one hundred and fifty-four (or
about one in twenty) have been adopted bodily into
our language in some Latin form, and a little over five
hundred have some English representative taken, or supposed to be taken, through the French. Thus we have
in the English vocabulary about one in four or five of
all the words found in the Latin lexicon under A. There
is no reason to suppose that this proportion would not
hold good approximately for the whole alphabet.'[6]

119. It must not be imagined that all the Latin
words as used in English conform exactly with the
rules of Latin pronunciation or with the exact classical

[6] *Words and their Ways*, 1902, p. 106.

meanings. 'My instructor,' says Fitzedward Hall,[7] 'took me to task for saying ¹*doctrinal*. "Where an English word is from Latin or Greek, you should always remember the stress in the original, and the quantity of the vowels there." I replied: "If others, in their solicitude to *pro¹pāgat* refinement, choose to be *ir¹ritated* or ¹*excīted*, because of what they take to be my *genu¹īne* *ig¹nōrance* in *ora¹tory,* they should at least be sure that their discomposure is not *gratu¹ītous.*" ' Among words used in English with a different signification from the classical one, may be mentioned *enormous* (Latin *enormis* 'irregular,' later also 'very big,' in English formerly also *enorm* and *enormious*) *item* (Latin *item* 'also,' used to introduce each article in a list, except the first), *ponder* (Lat. *ponderare* 'to weigh, examine, judge,' transitive), *premises* ('adjuncts of a building,' originally things set forth or mentioned in the beginning), *climax* (Greek *klĭmax* 'a ladder or gradation'; in the popular sense of culminating point it is found in Emerson, Dean Stanley, John Morley, Miss Mitford, and other writers of repute), *bathos* (Greek *báthos* 'depth'; in the sense of 'ludicrous descent from the elevated to the commonplace' it is due to Pope; the adjective *bathetic,* formed on the analogy of *pathetic,* was first used by Coleridge). It should be remembered, however, that when once a certain pronunciation or signification has been firmly established in a language, the word fulfils its purpose in spite of ever so many might-have-beens, and that, at any rate, correctness in one language should not be measured by the yard of another language. *Transpire* is perfectly legiti-

---

[7] Fitzedward Hall, *Two Trifles.* Printed for the Author, 1895. I have changed his symbol for stress, indicating here as elsewhere the beginning of the strong syllable by a prefixed little stroke.

mate in the sense 'to emit, or to be emitted through the pores of the skin' and in the derived sense 'to become known, to become public gradually' although there is no Latin verb *transpirare* in either of these senses; if, therefore, the occasional use of the verb in the sense of 'happen' (pretty frequent in newspapers, but also e.g. in Charlotte Brontë) is objectionable, it is not on account of any deviation from Latin usage, but because it has arisen through a vulgar misunderstanding of the *English* signification of an English word. Stuart Mill exaggerates the danger of such innovations when he writes: 'Vulgarisms, which creep in nobody knows how, are daily depriving the English language of valuable modes of expressing thought. To take a present instance: the verb *transpire* . . . Of late a practice has commenced of employing this word, for the sake of finery, as a mere synonym of *to happen:* "the events which have *transpired* in the Crimea," meaning the incidents of the war. This vile specimen of bad English is already seen in the despatches of noblemen and viceroys: and the time is apparently not far distant when nobody will understand the word if used in its proper sense . . . The use of "aggravating" for "provoking," in my boyhood a vulgarism of the nursery, has crept into almost all newspapers, and into many books; and when writers on criminal law speak of aggravating and extenuating circumstances, their meaning, it is probable, is already misunderstood.'[8] Let me add two small notes to Mill's remarks. First, that *aggravate* in the sense of 'exasperate, provoke' is exemplified in the NED. from Cotgrave (1611), T. Herbert (1634), Richardson (1748)—thus some time before Mill heard it in his nursery—and

[8] Stuart Mill, *A System of Logic,* People's edition, 1886, p. 451.

Thackeray (1848). And secondly, that the verb which Mill uses to explain it, *provoke*, is here used in a specifically English sense which is nearly as far removed from the classical signification as that of *aggravate* is. But we shall presently see that the English have taken even greater liberties with the classical languages.

120. When the influx of classical words began, it had its *raison d'être* in the new world of old but forgotten ideas, then first revealed to medieval Europe. Instead of their narrow circle of everyday monotonousness, people began to suspect new vistas, in art as well as in science, and classical literature became a fruitful source of information and inspiration. No wonder, then, that scores and hundreds of words should be adopted together with the ideas they stood for, and should seem to the adopters indispensable means of enriching a language which to them appeared poor and infertile as compared with the rich storehouses of Latin and Greek. But as times wore on, the ideas derived from classical authors were no longer sufficient for the civilized world, and, just as it will happen with children outgrowing their garments, the modern mind outgrew classicism, without anybody noticing exactly when or how. New ideas and new habits of life developed and demanded linguistic expression, and now the curious thing happened that classical studies had so leavened the minds of the educated classes that even when they passed the bounds of the ancient world they drew upon the Latin and Greek vocabulary in preference to their own native stock of words.

121. This is seen very extensively in the nomenclature of modern science, in which hundreds of chemical, botanical, biological and other terms have been

framed from Latin and Greek roots, most of them compound words and some extremely long compounds. It is
certainly superfluous here to give instances of such formations, as a glance at any page of a comprehensive
dictionary will supply a sufficient number of them, and
as one needs only a smattering of science to be acquainted with technical words from Latin and Greek
that would have struck Demosthenes and Cicero as bold,
many of them even as indefensible or incomprehensible
innovations. It is not, perhaps, so well known that quite
a number of words that belong to the vocabulary of
ordinary life and that are generally supposed to have the
best-ascertained classical pedigree, have really been
coined in recent times more or less exactly on classical
analogies. Some of them have arisen independently in
several European countries. Such modern coinages are,
for instance, *eventual* with *eventuality, immoral, frag-
mental* and *fragmentary, primal, annexation, fixation* and
affixation, climatic. There are scores of modern formations in *-ism,*[9] e.g. *absenteeism, alienism, classicism,
colloquialism, favouritism, individualism, mannerism,
realism,* not to speak of those made from proper names,
such as *Swinburnism, Zolaism,* etc. Among the innumerable words of recent formation in *-ist* may be mentioned
dentist, florist, jurist, oculist, copyist (formerly *copist* as
in some continental languages), *determinist, economist,
ventriloquist, individualist, plagiarist, positivist, socialist,
terrorist, nihilist, tourist.* For *calculist* the only author
quoted in the NED. is Carlyle. *Scientist* has often been
branded as an 'ignoble Americanism' or 'a cheap and
vulgar product of trans-Atlantic slang,' but Fitzedward
Hall has pointed out that it was fabricated and advo-

---

[9] See Fitzedward Hall, *Modern English,* p. 311. His lists have
also been utilized in the rest of this paragraph.

cated in 1840, together with *physicist,* by Dr. Whewell.
Whoever objects to such words as *scientist* on the plea
that they are not correct Latin formations, would have
to blot out of his vocabulary such well-established words
as *suicide, telegram, botany, sociology, tractarian, vege-
tarian, facsimile* and *orthopedic;* but then, happily, people are not consistent.

122. Authors sometimes coin quasi-classic words
without finding anybody to pass them on, as when
Milton writes 'our *inquisiturient* Bishops' (*Areop.,* 13).
Coleridge speaks of *'logodædaly* or verbal legerdemain.'
Thackeray of a lady's *'viduous* mansion' (*Newc.,* 794),
Dickens of *'vocular* exclamations' (*Oliver Twist);*
Tennyson writes in a letter (*Life,* I, 254) 'you range no
higher in my *andrometer';* Bulwer-Lytton says 'a cat the
most *viparious* [meaning evidently 'tenacious of life'] is
limited to nine lives'; and Mrs. Humphrey Ward, 'his air
of old-fashioned *punctilium.'*[10] I have here on purpose
mixed correct and incorrect forms, jocular and serious
words, because my point was to illustrate the love
found in most English writers of everything Latin or
Greek, however unusual or fanciful. Sometimes jocular
'classicisms' survive and are adopted into everybody's
language, such as *omnium gatherum* (whence Thackeray's bold heading of a chapter 'Snobbium Gatherum'),
circumbendibus (Goldsmith, Coleridge) and *tandem,*
which originated in a university pun on the two senses
of English 'at length.'

123. Hybrids, in which one of the component parts
was French and the other native English, have been
mentioned above (§ 106 f.). Here we shall give some

---

[10] Dictionaries recognize *punctilio,* a curious transformation of
the Spanish *puntillo;* there is a late Latin *punctillum,* but not
with the meaning of 'punctiliousness.'

examples of the corresponding phenomenon with Latin
and Greek elements, some of which may, however, have
been imported through French. The ending -*ation* is
found in *starvation, backwardation,* and others; note
also the American *thunderation* ('It was an accident,
sir.' 'Accident the thunderation,' Opie Read, *Toothpick
Tales,* Chicago, 1892, p. 35). *Johnsoniana, Miltoniana,*
etc., are quite modern; the ending *ana* alone is now also
used as a detached noun. In -*ist* we have *walkist,* which
is sometimes used to denote a *professional* walker, and
is therefore distinguished by the more learned ending.
Compare also *turfite* and the numerous words in -*ite*
derived from proper names: *Irvingite, Ruskinite,* etc.
The same ending is frequently used in mineralogy and
chemistry, one of the latest additions to these formations
being *fumelessite* = smokeless gunpowder. Hybrids in
-*ism* (cf. § 121) abound; *heathenism* has been used by
Bacon, Milton, Addison, Freeman and others; *witticism*
was first used by Dryden, who asks pardon for this new
word; *blockheadism* is found in Ruskin; further *funny-
ism, freelovism,* etc.; the curious *wegotism* may be
classed with the jocular *drinkitite* on the analogy of
appetite. *Girlicide,* after *suicide,* is another jocular formation (Smedley, *Frank Fairlegh* I, 190, not in NED.).
To the same sphere belong Byron's *weatherology* and
some words in -*ocracy,* such as *landocracy, shopocracy,
barristerocracy, squattocracy,* Carlyle's *strumpetocracy,*
and Meredith's *snipocracy* (*Evan Harrington,* 174,
from *snip* as a nickname for a tailor). On the other hand
squirearchy (with *squirearchical*) seems to have quite
established itself in serious language. Among verbal
formations must be mentioned those in -*ize:* he *woman-
ized* his language (Meredith, *Egoist,* 32), *Londonizing*
(ibid., 80), *soberize,* etc. Adjectives are formed in

-*ative: talkative, babblative, scribblative,* and *soothative,*
of which only the first is recognized; in -*aceous: gossip-
aceous* (Darwin, *Life and Letters,* I, 375); in -*arious:
burglarious* (Stevenson, *Dynamiter,* 130), and -*iacal:
dandiacal* (Carlyle, *Sartor,* 188). Even if many of these
words are 'nonce-words,' it cannot be denied that the
process is genuinely English and perfectly legitimate—
within reasonable limits at any rate.

124. Some Latin and Greek prepositions have in
recent times been extensively used to form new words.
Ex-, as in *ex-king, ex-head-master,* etc.,[11] seems first to
have been used in French, but it is now common to
most or all Germanic languages as well; in English this
formation did not become popular till the end of the
18th century. *Anti:* the anti-taxation movement; an
antiforeign party; 'Mr. Anti-slavery Clarkson' (De
Quincey, *Opium-Eater,* 197); 'chairs unpleasant to sit
in—anticaller chairs they might be named' (H. Spencer,
Facts and Comments, 85). *Co-:* 'a friend of mine, co-
godfather to Dickens's child with me' (Tennyson, *Life,*
II, 114); 'Wallace, the co-formulator of the Darwinian
theory' (Clodd, *Pioneers of Evolution,* 68). *De-,* especially with verbs in -*ize:* de-anglicize, de-democratize,
deprovincialize, denationalize; less frequently as in de-
tenant, de-miracle (Tennyson). *Inter-:* intermingle, in-
termix, intermarriage, interbreed, intercommunicate,
interdependence, etc. *International* was coined by Bent-
ham in 1780: it marks linguistically the first beginning
of the era when relations between nations came to be
considered like relations between citizens, capable of
peaceful arrangement according to right rather than according to might. A great many other similar adjectives
have since been formed: *intercollegiate, interracial,*

[11] 'A pair of ex-white satin shoes' (Thackeray).

interparliamentary, etc. Where no adjective existed, the substantive is used unchanged, but the combination is virtually an adjective: *interstate* affairs; an *inter-island* steamer; 'international, inter-club, inter-team, inter-college or inter-school contests' (quoted in NED.); 'in short inter-whiff sentences' (Kinglake, *Eothen,* 125). *Pre-:* the pre-Darwinian explanations; prenuptial friend-ships (Pinero, *Second Mrs. Tanqueray,* p. 6, what are called on p. 8 'ante-nuptial acquaintances'); 'in the pre-railroad, pre-telegraphic period' (G. Eliot); the pre-railway city; the pre-board school; a bunch of pre-Johannesburg Transvaals; the pre-mechanical civilized state (all these are quotations from H. G. Wells); in your pre-smoking days (Barrie); pre-war prices. *Pro-:* the pro-Boers; pro-foreign proclivities; a pro-Belgian, or rather pro-King Leopold speaker. As any number of such derivatives or compounds can be formed with the greatest facility, the utility and convenience of these cer-tainly not classical expedients cannot be reasonably denied, though it may be questioned whether it would not have been better to utilize English prepositions for the same purposes, as is done with *after-* (an after-dinner speech) and sometimes with *before-* ('the before Alfred remains of our language,' Sweet; 'smoking his before-breakfast pipe,' Conan Doyle).[12] A few words must be added on *re-,* which is used in a similar man-ner in any number of free compounds, such as *rebirth,* and especially verbs: re-organize, re-sterilize, re-submit, re-pocket, re-leather, re-case, etc. Here *re-* is always strongly stressed and pronounced with a long vowel [i·], and by that means these recent words are in the spoken language easily distinguished from the older set of *re-* words, where *re* is either weakly stressed or else, when

[12] Cf. my *Mod. E. Grammar,* II, p. 343.

strongly stressed, pronounced with short [e]. We have therefore such pairs as *recollect* = to remember, and *re-collect* = to collect again; he *recovered* the lost umbrella and had it *re-covered; reform* and *re-form* (reformation and re-formation), *recreate and re-create, remark* and *re-mark, resign* and *re-sign, resound* and *re-sound, resort* and *re-sort*. In the written language the distinction is not always observed.

125. Latin has influenced English not only in vocabulary, but also in style and syntax. The absolute participle (as in 'everything considered,' or 'this being the case') was introduced at a very early period in imitation of the Latin construction.[13] It is comparatively rare in Old English, where it occurs chiefly in close translations from Latin. In the first period of Middle English it is equally rare, but in the second period it becomes a little more frequent. Chaucer seems to have used it chiefly in imitation of the Italian construction, but this Italian influence died out with him, and French influence did very little to increase the frequency of the construction. In the beginning of the Modern English period the absolute participle, though occurring more often than formerly, 'had not become thoroughly naturalized. It limited itself to certain favorite authors where the classical element largely predominated, and was used but sparingly by authors whose style was essentially English' (Ross, p. 38). But after 1660, when English prose style developed a new phase, which was saturated with classical elements, the construction rapidly gained ground and was finally fixed and naturalized in the language. There are some other Latin idioms which authors tried

[13] Morgan Callaway, *The Absolute Participle in Anglo-Saxon* (Baltimore, 1889). Charles Hunter Ross, *The Absolute Participle in Middle and Modern English* (Baltimore, 1893).

to imitate, but which have always been felt as unnatural, so that now they have been dropped, for instance *who* for *he who* or *those who* as in 'sleeping found by whom they dread' (Milton, *P.L.,* I, 1333), further such interrogative and relative constructions as those found in the following quotations: 'To do what service am I sent for hither?' (Shakesp. R 2, IV, 1, 176) and 'a right noble and pious lord, who had he not sacrific'd his life . . . we had not now mist and bewayl'd a worthy patron' (Milton, *Areop.,* 51).

126. Latin grammar was the only grammar taught in those days, and the only grammar found worthy of study and imitation. 'That highly disciplined syntax which Milton favoured from the first, and to which he tended more and more, was in fact the classical syntax, or, to be more exact, an adaptation of the syntax of the Latin tongue,' says D. Masson,[14] and when he adds, 'It could hardly fail to be so . . . Even now, questions in English syntax are often settled best practically, if a settlement is wanted, by a reference to Latin construction,' he expressed a totally erroneous conception which has been, and is, unfortunately too common, although very little linguistic culture would seem to be needed to expose its fallacy. Nowhere, perhaps, has this misconception been more strongly expressed than in Dryden's preface to *Troilus and Cressida,* where he writes: 'How barbarously we yet write and speak your Lordship knows, and I am sufficiently sensible in my own English. For I am often put to a stand in considering whether what I write be the idiom of the tongue, or false grammar and nonsense couched beneath that specious name of Anglicism, and have no other way to clear my doubts but by translating my English into Latin, and thereby trying

[14] *Poetical Works of Milton,* 1890, vol. III, p. 74–5.

what sense the words will bear in a more stable language.' I am afraid that Dryden would never have become the famous writer he is, had he employed this practice as often as he would have us imagine. But it was certainly in deference to Latin syntax that in the later editions of his *Essay on Dramatic Poesy* he changed such phrases as 'I cannot think so contemptibly of the age I live in' to 'the age in which I live'; he speaks somewhere[15] of the preposition at the end of the sentence as a common fault with Ben Jonson 'and which I have but lately observed in my own writings.' The construction Dryden here reprehends is not a 'fault' and is not confined to Ben Jonson, but is a genuine English idiom of long standing in the language and found very frequently in all writers of natural prose and verse. The omission of the relative pronoun, which Dr. Johnson terms 'a colloquial barbarism' and which is found only seven or eight times in all the writings of Milton, and according to Thum only twice in the whole of Macaulay's History, abounds in the writings of such authors as Shakespeare, Bunyan, Swift, Fielding, Goldsmith, Sterne, Byron, Shelley, Dickens, Thackeray, Tennyson, Ruskin, etc., etc. In Addison's well-known *Humble Petition of Who and Which*[16] these two pronouns complain of the injury done to them by the recent extension of the use of *that*. 'We are descended of ancient Families, and kept up our Dignity and Honour many Years till the Jacksprat *that* supplanted us.' Addison here turns all historical truth topsy-turvy, for *that* is much older as a relative than either *who* or *which;* but the real reason of his predilection for the latter two was certainly their

---

[15] I quote this second-hand, see J. Earle, *English Prose*, 267; Hales, Notes to Milton's *Areopagitica*, p. 103.

[16] The *Spectator*, No. 78, May 30, 1711.

conformity with Latin relative pronouns, and there can
be no doubt that his article, assisted by English grammars and the teaching given in schoolrooms, has contributed very much to restricting the use of *that* as a
relative word—in writing at least. Addison himself,
when editing the *Spectator* in book-form, corrected many
a natural *that* into a less natural *who* or *which*.

127. As to the more general effect of classical
studies on English style, I am very much inclined to
think that Darwin and Huxley are right as against most
schoolmasters. Darwin 'had the strongest disbelief in the
common idea that a classical scholar must write good
English; indeed, he thought that the contrary was the
case.'[17] Huxley wrote to *The Times,* Aug. 5, 1890:[18]
'My impression has been that the Genius of the English
language is widely different from that of Latin; and that
the worst and the most debased kinds of English style
are those which ape Latinity. I know of no purer English
prose than that of John Bunyan and Daniel Defoe; I
doubt if the music of Keats's verse has ever been sur-
passed; it has not been my fortune to hear any orator
who approached the powerful simplicity, the limpid
sincerity, of the speech of John Bright. Yet Latin literature and these masters of English had little to do with
one another.' As 'in diesem Bund der dritte' might be
mentioned Herbert Spencer, who expressed himself
strongly to the same effect in his last book.[19]

128. To return to the vocabulary. We may now
consider the question: Is the Latin element on the whole
beneficial to the English tongue or would it have been
better if the free adoption of words from the classical

[17] *Life and Letters* of Ch. Darwin, 1887, I, p. 155.
[18] Quoted by J. Earle, *English Prose,* 487.
[19] *Facts and Comments,* 1902, p. 70.

languages had been kept within much narrower limits? A perfectly impartial decision is not easy but it is hoped that the following may be considered a fair statement of the most important pros and cons. The first advantage that strikes the observer is the enormous addition to the English vocabulary. If the English boast that their language is richer than any other, and that their dictionaries contain a far greater number of words than German and French ones, the chief reason is, of course, the greater number of foreign and especially of French and Latin words adopted. 'I trade,' says Dryden, 'both with the living and the dead for the enrichment of our native language.'

129. But this wealth of words has its seamy side too. The real psychological wealth is wealth of ideas, not of mere names. 'We have more words than notions, half a dozen words for the same thing,' says Selden (*Table Talk*, LXXVI). Words are not material things that can be heaped up like money or stores of food and clothes, from which you may at any time take what you want. A word to be yours must be learnt by you, and possessing it means reproducing it. Both the process of learning and that of reproducing it involve labour on your part. Some words are easy to handle, and others difficult. The number of words at your disposal in a given language is, therefore, not the only thing of importance; their quality, too, is to be considered, and especially the ease with which they can be associated with the ideas they are to symbolize and with other words. Now many of the Latin words are deficient in that respect, and this entails other drawback to speakers of English, as will presently appear.

130. It will be argued in favour of the classical elements that many of them fill up gaps in the native stock of words, so that they serve to express ideas which would have been nameless but for them. To this it may be objected that the resources of the original language should not be underrated. In most, perhaps in all, cases it would have been possible to find an adequate expression in the vernacular or to coin one. The tendency to such economy in Old English and the ease with which felicitous terms for new ideas were then framed by means of native speech-material, have been mentioned above. But little by little English speakers lost the habit of looking first to their own language and utilizing it to the utmost before going abroad for new expressions. People who had had their whole education in Latin and had thought all their best thoughts in that language to an extent which is not easy for us moderns to realize, often found it easier to write on abstract or learned subjects in Latin than in their own vernacular, and when they tried to write on these things in English Latin words would constantly come first to their minds. Mental laziness and regard to their own momentary convenience therefore led them to retain the Latin word and give it only an English termination. Little did they care for the convenience of their readers, if they should happen to be ignorant of the classics, or for that of unborn generations, whom they forced by their disregard for their own language to carry on the burden of committing to memory words and expressions that were really foreign to their idiom. If they have not actually dried up the natural sources of speech—for these run on as fresh as ever—yet they have accustomed their countrymen to cross the stream in search of water, to use an expressive Danish locution.

131. There is one class of words which seems to be rather sparingly represented in the native vocabulary,

so that classical formations are extremely often resorted to, namely, the adjectives. It is, in fact, surprising how many pairs we have of native nouns and foreign adjectives, e.g. mouth: *oral;* nose: *nasal;* eye: *ocular;* mind: *mental;* son: *filial;* ox: *bovine;* worm: *vermicular;* house: *domestic;* the middle ages: *medieval;* book: *literary;* moon: *lunar;* sun: *solar;* star: *stellar;* town: *urban;* man: *human, virile,* etc., etc. In the same category we may class such pairs as money: *monetary, pecuniary;* letter: *epistolary;* school: *scholastic,* as the nouns, though originally foreign, are now for all practical purposes to be considered native. We may note here English proper names and their Latinized adjectives, e.g. Dorset: *Dorsetian;* Oxford: *Oxonian;* Cambridge: *Cantabrigian;* Gladstone: *Gladstonian.* Lancaster has even two adjectives, *Lancastrian* (in medieval history) and *Lancasterian* (schools, Joseph Lancaster, 1771–1838). It cannot be pretended that all these adjectives are used on account of any real deficiency in the English language, as it has quite a number of endings by which to turn substantives into adjectives: *-en* (silken), *-y* (flowery), *-ish* (girlish), *-ly* (fatherly), *-like* (fishlike), *-some* (burdensome), *-ful* (sinful), and these might easily have been utilized still more than they actually have been. In point of fact, we possess not a few native adjectives by the side of more learned ones, e.g. *fatherly: paternal; motherly: maternal; brotherly: fraternal* (but only *sisterly,* as *sororal* is so rare as to be left out of account); further *watery: aquatic* or *aqueous; heavenly: celestial; earthy, earthly, earthen: terrestrial; timely: temporal; daily: diurnal; truthful: veracious;* etc. In some cases the meanings of these have become more or less differentiated, the English words having often lost an abstract sense which they formerly had and which might have been retained with advantage. If the word *sangui-nary* is now extensively used it is due to the curious twist-ing of the meaning of *bloody* in vulgar speech (cf. 244). *Kingly, royal* and *regal:* who is able to tell exactly how these adjectives differ in signification? And might not English like other languages (*royal* in French, *kongelig* in Danish, *königlich* in German) have been content with one word instead of three?

132. Besides, in a great many cases it is really con-trary to the genius of the language to use an adjective at all. Where Romanic and Slavic languages very often prefer a combination of a noun and an adjective the Germanic languages combine the two ideas into a com-pound noun. *Birthday* is much more English than *natal day* (which is used, for instance, in Wordsworth's 75th Sonnet), and *eyeball* than *ocular globe,* but physiologists think it more dignified to speak of the *gustatory nerve* than of the *taste nerve* and will even say *mental nerve* (Lat. mentum 'chin') instead of *chin nerve* in spite of the unavoidable confusion with the familiar adjective *mental.* Mere position before another noun is really the most English way of turning a noun into an adjective, e.g. the *London* market, a *Wessex* man, *Yorkshire* pud-ding, a strong *Edinburgh* accent, a *Japan* table, *Venice* glasses, the *Chaucer* Society, the *Droeshout* picture, a *Gladstone* bag, imitation *Astrakhan,* 'Every *tiger* mad-ness muzzled, every *serpent* passion kill'd' (Tenny-son).[20] It is worth noting that the English adjective corresponding to *family* is not *familiar,* which has been somewhat estranged from its kindred, but *family;* family reasons, family affairs, family questions, etc. The un-

---

[20] Shakespeare did not scruple to write 'the Carthage queen,' 'Rome gates,' 'Tiber banks,' even 'through faire Verona streets.' Cf. below, § 194, and *Mod. Engl. Grammar,* II, ch. XIII.

naturalness of forming Latin adjectives is, perhaps, also
shown by the vacillation often found between different
endings, as in *feudatary* and *feudatory, festal* and *festive.*
From *labyrinth* no less than six adjectives have been
found: *labyrinthal, labyrinthean, labyrinthian, labyrin-
thic, labyrinthical* and *labyrinthine.* Many adjectives are
quite superfluous; Shakespeare never used either *au-
tumnal, hibernal, vernal* or *estival,* and he probably
never missed them. Instead of *hodiernal* and *hesternal*
we have luckily other expressions (to-day's post; the
questions of the day; yesterday's news). Most of us can
certainly do without *gressorial* (birds), *avuncular* (a
favourite with Thackeray: 'Clive, in the avuncular gig';
'the avuncular banking house'; 'the avuncular quarrel,'
all from *The Newcomes*), *osculatory* (processes = kiss-
ing; ib.), *lachrymatory* (he is great in the l. line; ib.),
aquiline ('What! am I an eagle too? I have no aquiline
pretensions at all,' ib.[21])—and a great many similarly
purposeless adjectives.

133. More than in anything else the richness of the
English language manifests itself in its great number of
synonyms, whether we take his word in its strict sense
of words of exactly the same meaning or in the looser
sense of words with nearly the same meaning. It is
evident that the latter class must be the most valuable,
as it allows speakers to express subtle shades of thought.
Juvenile does not signify the same thing as *youthful,
ponderous* as *weighty, portion* as *share, miserable* as
wretched. Legible means 'that can be read,' *readable*
generally 'worth reading.' Sometimes the Latin word is
used in a more limited, special or precise sense than the
English, as is seen by a comparison of *identical* and

[21] Thus used in a different manner from the familiar *aquiline*
nose.

same, science and *knowledge, sentence* and *saying, latent* or *occult* and *hidden. Breath* can hardly now be called a synonym of *spirit* ('The spirit does not mean the breath,' Tennyson), and similarly *edify,* which is still used by Spenser in the concrete sense of 'building up,' is now used exclusively with a spiritual signification, which its former synonym *build* can never have. *Homicide* is the learned, abstract, colourless word, while *murder* denotes only one kind of *manslaughter,* and *killing* is the everyday word with a much vaguer signification (being applicable also to animals); there is a very apposite quotation from Coleridge in the NED.: '[He] is acquitted of murder—the act of manslaughter only, or it was justifiable homicide.' The learned word *magnitude* is more specialized than *greatness* or *size* (which is now thoroughly English, but is a very recent development of *assize* in a curiously modified sense). *Popish* has an element of contempt which the learned *papal* does not share. The Latin *masculine* is more abstract than the English *manly,* which generally implies an emotional element of praise, the French *male* has not exactly the same import as either, and the Latin *virile* represents a fourth shade, while for the other sex we have *female, feminine, womanly* and *womanish,* the differences between which are not parallel to those between the first series of synonyms.

134. These examples will suffice to illustrate the synonymic relations between classical and other words. It will be seen that it is not always easy to draw a line or to determine exactly the different shades of meaning attached to each word; indeed, a comparison of the definitions given in various essays on synonyms and in dictionaries, and especially a comparison of these definitions with the use as actually found in various writers, will show that it is in many cases a hopeless task to assign definite spheres of signification to these words. Sometimes the only real difference is that one term is preferred in certain collocations and another in others. Still, it is indubitable that very often the existence of a double or triple assortment of expressions will allow a writer to express his thoughts with the greatest precision imaginable. But on the other hand, only those whose thoughts are accurate and well disciplined attain to the highest degree of linguistic precision, and the use in speech and writing of the same set of words by loose and inexact thinkers will always tend to blur out any sharp lines of demarcation that may exist between such synonymous terms as do not belong to their everyday stock of language.

135. However, even where there is no real difference in the value of two words or where the difference is momentarily disregarded, their existence may not be entirely worthless, as it enables an author to avoid a trivial repetition of the same word, and variety of expressions is generally considered one of the felicities of style. We very often see English authors use a native and a borrowed word side by side simply, it would seem, to amplify the expression, without modifying its meaning. Thus 'of blind *forgetfulnesse* and dark *oblivion*' (Shakespeare, in Buckingham's strongly rhetorical speech, R 3, III, 7, 129). 'The *manifold multiform* flower' (Swinburne, *Songs bef. Sunr.*, 106). A perfectly natural variation of three expressions is seen in: 'the Bushman story is just the *sort* of *story* we *expect* from Bushmen, whereas the Hesiodic story is not at all the *kind* of *tale* we *look for* from Greeks.' (A. Lang, *Custom and Myth*, 54.) Further examples: 'I *went upstairs* with my candle directly. It appeared to my childish fancy,

as I *ascended* to the bedroom . . .' 'He asked me if it
would suit my convenience to have the light *put out;*
and on my answering "yes," instantly *extinguished* it.'
'The phantom slowly *approached.* When it *came near*
him, Scrooge bent down'; 'they are *exactly unlike.* They
are *utterly dissimilar* in all respects' (all these from
Dickens). 'We who boast of our *land* of *freedom,* we
who live in the *country* of *liberty.*' 'I could not repress
a *half smile* as he said this; a similar *demi-manifestation
of feeling* appeared at the same moment on Hunsden's
lips.' This kind of variation evidently does not *always*
lead to the highest excellence of style. I quote from
Minto[22] Samuel Johnson's comparison between punch
and conversation: 'The spirit, volatile and fiery, is *the
proper emblem* of vivacity and wit; the acidity of the
lemon will very *aptly figure* pungency of raillery and
acrimony of censure; sugar is the *natural representative*
of luscious adulation and gentle complaisance; and water
is the *proper hieroglyphic* of easy prattle, innocent and
tasteless.' This is not far from Mr. Micawber's piling up
of words ('to the best of my knowledge, information and
belief . . . to wit, in manner following, that is to say'),
which gives Dickens the occasion for the following out-
burst:

'In the taking of legal oaths, for instance, deponents
seem to enjoy themselves mightily when they come to
several good words in succession, for the expression of
one idea; as, that they utterly detest, abominate, and
abjure, or so forth; and the old anathemas were made
relishing on the same principle. We talk about the
tyranny of words, but we like to tyrannize over them
too; we are fond of having a large superfluous establish-
ment of words to wait upon us on great occasions; we

[22] *Manual of English Prose Literature,* 3rd ed., 1896, p. 418.

think it looks important, and sounds well. As we are not particular about the meanings of our liveries on state occasions, if they be but fine and numerous enough, so the meaning or necessity of our words is a secondary consideration if there be but a great parade of them. And as individuals get into trouble by making too great a show of liveries, or as slaves when they are too numerous rise against their masters, so I think I could mention a nation that has got into many great difficulties, and will get into many greater, from maintaining too large a retinue of words.' (*David Copperfield*, p. 702.)[23]

136. No doubt many of the synonymous terms introduced from Latin and Greek had best been let alone. No one would have missed *pharos* by the side of *lighthouse,* or *nigritude* by the side of *blackness*. The native words *cold, cool, chill, chilly, icy, frosty* might have seemed sufficient for all purposes, without any necessity for importing *frigid, gelid,* and *algid,* which as a matter of fact are found neither in Shakespeare nor in the Authorized Version of the Bible nor in the poetical works of Milton, Pope, Cowper and Shelley.

137. Apart from the advantage of being able constantly to make a choice between words possessing a different number of syllables and often also presenting a difference in the place of the accent, poets will often find the sonorous Latin words better for their purposes than the short native ones. In some kinds of prose writing, too, they are felt to heighten the tone, and add dignity, even majesty, to the structure of the sentence. The chief reason of this seems to be that the long word takes up more time. Instead of hurrying the reader or

---

[23] Mr. Micawber also has the following delightful piece of bathos: 'It is not an avocation of a remunerative description—in other words, it does *not* pay.'

listener on to the next idea, it allows his mind to dwell
for a longer time upon the same idea; it gives time for
his reflexion to be deeper and especially for his emotion
to be stronger. This seems to me more important than
the two other reasons given by H. Spencer (*Essays*, II,
p. 14) that 'a voluminous, mouth-filling epithet is, by its
very size, suggestive of largeness or strength' and that
'a word of several syllables admits of more emphatic
articulation (?); and as emphatic articulation is a sign
of emotion, the unusual impressiveness of the thing
named is implied by it.' Let me quote here also a quaint
passage (not to be taken too seriously) from Howell
(*New English Grammar,* 1662, p. 40): 'The Spanish
abound and delight in words of many syllables and
where the English expresseth himself in one syllable, he
doth in 5 or 6, as thoughts pensamientos, fray levanta-
miento, &c., which is held a part of wisdom, for while
they speak they take time to consider of the matter.'

138. It is often said that the classical elements are
commendable on the score of international intelligibility, and it is certain that many of them, even of those
formed during the last century on more or less exact
Latin and Greek analogy, are used in many other
civilized countries as well as in England. The utility
of this is evident in our days of easy communication
between the nations; but on the whole its utility should
not be valued beyond measure. If the thing to be named
is one of everyday importance, national convenience
should certainly be considered before international ease:
therefore *to wire* and *a wire* are preferable to *telegraph*
and *telegram*.[24] Scientific nomenclature is to a great extent universal, and there is no reason why each nation

[24] Nowadays also *wireless* both as a noun and as a verb: 'I
sent him a wireless'; 'they wirelessed for help.'

should have its own name for *foraminifera* or *mono-cotyledones*. But so much of science is now becoming more and more the property of everybody and influences daily life so deeply that the endeavour should rather be to have popular than learned names for whatever in science is not intended exclusively for the specialist. *Sleeplessness* is a better name than *insomnia,* and foreigners who know English enough to read a medical treatise in it will be no more perplexed by the word than an Englishman reading German is by *Schlaflosigkeit.* Foreign phoneticians have had no difficulty in understanding Melville Bell's excellent nomenclature and have even to a great extent adopted the English terms of *front, mixed, back,* etc., in preference to the more cumbersome *palatal, gutturopalatal,* and *guttural.* It is a pity that *half-vowel* (Googe, 1577) and *half-vowelish* (Ben Jonson) should have been superseded by *semi-vowel* and *semi-vowel-like.* Among English words that have been in recent times adopted by many foreign languages may be mentioned *cheque, box* (in a bank), *trust, film* (in photography), *sport, jockey, sulky, gig, handicap, dock, waterproof, tender, coke* (German and Danish *koks* or sometimes with pseudo-English spelling *coaks*), so that even to obtain international currency a word need not have a learned appearance or be derived from Greek and Latin roots. Besides, many of the latter class are not quite so international as might be supposed, as their English significations are unknown on the continent (*pathos, physic, concurrent, competition, actual, eventual, injury*); sometimes, also, the ending is different, as in *principle* (Fr. principe, etc.), *individual* (Fr. individu, Dan. individ, German Individuum), *chemistry* (chimie, chemie), *botany* (botanique), *fanaticism* (fanatisme).

139. It is possible to point out a certain number of inherent deficiencies which affect parts of the vocabulary borrowed from the classical language. Mention has already been made (§ 26) of the stress-shifting which is so contrary to the general spirit of Germanic tongues and which obscures the relation between connected words, especially in a language where unstressed syllables are generally pronounced with such indistinct vowel sounds as in English. Compare, for instance, *solid* and *solidity, pathos* and *pathetic, pathology* and *pathologic, pacify* and *pacific* (note that the first two syllables of *pacification,* where the strongest stress is on the fourth syllable, vacillate between the two corresponding pronunciations). The incongruity is especially disagreeable when native names are distorted by means of a learned derivative ending, as when *Milton* has the stress shifted on to the second syllable and the vowel changed (in two different ways) in *Miltonic* and *Miltonian;* cf. also *Baconian, Dickensian, Taylorian, Spenserian, Canadian, Dorsetian,* etc.

140. Another drawback is shown in the relation between *emit* and *immit, emerge* and *immerge.* While in Latin *emitto* and *immitto, emergo* and *immergo* were easily kept apart, because the vowels were distinct and double consonants were rigorously pronounced double and so kept apart from single ones, the natural English pronunciation will confound them, just as it confounds the first syllables of *immediate* and *emotion.* Now, as the meaning of *e-* is the exact opposite of *in-*, the two pairs do not go well together in the same language. The same is true of *illusion* and *elusion.*[25] A still greater

---

[25] Illiterate spellers will often write *illicit* for *elicit, enumerable* for *innumerable,* etc. Many words have had, and some still have, two spellings, with *en-* (*em-*) from the French, and with *in-* (*im-*) from the Latin (*enquire, inquire,* etc.).

drawback arises from the two meanings of initial *in,* which is sometimes the negative prefix and sometimes the preposition. According to dictionaries *infusible* means (1) that may be infused or poured in, (2) incapable of being fused or melted. *Importable,* which is now only used as derived from *import* (capable of being imported), had formerly also the meaning 'unbearable,' and *improvable* similarly had the meaning of 'incapable of being proved' though it only retains that of 'capable of being improved.' What Shakespeare in one passage (Temp. II, 1, 37) expresses in accordance with modern usage by the word *uninhabitable* he elsewhere calls *inhabitable* ('Even to the frozen ridges of the Alpes, Or any other ground inhabitable,' R 2, I, 1, 65), and the ambiguity of the latter word has now led to the curious result that the positive adjective corresponding to *inhabit* is *habitable* and the negative *uninhabitable.* The first syllable of *inebriety* is the preposition *in-,* so that it means the same thing as the rare *ebriety* 'drunkenness,' but T. Hook mistook it for the negative prefix and so, subtracting *in-,* made *ebriety* mean 'sobriety.'[26] *Illustrious* is used in Shakespeare's Cymb. I, 6, 109, as the negative of *lustrous,* while elsewhere it has the exactly opposite signification. Fortunately this ambiguity is limited to a comparatively small portion of the vocabulary.[27]

141. Loan-words do not necessarily make a language inharmonious. In Finnish, for instance, in spite of numerous loans from a variety of languages, the prevailing impression is one of unity, apart perhaps

[26] See quotation in Davies, *Supplementary English Glossary,* 1881.

[27] If *invaluable* means generally 'very valuable' and sometimes 'valueless,' the case is obviously different from the above.

from some of the most recent Swedish words. The
foreign elements have been so assimilated in sound
and inflexion as to be recognizable as foreign only to
the eye of a philologist. The same may be said of the
pre-Conquest borrowings from Latin into English, of
the Scandinavian and of the most important among the
French loans, nay even of a great many recent loans
from exotic languages. *Wine* and *tea, bacon* and *eggs,
orange* and *sugar, plunder* and *war, prison* and *judge*—
all are not only indispensable, but harmonious elements
of English. But while most people are astonished on
first hearing that such words have not always belonged
to their language, no philological training is required
to discover that *phenomenon* or *diphtheria* or *intellectual*
or *latitudinarian* are out of harmony with the real core
or central part of the language. Every one must feel
the incongruity of such sets of words as *father*—*paternal*
—*parricide*, or of the abnormal plurals which break the
beautiful regularity of nearly all English substantives—
phenomena, nuclei, larvæ, chrysalides, indices, etc. The
occasional occurrence of such blundering plurals as
animalculæ and *ignorami* is an unconscious protest
against the prevalent pedantry of schoolmasters in this
respect.[28]

142. The unnatural state into which the language

---

[28] 'He may also see giraffes, lions or rhinoceros. The mention
of this last word reminds me of a problem, which has tormented
me all the time that I have been in East Africa, namely, what is
the plural of rhinoceros? The conversational abbreviations,
"rhino," "rhinos," seem beneath the dignity of literature, and to
use the sporting idiom by which the singular is always put for
the plural is merely to avoid the difficulty. Liddell and Scott
seem to authorize "rhinocerotes" which is pedantic, but "rhi-
noceroses" is not euphonious.' Sir Charles Eliot, *The East
Africa Protectorate* (1905), 266. Cf. *Mod. Engl. Grammar* II,
ch. III.

has been thrown by the wholesale adoption of learned words is further manifested by the fact that not a few of them have no fixed pronunciation; they are, in fact, eye-words that do not really exist in the language. Educated people freely write them and understand them when they see them written, but are more or less puzzled when they have to pronounce them. Dr. Murray relates how he was once present at a meeting of a learned society, where in the course of discussion he heard the word *gaseous* systematically pronounced in six different ways by as many eminent physicists. (NED., Preface.) *Diatribist* is by Murray and the Century Dictionary stressed on the first, by Webster on the second syllable, and the same hesitation is found with *phonotypy, photochromy,* and many similar words. This is, however, beaten by two so well-known words as *hegemony* and *phthisis,* for each of which dictionaries record no less than nine possible pronunciations without being able to tell us which of these is the prevalent or preferable one. I doubt very much whether analogous waverings can be found in any other language.

143. The worst thing, however, that can be said against the words that are occupying us here is their difficulty and the undemocratic character which is a natural outcome of their difficulty. A great many of them will never be used or understood by anybody that has not had a classical education.[29] There are usually

[29] Sometimes they are not even understood by the erudite themselves. *Gestic* in Goldsmith's 'skill'd in gestic lore' (*Traveller,* 253) is taken in many dictionaries as meaning 'legendary, historical' as if from *gest,* OFr. *geste,* 'story, romance'; but the context shows conclusively that 'pertaining to bodily movement, esp. dancing' (NED.) must be the meaning; Cf. Lat. *gestus,* 'gesture.' *Aristarchy* has been wrongly interpreted in most dictionaries as 'a body of good men in power,' while it is derived

no associations of ideas between them and the ordinary
stock of words, and no likenesses in root or in the
formative elements to assist the memory. We have here
none of those invisible threads that knit words together
in the human mind. Their great number in the language
is therefore apt to form or rather to accentuate class
divisions, so that a man's culture is largely judged by
the extent to which he is able correctly to handle these
hard words in speech and in writing—certainly not the
highest imaginable standard of a man's worth. No literature in the world abounds as English does in characters
made ridiculous to the reader by the manner in which
they misapply or distort 'big' words. Shakespeare's
Dogberry and Mrs. Quickly, Fielding's Mrs. Slipslop,
Smollett's Winifred Jenkins, Sheridan's Mrs. Malaprop,
Dickens's Weller senior, Shillaber's Mrs. Partington, and
footmen and labourers innumerable made fun of in
novels and comedies might all of them appear in court
as witnesses for the plaintiff in a law-suit brought against
the educated classes of England for wilfully making the
language more complicated than necessary and thereby
hindering the spread of education among all classes of
the population.

144. Different authors vary very greatly with regard to the extent to which they make use of such
'choice words, and measured phrase above the reach
of ordinary men.' So much is said on this head in easily
accessible textbooks on literature that I need not repeat
it here. Unfortunately the statistical calculations given
there of the percentage of native and of foreign words
in different writers are not quite to the point, for while
they generally include Scandinavian loans among native

from the proper name Aristarch and means 'a body of severe
critics.' (Fitzedward Hall, *Modern English*, 143.)

words, they reckon together all words of classical origin, although such popular words as *cry* or *crown* have evidently quite a different standing in the language from learned words like *auditory* or *hymenoptera*. The culmination with regard to the use of learned words in ordinary literary style was reached in the time of Dr. Samuel Johnson. I can find no better example to illustrate the effect of extreme 'Johnsonese' than the following:

'The proverbial oracles of our parsimonious ancestors have informed us, that the fatal waste of our fortune is by small expenses, by the profusion of sums too little singly to alarm our caution, and which we never suffer ourselves to consider together. Of the same kind is the prodigality of life; he that hopes to look back hereafter with satisfaction upon past years, must learn to know the present value of single minutes and endeavour to let no particle of time fall useless to the ground.'[30]

145. In his Essay on Madame D'Arblay, Macaulay gives some delightful samples of this style as developed by that ardent admirer of Dr. Johnson. Sheridan refused to permit his lovely wife to sing in public, and was warmly praised on this account by Johnson. 'The last of men,' says Madame D'Arblay, 'was Doctor Johnson to have abetted squandering the delicacy of integrity by nullifying the labours of talent.' To be starved to death is 'to sink from inanition into nonentity.' Sir Isaac Newton is 'the developer of the skies in their embodied movements,' and Mrs. Thrale, when a party of clever

---

[30] Minto (*Manual of Engl. Prose Lit.*, 422) translates this as follows: 'Take care of the pennies,' says the thrifty old proverb, 'and the pounds will take care of themselves.' In like manner we might say, 'Take care of the minutes, and the years will take care of themselves.'

people sat silent, is said to have been 'provoked by the
dulness of a taciturnity that, in the midst of such renowned interlocutors, produced as narcotic a torpor as
could have been caused by a death the most barren of
all human faculties.' (Macaulay, *Essays,* Tauchn. ed.
V., p. 65.)[31]

146. In the nineteenth century a most happy
reaction set in in favour of 'Saxon' words and natural
expressions; and it is highly significant that Tennyson,
for instance, prides himself on having in the *Idylls of
the King* used Latin words more sparingly than any
other poet. But still the malady lingers on, especially
with the half-educated. I quote from a newspaper the
following story: The young lady home from school was
explaining. 'Take an egg,' she said, 'and make a perfora-
tion in the base and a corresponding one in the apex.
Then apply the lips to the aperture, and by forcibly in-
haling the breath the shell is entirely discharged of its
contents.' An old lady who was listening exclaimed: 'It
beats all how folks do things nowadays. When I was a
gal they made a hole in each end and sucked.' To a
different class belongs that master of Saxon English,
Charles Lamb, who begins his 'Chapter on Ears' in the
following way: 'I have no ear. Mistake me not, reader,
nor imagine that I am by nature destitute of those exterior twin appendages, hanging ornaments, and (archi-
tecturally speaking) handsome volutes to the human
capital. Better my mother had never borne me. I am,
I think, rather delicately than copiously provided with
those conduits; and I feel no disposition to envy the
mule for his plenty, or the mole for her exactness, in

---

[31] My brother and I meet every week, by an alternate reciproca-
tion of intercourse, as Sam Johnson would express it' (Cowper, *Letters,* I, 18).

those labyrinthine inlets—those indispensable side-intelligencers.'

147. Of course, the author of the last sample aims here at a certain humorous effect, and very often similar circumlocutions are consciously resorted to in conversation to obtain a ludicrous effect, as 'he amputated his mahogany' (cut his stick, went off), 'to agitate the communicator' (ring the bell), 'a sanguinary nasal protuberance,' 'the Recent Incision' (the New Cut, a street in London), 'the Grove of the Evangelist' (St. John's Wood in London), etc. When Mr. Bob Sawyer asked 'I say, old boy, where do you hang out?' Mr. Pickwick replied that he was at present *suspended* at the George and Vulture. (Dickens, *Pickw.* II, 13.) *Punch* somewhere gives the following paraphrases of well-known proverbs: 'Iniquitous intercourses contaminate proper habits. In the absence of the feline race, the mice give themselves up to various pastimes. Casualties will take place in the most excellently conducted family circles. More confectioners than are absolutely necessary are apt to ruin the potage.' (Quoted in Fitzgerald's *Miscellanies,* p. 166.) Similarly 'A rolling stone gathers no moss' is paraphrased 'Cryptogamous concretion never grows on mineral fragments that decline repose.' Some Latin and Greek words will scarcely ever be used except in jocular or ironical speech, such as *sapient* (wise), *histrion* (actor), *a virgin aunt* (maiden aunt), *hylactism* (barking), *edacious* (greedy), the *genus Homo* (mankind), etc.

148. But how many words are there not which belong virtually to the same class, but are used in dead earnest by people who know that many big words are found in the best authors and who want to show off their education by avoiding plain everyday expressions

and couching their thoughts in a would-be refined style?
When Canning wrote the inscription graven on Pitt's
monument in the London Guildhall, an Alderman felt
much disgust at the grand phrase, 'he died poor,' and
wished to substitute 'he expired in indigent circumstances' (quoted by Kington Oliphant).[32] James Russell
Lowell, in the Introduction to the Second Series of his
Biglow Papers, has a list of what he calls the old and the
new styles of newspaper writing, which I find so characteristic that I select a few samples:

Old Style.	New Style.
A great crowd came to see.	A vast concourse was assembled to witness.
Great fire.	Disastrous conflagration.
The fire spread.	The conflagration extended its devastating career.
Man fell.	Individual was precipitated.
Sent for the doctor.	Called into requisition the services of the family physician.
Began his answer.	Commenced his rejoinder.
He died.	He deceased, he passed out of existence, his spirit quitted its earthly habitation, winged its way to eternity, shook off its burden, etc.

149. I do not deny that somewhat parallel instances of stilted language might be culled from the daily

[32] Cf. the following passage from Arnold Bennett's *Clay-
hanger:* Edwin began to write: 'Dear James, my father passed
peacefully away at —' Then, with an abrupt movement, he tore
the sheet in two and began again: 'Dear James, my father died
quietly at eight o'clock to-night.' Which of the two bills is
preferable, 'Expectoration is strictly prohibited' or 'Don't spit'?

press of most other nations, but nowhere else are they found in such plenty as in English, and no other language lends itself by its very structure to such vile stylistic tricks as English does. Wordsworth writes: 'And sitting on the grass partook The fragrant beverage drawn from China's herb,' to which Tennyson remarked: 'Why could he not have said, "And sitting on the grass had tea"?'[33] Gissing in one of his novels says of a clergyman: 'One might have suspected that he had made a list of uncommon words wherewith to adorn his discourse, for certain of these frequently recurred. "Nullifidian," "mortific," "renascent," were among his favourites. Once or twice he spoke of "psychogenesis," with an emphatic enunciation which seemed to invite respectful wonder.'[34] And did not little Thomas Babington Macaulay, when four years old, reply to a lady who took pity on him after he had spilt some hot coffee over his legs, 'Thank you, madam, the agony is abated'? And does not a language which possesses, besides the natural expression for each thing, two or three sonorous equivalents, tempt a writer into what Lecky hits off so well when he says of Gladstone: 'He seemed sometimes to be labouring to show with how many words a simple thought could be expressed or obscured'?[35]

150. To sum up: the classical words adopted since the Renaissance have enriched the English language very greatly and have especially increased its number of synonyms. But it is not every 'enrichment' that is an advantage, and this one comprises much that is really superfluous, or worse than superfluous, and has, moreover, stunted the growth of native formations. The

[33] *Life and Letters,* III, 60.
[34] *Born in Exile,* p. 380.
[35] *Democracy and Liberty,* I, p. xxi.

international currency of many words is not a full compensation for their want of harmony with the core of the language and for the undemocratic character they give to the vocabulary. While the composite character of the language gives variety and to some extent precision to the style of the greatest masters, on the other hand it encourages an inflated turgidity of style. Without siding completely with Milton's teacher Alexander Gill, who says that classical studies have done the English language more harm than ever the cruelties of the Danes or the devastations of the Normans,[36] we shall probably be near the truth if we recognize in the latest influence from the classical languages 'something between a hindrance and a help.'

[36] 'Ad Latina venio. Et si uspiam querelæ locus, hîc est; quòd otium, quòd literæ, maiorem cladem sermoni Anglico intulerint quam ulla Danorum sævitia, ulla Normannorum vastitas unquam inflixerit.' *Logonomia Anglica*, 1621 (Jiriczek's reprint, Strassburg, 1903, p. 43).

CHAPTER VII

Various Sources

151. Although English has borrowed a great many
words from other languages than those mentioned in the
preceding chapters, these borrowings need not occupy
us long here. For only Scandinavian, French and Latin
have left a mark on English deep enough to modify its
character and to change its structure, and the language
would remain the same in every essential respect even
were all the other loan-words to disappear to-morrow.

There is, of course, nothing peculiarly English in
the adoption of words denoting animals, plants, products, or institutions originally peculiar to one part of
the world, but later known in many countries, such as
gondola, maccaroni and *lava* from Italian, *matador,
siesta* and *sherry* from Spanish, *steppe* and *verst* from
Russian, *caravan* and *dervish* from Persian, *hussar* and
shako from Hungarian, *bey* and *caftan* from Turkish,
harem and *mufti* from Arabic, *bamboo* and *orang-
outang* from Malay, *taboo* from Polynesian, *boomerang*
and *wombat* from Australian, *chocolate* and *tomato*
from Mexican, *moccasin, tomahawk* and *totem* from
other American languages. As a matter of fact, all these
words now belong to the whole of the civilized world:
like such classical or pseudo-classical words as *nationality, telegram* and *civilization,* they bear witness to the
sameness of modern culture everywhere: the same

products and to a great extent the same ideas are now
known all over the globe and many of them have in
many languages identical names.

With regard to these as well as to other loan-words
it should always be remembered that the ultimate origin
of a word is not always the source whence it has penetrated into English. Many exotic words have come to
England through Spanish or Portuguese. *Paradise,* originally a Persian word, has come through French; so
have *shallop, chaloupe,* originally Dutch *sloep,* in English spelt *sloop,* and *fuchsia,* as shown by the pronunciation: it is derived from the name of a German botanist
Fuchs.

152. It will be worth our while to consider the
loans from a few languages, as they have great cultural
importance. First the Dutch.[1] It is significant that this
word in English means not German (deutsch), but the
inhabitants and the language of the Netherlands, with
which the English came into more intimate relations
than with the Germans themselves. The Dutch have
always been a seafaring nation; hence it is no wonder
that many nautical words have come from that source:
*yacht, yawl, schooner, bowline, deck, cruise, iceberg;
euphroe,* a learned spelling of Du. *juffrouw* 'a crowfoot
dead-eye,' must have been taken over by word of mouth.
There are also some military words: *furlough, tattoo,
onslaught.* But the most interesting group of Dutch
words relates to the fine arts, which flourished in the

---

[1] See J. F. Bense, *The Anglo-Dutch Relations* ('s-Gravenhage,
1924); Bense, *A Dictionary of the Dutch Element in the English
Vocabulary* (The Hague, 1926–1935. A standard work); E. C.
Llewellyn, *The Influence of Low Dutch on the English Vocabulary* (Oxford, 1936; based chiefly on Bense); G. N. Clark, *The
Dutch Influence on the English Vocabulary* (S.P.E., 44, Oxford, 1935).

Low Countries in the 16th and 17th centuries and exercised a strong influence on English artists. Hence such words as *easel, etch, sketch, maulstick, landscape* (whence such English new-formed words as *seascape, cloudscape,* and finally the isolated *scape*). On South African words see § 160.

153. This leads us naturally to the other great influence on the artistic vocabulary, namely Italian.[2] Attention has already been called to the great number of musical terms derived from Italian (§ 31). A great many terms of architecture and of the fine arts in general derive from Italy: *balcony, colonnade, cornice, corridor, grotto, loggia, mezzanine, niche, parapet, pilaster, profile;* further *fresco, miniature; improvisatore, dilettante, opera, sonnet.* From related cultural domains we may mention *casino, carnival, milliner* (orig. modistes from Milan). Commercial relations have given us such words as *traffic, risk, magazine, bank* and what belongs to that: *bankrupt* (Latinized from *bancarotta*), *agio, Lombard.* Among military terms may be mentioned *alarm, colonel* (the pronunciation goes back to the form *coronel*), *arsenal, pistol.*

154. From Spanish we may mention the military words *armada, escapade* and *embargo,* further designations for persons like *don* (note the curious use in English universities) and *hidalgo; padre* obtained a certain vogue during the first world war. In the world of games we have *quadrille, spade* and other terms for cards. Commerce brought *anchovy, cargo, cordovan* and *lime* (the fruit). In recent times the Californian *cafeteria* has proved exceedingly productive in linguistic offspring: *drugteria, sodateria, fruiteria, shaveteria,*

[2] See Mario Praz, *The Italian Element in English* (Essays and Studies, XV, 20 ff.).

shoeteria, and other more or less ridiculous American words.

155. Among Arabic words in English[3]—some of them easily recognizable through the definite article *al* —we must specially mention those relating to mathematics, astronomy, and science in general: *algebra, cipher, zero, nadir, zenith, alchemy, alcohol, alkali, bismuth, elixir, natron.* Some English scientific terms are Arabic in meaning, but not in form, thus the mathematical *sine* from Latin *sinus* 'fold,' translating Arabic *jaib;* x as a sign for an unknown quantity 'was no doubt used first in Spain because it is the letter corresponding etymologically in Spanish to Arabic *shîn,* used in this sense as an abbreviation of the word *shai* thing.' Other Arabic words are *alcove, sofa, sash, caraway, sherbet.*

156. The British Empire has caused contact with a great many peoples and in consequence loans from many languages. From India we have, among other words, *sahib, begum, maharajah, pundit, baboo* (the curious language spoken by some Hindus is often called Baboo English), *thug; durbar, Swaraj; cot, bungalow, pucka, coolie, pariah, chit, Choki,* originally meaning customs-house, is used for 'prison' (folk-etymological connexion with E. choke?). For articles of apparel we have *topi, pyjamas* and *bandana. Loot* is an interesting parallel to *plunder* (§ 157). The notorious *dumdum* bullets are named from a place Dum Dum, near Calcutta. Some originally Indian words have come to English through Persian: *divan, khaki, zenana, purdah.* From African languages we have, e.g., *impi* 'regiment,' *indaba* 'conference.' From Chinese *kowtow.* But some

[3] Walt Taylor, *Arabic Words in English* (S.P.E., 38, Oxford, 1933).

of these words can hardly be said to belong to ordinary English.

157. There are surprisingly few German loan-words in English,[4] and very little can be inferred from them with regard to cultural relations, apart, perhaps, from some philosophical terms the meaning of which was stamped by Kant and his English followers. *Plunder* is due to the English soldiers in the thirty years' war, and *swindler* is said to have been introduced by German Jews ab. 1726. Some mining terms, such as *feldspar, gneiss* and *quartz,* come from Germany. There are some translation-loans, e.g. *home-sickness* and *one-sided,* also the place-name the *Black Forest,* but otherwise the tendency is to swallow German words raw, even where a translation would have been easy: the *Siebengebirge* and the *Riesengebirge* are much more commonly used than the *Seven Mountains* and the *Giant Mountains.* Thus we have *kindergarten* unchanged, while for the same institution Danish has the literal translation *börne-have* and Norwegian *barnehave.* Similarly English has *rinderpest, landsturm, zollverein, weltpolitik, weltan-schauung* and *hinterland*—which may even be used as in 'a residential hinterland' (of a town, Kaye-Smith, *Tamarisk Town,* 105), and 'a vast hinterland of thoughts and feelings' (Wells, *Marriage,* 2, 121). Here we have come upon something which seems to be characteristic of the English in their relation to foreign words.

158. An interesting contrast may be seen between the linguistic behaviour of the Dutch and the English in South Africa. The former, finding there a great many natural objects which were new to them, designated

[4] See Charles T. Carr, *The German Influence on the English Vocabulary* (S.P.E., 42, Oxford, 1934).

them either by means of existing Dutch words whose
meanings were, accordingly, more or less modified, or
else by coining new words, generally compounds. Thus
sloot 'ditch' was applied to the peculiar dry rivers of
that country, *veld* 'field' to the open pasturages, and
kopje 'a little head or cup' to the hills, etc.; different
kinds of animals were called *roodebok* 'red-buck,' *steen-
bok* 'stonebuck,' *springbok* 'hopbuck,' *springhaas* 'hop-
hare,' *hartebeest* 'hartbeast'; a certain bird was called
slangvreter 'serpent-eater,' a certain large shrub *spek-
boom* 'bacon-tree,' etc. The English, on the other hand,
instead of imitating this principle, have simply taken
over all these names into their own language, where
they now figure[5] together with some other South African
Dutch words, among which may be mentioned *trek* and
spoor in the special significations of 'colonial migration'
and 'track of wild animal,' while the Dutch words are
much less specialized (*trekken* 'to draw, pull, travel,
move'; *spoor* 'trace, track, trail'). These examples of
borrowings might easily be multiplied from other domains, and we may say of the English what Moth says
of Holofernes and Sir Nathaniel that 'they have been at
a great feast of languages, and stolen the scraps' (Love's
L. L. V, 1, 39). It will therefore be natural to inquire
into the cause of this linguistic omnivorousness.

159. It would, of course, be irrational to ascribe
the phenomenon to a greater natural gift for learning
languages, for in the first place, the English are not
usually credited with such a gift, and secondly the best
linguists are generally inclined to keep their own language pure rather than adulterate it with scraps of other

---

[5] *Roodebok* often spelt in accordance with the actual Dutch
pronunciation *rooibok, rooyebok*. *Sloot* often appears in the un-
Dutch spelling *sluit*.

languages. Consequently, we should be nearer the truth
if we were to give as a reason the linguistic incapacity
of the average Englishman. As a traveller and a colo-
nizer, however, he is thrown into contact with people
of a great many different nations and thus cannot help
seeing numerous things and institutions unknown in
England. R. L. Stevenson says somewhere about the
typical John Bull, that 'his is a domineering nature,
steady in fight, imperious to command, but neither
curious nor quick about the life of others.'[6] And perhaps
the loan-words we are considering testify to nothing but
the most superficial curiosity about the life of other
nations and would not have been adopted if John Bull
had really in his heart cared any more than this for the
foreigners he meets. He is content to pick up a few
scattered fragments of their speech—just enough to impart a certain local colouring to his narratives and
political discussions, but he goes no further.

160. The tendency to adopt words from other
languages is due, then, probably to a variety of causes.
Foremost among these I think it is right to place the
linguistic laziness mentioned in § 159 and fostered
especially by the preference for words from the classical
languages. That the borrowing is not occasioned by an
inherent deficiency in the *language* itself is shown by
the ease with which new terms actually *are* framed
whenever the need of them is really felt, especially by
uneducated people who are not tempted to go outside
their own language to express their thoughts. Interesting examples of this natural inventiveness may be found
in Mr. Edward E. Morris's *Austral English, A dictionary of Australasian words, phrases and usages*. As
Mr. Morris says in his preface, 'Those who, speaking

[6] *Memories and Portraits*, p. 3.

the tongue of Shakespeare, of Milton, and of Dr. Johnson, came to various parts of Australasia, found a Flora and a Fauna waiting to be named in English. New birds, beasts and fishes, new trees, bushes and flowers, had to receive names for general use. It is probably not too much to say that there never was an instance in history when so many new names were needed, and that there never will be such an occasion again, for never did settlers come, nor can they ever again come, upon Flora and Fauna so completely different from anything seen by them before.' The gaps were filled partly by adopting words from the aboriginal languages, e.g. *kangaroo, wombat,* partly by applying English words to objects bearing a real or fancied resemblance to the objects denoted by them in England, e.g. *magpie, oak, beech,* but partly also by new English formations. Accordingly, in turning over the leaves of Mr. Morris's Dictionary we come across numerous names of birds like *friar-bird, frogs-mouth, honey-eater, ground-lark, forty-spot,*[7] of fishes like *long-fin, trumpeter,* of plants like *sugar-grass, hedge-laurel, ironheart, thousand-jacket.* Most of these show that 'the settler must have had an imagination. Whip-bird, or Coach-whip, from the sound of the note, Lyre-bird from the appearance of the outspread tail, are admirable names.' (Morris, l. c.). It certainly seems a pity that book-learned people when wanting to enrich their mother tongue have not, as a rule, drawn from

---

[7] One story of a curious change of meaning must be recounted in Mr. Morris's words: 'The settler heard a bird laugh in what he thought an extremely ridiculous manner, its opening notes suggesting a donkey's bray—he called it the "laughing jackass." His descendants have dropped the adjective, and it has come to pass that the word "jackass" denotes to an Australian something quite different from its meaning to other speakers of our English tongue.'

the same source or shown the same talent for picturesque and 'telling' designations.

161. Many of our times' new inventions and other innovations have enriched the language.[8] Cinematograph is generally shortened into *cinema*, even *cine*, but people often speak of the *movies*. We have the curious differentiation of *radium* and *radio*: the latter has given a new sense to the old *broadcast* (B.B.C. = British Broadcasting Corporation). For *automobile* the simple word *car* is generally said, or else *motor-car*. We have *aeroplane*, for which some people prefer the form *airplane*; it is also shortened into *plane*, and we have the new *aquaplane* and *seaplane*; further, *airship*, *aircraft*, *airman*, etc., also *aerodrome*; *taxi* is used for crawling along the ground before or after alighting in a plane. Some of the new words introduced with these inventions have taken some time, before their spoken forms in English were quite fixed: *chauffeur* from [ʃou'fə·] has now usually become ['ʃoufə]; *hangar* and *garage* were at first spoken with long [a·] in the last syllable, but now they are generally Anglicized [hæŋgə] or [hænə], [gæridʒ]. The learned *television* has brought about the verb *televise*, and *televisor* for the apparatus. Let me finally mention *tango* and *jazz*.

162. A great many words are nowadays coined by tradespeople to designate new articles of merchandise. Very little regard is generally paid to correctness of formation, the only essential being a name that is good for advertising purposes. Sometimes a mere arbitrary collection of sounds or letters is chosen, as in the case

---

[8] Recent linguistic innovations are dealt with in H. Spies, *Kultur und Sprache im neuen England* (Leipzig, 1925); R. Hittmair, *Wortbildende Kräfte im heutigen Englisch* (Leipzig, 1937); W. E. Collinson, *Contemporary English* (Leipzig, 1927).

of *kodak,* and sometimes the inventor contents himself
with some vague resemblance to some other word, which
may assist the buyer to remember the name. A few
examples may be given: *bovril* (Latin bos + vril, an
electrical fluid mentioned in an old novel by Lytton),
vapo-cresolene (cresolene vaporized), *harlene* (hair),
wincarnis (a tonic, wine, Latin caro?), *rinso* (for clean-
ing, rinse), *redux* (reducing herbal tea), *yeast-vite*
(tonic), *ceilingite* (whitewash), *elasto* . . . Sometimes
these trade names are merely ordinary words disguised
by fancy spellings, e.g. *Phiteesi* boots, *Stickphast,
Uneeda* cigar (= you need a cigar) in England, *Uneeda*
biscuit in America. Many such names are very short-
lived, but some are there to stay and may even pass into
common use outside the sphere for which they were
originally invented. This is the case with *kodak.*[9]

163. The Great War (1914–1918) left its mark
on language as on everything.[10] It introduced a certain
number of foreign words, e.g. *camouflage* (in English
also as a verb = Fr. camoufler), in the navy called
dazzle-painting; from German we had *U-boat* = sub-
marine, and the stupid *strafe* (from 'Gott strafe England,' at the time often pronounced [streif]; the curious
blighty is from Hindu *bilayati* 'foreign,' used by soldiers
on foreign service for 'home, i.e. England.' Old words
were provided with new meanings: *ace* like Fr. *as* came
to mean an airman who had brought down a certain
number of foreign men; *bus* = aeroplane, further *gas*
(be gassed) and *tank; go West* was used as a euphemism

[9] Additional examples in Louise Pound, *Word-Coinage and
Modern Trade Names* (Dialect Notes, LV, 1913), and H. L.
Mencken, *The American Language,* 4th ed., 171 ff.

[10] See besides the works by Spies, Collinson and Hittmair
mentioned above, A. Smith, *New Words Self-Defined* (New
York, 1920).

for 'die, be lost.' The war even produced a new numeral: *umpteen*, used to disguise the number of a brigade, later in the sense of a considerable number. The tendency to shorten words (cf. 186) is seen in *conchy* = conscientious objector, *zepp* = Zeppelin, etc. But most of the war words belong to slang and as such fall outside the scope of this work.

CHAPTER VIII

Native Resources

164. However important foreign loan-words are, the chief enrichment of the language is due to those regular processes which are so familiar that any new word formed by means of them seems at once an old acquaintance. The whole history of English word-formation may be summed up as follows—that some formative elements have been gradually discarded, especially those that presented some difficulty of application, while others have been continually gaining ground, because they have admitted of being added to all or nearly all words without occasioning any change in the kernel of the word. Among the former I shall mention *-en* to denote female beings (cf. German *-in*). In Old English this had already become very impracticable because sound changes had occurred which obscured the connexion between related words. Corresponding to the masculine *þegn* 'retainer,' *þeow* 'slave,' *wealh* 'foreigner,' *scealc* 'servant,' *fox*, we find the feminine *þignen*, *þiewen*, *wielen*, *scielcen*, *fyxen*. It seems clear that new generations would find difficulties in forming new feminines on such indistinct analogies, so we cannot wonder that the ending ceased to be productive and that the French ending *-ess*, which presented no difficulties, came to be used extensively (107). Of the words in *-en* mentioned, *fyxen* is the only one surviving, and its connexion with *fox* is now loosened, both through the form *vixen* (with its *v* from Southern dialects) and through the meaning, which is now most often 'a quarrelsome woman.'

165. A much more brilliant destiny was reserved for the Old English ending *-isc*. At first it was added only to nouns indicating nations, whose vowel it changed by mutation; thus *Englisc,* now *English,* from *Angle,* etc. In some adjectives, however, no mutation was possible, e.g. *Irish,* and by analogy the vowel of the primitive word was soon introduced into some of the adjectives, e.g. *Scottish* (earlier *Scyttisc*), *Danish* (earlier *Denisc*). The ending was extended first to words whose meaning was cognate to these national names, *heathenish,* OE. *folcisc* or *þeodisc* 'national' (from *folc* or *þeod* 'people'); then gradually came *childish, churlish,* etc. Each century added new extensions; *foolish* and *feverish,* for instance, date from the 14th, and *boyish* and *girlish* from the 16th century, until now *-ish* can be added to nearly any noun and adjective (swinish, bookish, greenish, biggish, etc.).

166. We shall see in a later section (§ 206) that the ending *-ing* has still more noticeably broken the bounds of its originally narrow sphere of application. Another case in point is the verbal suffix *-en*. It is now possible to form a verb from any adjective fulfilling certain phonetic conditions by adding *-en* (harden, weaken, sweeten, sharpen, lessen). But this suffix was not used very much before 1500, indeed most of the verbs formed in *-en* belong to the last three centuries. Another extensively used ending is *-er*. Old English had various methods of forming substantives to denote agents; from the verb *huntan* 'hunt' it had the noun *hunta* 'hunter'; from *beodan* 'announce,' *boda* 'messenger, herald'; from *wealdan* 'rule,' *weada;* from *beran* 'bear,' *bora;* from *sceþþan* 'injure,' *sceaþa;* from *weorcan*

'work,' *wyrhta* 'wright' (in *wheelwright,* etc.), though
some of these were used in compounds only; some nouns
were formed in *-end: rædend* 'ruler,' *scieppend* 'creator,'
and others in *-ere: blawere* 'one who blows,' *blotere*
'sacrificer,' etc. But it seems as if there were many verbs
from which it was impossible to form any agent-noun
at all, and the reader will have noticed that even the
formation in *a* presented some difficulties, as the vowel
was modified according to complicated rules. When the
want of new substantives was felt, it was, therefore,
more and more the ending *-ere* that was resorted to. But
the curious thing is that the function of this ending was
at first to make nouns, not from verbs, but from other
nouns, thus OE. *bocere* 'scribe' from *boc* 'book' (already
Gothic *bokareis*), compare modern *hatter, tinner, Lon-
doner, New Englander, first-nighter.* As, however, such
a word as fisher, OE. *fiscere,* which is derived from the
noun a *fish,* OE. *fisc,* might just as well be analysed as
derived from the corresponding verb to *fish,* OE. *fiscian,*
it became usual to form new agent-denoting nouns in *-er*
from verbs, and in some cases these supplanted older
formations (OE. *hunta,* now *hunter*). Now we do not
hesitate to make new words in *-er* from any verb, e.g.,
a *snorer,* a *sitter,* odd *comers* and *goers,* a total *abstainer,*
etc. Combinations with an adverb (a *diner-out,* a *looker-
on*) go back to Chaucer (A somnour is a renner up and
down With mandements for fornicacioun, D 1284), but
do not seem to be very frequent before the Elizabethan
period. Note also the extensive use of the suffix to denote
instruments and things, as in *slipper, rubber, typewriter,
sleeper* (American = sleeping car). A variant of *-er* is
-eer, which is liable, but only after *t,* to impart a dis-
paraging meaning: this starts perhaps from *garreteer*
and *pamphleteer,* hence the contemptuous *sonneteer,*

profiteer, famous or infamous during the war, and *patrioteering* (my *Language,* p. 388, not in NED.). Another variant of *-er* is *-ster,*[1] which is often wrongly supposed to be a specially feminine suffix, though from the earliest times it has been used of men as well as of women, from the old *demestre,* now *deemster* or *dempster* 'a judge,' and family names like *Baxter, Webster,* down to the more modern *punster, gangster, fibster, youngster,* etc. A *spinster* originally meant one who spins, but is now restricted to unmarried (old) maids. Special feminines are formed in *-stress: seamstress* (*sempstress*), *songstress.*

167. Other much-used suffixes for substantives are: *-ness* (goodness, truthfulness), *-dom* (Christendom, boredom, 'Swelldom,' Thackeray), *-ship* (ownership, companionship, horsemanship), for adjectives: *-ly* (lordly, cowardly), *-y* (fiery, churchy, creepy), *-less* (powerless, dauntless), *-ful* (powerful, fanciful), and *-ed* (blue-eyed, good-natured, renowned, conceited, talented; broad-breasted; level-browed, like the horizon '—thighed and shouldered like the billows—footed like their stealing foam,' Ruskin). Prefixes of wide application are *mis-, un-, be-,* and others. By means of these formatives the English vocabulary has been and is being constantly enriched with thousands and thousands of useful new words.

168. There is one manner of forming verbs from nouns and vice versa which is specifically English and which is of the greatest value on account of the ease with which it is managed, namely that of making them exactly like one another. In Old English there were a certain number of verbs and nouns of the same 'root,' but distinguished by the endings. Thus 'I love' through

[1] Jespersen, *Linguistica* (Copenhagen, 1933), p. 420 ff.

the three persons singular ran *lufie, lufast, lufaþ,* plural *lufiaþ;* the infinitive was *lufian,* the subjunctive *lufie,* pl. *lufien,* and the imperative was *lufa,* pl. *lufiaþ.* The substantive 'love' on the other hand was *lufu,* in the other cases *lufe,* plural *lufa* or *lufe, lufum, lufena* or *lufa.* Similarly 'to sleep' was *slæpan,* pres. *slæpe, slæpest, slæp(e)þ, slæpaþ,* subjunctive *slæpe, slæpen,* imperative *slæp, slæpaþ,* while the substantive had the forms *slæp, slæpe* and *slæpes* in the singular and *slæpas, slæpum, slæpa* in the plural. If we were to give the corresponding forms used in the subsequent centuries, we should witness a gradual simplification which had as a further consequence the mutual approximation of the verbal and nominal forms. The *-m* is changed into *-n,* all the vowels of the weak syllables are levelled to one uniform *e,* the plural forms of the verbs in *-þ* give way to forms in *-n,* and all the final *n*'s eventually disappear, while in the nouns *s* is gradually extended so that it becomes the only genitive and almost the only plural ending. The second person singular of the verbs retains its distinctive *-st,* but towards the end of the Middle English period *thou* already begins to be less used, and the polite *ye, you,* which becomes more and more universal, claims no distinctive ending in the verb. In the fifteenth century, the *e* of the endings, which had hitherto been pronounced, ceased to be sounded, and somewhat later *s* became the ordinary ending of the third person singular instead of *th.* These changes brought about the modern scheme:

noun: *love loves—sleep sleeps*
verb: *love loves—sleep sleeps*

where we have perfect formal identity of the two parts of speech, only with the curious cross-relation between them that *s* is the ending of the plural in the nouns and of the singular (third person) in the verbs—an accident which might almost be taken as a device for getting an *s* into most sentences in the present tense (the lover love*s*; the lover*s* love) and for showing by the place of the *s* which of the two numbers is intended.

169. As a great many native nouns and verbs had thus come to be identical in form (e.g. *blossom, care, deal, drink, ebb, end, fathom, fight, fish, fire*), and as the same thing happened with numerous originally French words (e.g., *accord,* OFr. acord and acorder, *account, arm, blame, cause, change, charge, charm, claim, combat, comfort, copy, cost, couch*), it was quite natural that the speech-instinct should take it as a matter of course that whenever the need of a verb arose, it might be formed without any derivative ending from the corresponding substantive.[2] Among the innumerable nouns from which verbs have been formed in this manner, we may mention a few: *ape, awe, cook, husband, silence, time, worship.* Nearly every word for the different parts of the body has given rise to a homonym verb, though

[2] It is often said, even by some of the most famous recent writers, that Modern English has given up the sharp division into different parts of speech which was characteristic of the earlier stages of our family of speech. This is entirely wrong: even if the same form *love* or *sleep* may be said to belong to more than one word-class, this is true of the isolated form only: in each separate case in which the word is used in actual speech it belongs definitely to one class and to no other. The form *round* is a substantive in 'a round of the ladder,' 'he took his daily round,' an adjective in 'a round table,' a verb in 'he failed to round the lamp-post,' an adverb in 'come round to-morrow,' and a preposition in 'he walked round the house.' Many people will say that in the sentence 'we tead at the vicarage' we have a case of a substantive used as a verb. The truth is that we have a real verb, just as real as *dine* or *eat,* though derived from the substantive *tea,* and derived without any distinctive ending in the infinitive. Cf. *Philosophy of Grammar,* p. 52 and 61 f.

true it is that some of them are rarely used: *eye, nose*
('you shall nose him as you go up the stairs,' *Hamlet*),
lip (= kiss, Shakesp.), *beard, tongue, brain* ('such stuffe
as madmen tongue and braine not,' Shakesp. *Cym-
beline*), *jaw* (= scold, etc.), *ear* (rare = give ear to),
chin (American = to chatter), *arm* (= put one's arm
round), *shoulder* (arms), *elbow* (one's way through the
crowd), *hand, fist* ('fisting each other's throat,'
Shakesp.), *finger, thumb, breast* (= oppose), *body*
(forth), *skin, stomach, limb* ('they limb themselves,'
Milton), *knee* (= kneel, Shakesp.), *foot*. It would be
possible in a similar way to go through a great many
other categories of words; everywhere we should see the
same facility of forming new verbs from substantives.

170. The process is also very often resorted to for
'nonce-words' in speaking and in writing. Thus, a common form of retort is exemplified by the following quotations: 'Trinkets! a bauble for Lydia! . . . So this was
the history of his trinkets! I'll *bauble* him!' (Sheridan,
Rivals, V, 2). 'I was explaining the Golden Bull to his
Royal Highness.' 'I'll *Golden Bull* you, you rascal!'
roared the Majesty of Prussia (Macaulay, *Biographical
Ess.*). 'Such a savage as that, as has just come home
from South Africa. Diamonds indeed! I'd *diamond* him'
(Trollope, *Old Man's Love*)—and in a somewhat different manner: 'My gracious Uncle.—Tut, tut, Grace me
no Grace, nor Uncle me no Uncle' (Shaksp. R 2, cf.
also Romeo III, 5, 143). 'I heartily wish I could, but—'
'Nay, but me no buts—I have set my heart upon it'
(Scott, *Antiq.*, ch. XI). 'Advance and take thy prize,
The diamond; but he answered, Diamond me No diamonds! For God's love, a little air! Prize me no prizes,
for my prize is death' (Tennyson, *Lancelot and Elaine*).

171. A still more characteristic peculiarity of the English language is the corresponding freedom with which a form which was originally a verb is used unchanged as a substantive. This was not possible till the disappearance of the final -e which was found in most verbal forms, and accordingly we see an ever increasing number of these formations from about 1500. I shall give some examples in chronological order, adding the date of the earliest quotation for the noun in the NED.: *glance* 1503, *bend* 1529, *cut* 1530, *fetch* 1530, *hearsay* 1532, *blemish* 1535, *gaze* 1542, *reach* 1542, *drain* 1552, *gather* 1555, *burn* 1563, *lend* 1575, *dislike* 1577, *frown* 1581, *dissent* 1585, *fawn* (a servile cringe) 1590, *dismay* 1590, *embrace* 1592, *hatch* 1597, *dip* 1599, *dress* (personal attire) 1606, *flutter* 1641, *divide* 1642, *build* 1667 (before the 19th century apparently used by Pepys only), *harass* 1667, *haul* 1670, *dive* 1700, *go* 1727 (many of the most frequent applications date from the 19th century), *hobble* 1727, *lean* (the act or condition of leaning) 1776, *bid* 1788, *hang* 1797, *dig* 1819, *find* 1825 (in the sense of that which is found, 1847), *crave* 1830, *kill* (the act of killing) 1825, (a killed animal) 1878. It will be seen that the 16th century is very fertile in these nouns, which is only a natural consequence of the phonological reason given above. As, however, some of the verb-nouns found in Elizabethan authors have in modern times disappeared or become rare, some grammarians have inferred that we have here a phenomenon peculiar to that period and due to the general exuberance of the Renaissance which made people more free with their language than they have since been. A glance at our list will show that this is a wrong view; indeed, we use a great many formations of this kind which were unknown to Shakespeare; he had only the substantive *a visitation*, where we say *a visit*, nor did he know our *worries*, our *kicks*, and *moves*, etc., etc.

172. In some cases a substantive is formed in this manner in spite of there being already another noun derived from the same verb; thus *a move* has nearly the same meaning as *removal*, *movement* or *motion* (from which latter a new verb *to motion* is formed); a *resolve* and *resolution*, a *laugh* and *laughter* are nearly the same thing (though an *exhibit* is only one of the things found at an *exhibition*). Hence we get a lively competition started between these substantives and forms in -*ing*: *meet* (especially in the sporting world) and *meeting*, *shoot* and *shooting*, *read* (in the afternoon I like a rest and a read) and *reading*,[3] *row* (let us go out for a row) and *rowing* (he goes in for rowing), *smoke* and *smoking*, *mend* and *mending*, *feel* (there was a soft feel of autumn in the air) and *feeling*. The *build* of a house and the *make* of a machine are different from the *building* of the house and the *making* of the machine. The *sit* of a coat may sometimes be spoilt at one *sitting*, and we speak of *dressing*, not of *dress*, in connexion with a salad, etc. The enormous development of these convenient differentiations belongs to the most recent period of the language. Compared with the sets of synonyms mentioned above (§ 133: one of the words borrowed from Latin, etc.) this class of synonyms shows a decided superiority, because here small differences in sense are expressed by small differences in sound, and because all these words are formed in the most regular and easy manner; con-

---

[3] Darwin says in one of his letters: 'I have just finished, after several reads, your paper'; this implies that he did not read it from beginning to end at one sitting; if he had written 'after several readings' he would have implied that he had read it through several times.

sequently there is the least possible strain put on the memory.

173. In early English a noun and the verb corresponding to it were often similar, although not exactly alike, some historical reason causing a difference in either the vowel or the final consonant or both. In such pairs of words as the following the old relation is kept unchanged: a *life*, to *live*; a *calf*, to *calve*; a *grief*, to *grieve*; a *cloth*, to *clothe*; a *house*, to *house*; a *use*, to *use* —in all these the noun has the voiceless and the verb the voiced consonant. The same alternation has been imitated in a few words which had originally the same consonant in the noun as in the verb; thus *belief*, *proof*, and *excuse* (with voiceless *s*) have supplanted the older substantives in *-ve* and voiced *-se* and inversely the verb *grease* has now often voiced *s* [z] alternating with a voiceless *s*. But in a far greater number of words the tendency to have nouns and verbs of exactly the same sound has prevailed, so that we have to *knife*, to *scarf* (Shakesp.), to *elf* (id.), to *roof*, and with voiceless *s*, to *loose*, to *race*, to *ice*, to *promise*, while the nouns *repose*, *cruise* (at sea), to *reprieve*, owe their voiced consonants to the corresponding verbs. In this way we get some interesting doublets. Besides the old noun *bath* and verb *bathe* we have the recent verb to *bath* (will you bath baby to-day?) and the substantive *bathe* ('I walked into the sea by myself and had a very decent bathe,' Tennyson). Besides *glass* (noun) and *glaze* (verb) we have now also *glass* as a verb and *glaze* as a noun; so also in the case of *grass* and *graze*, *price* and *prize* (where *praise* verb and noun should be mentioned as etymologically the same word).

174. The same forces are at work in the smaller class of words in which the distinction between the noun

and the verb is made by the alternation of *ch* and *k,* as
in *speech—speak.* Side by side with the old *batch* we
have a new noun, a *bake,* besides the noun *stitch* and
the verb *stick* we have now also a verb to *stitch* (a book,
etc.) and the rare noun a *stick* (the act of sticking);
besides the old noun *stench* we have a new one from the
verb *stink.* The modern word *ache* (in toothache, etc.)
is a curious cross of the old noun, whose spelling has
been kept, and the old verb, whose pronunciation (with
k) has prevailed. Baret (1573) says expressly, '*Ake* is
the verb of this substantive *ache, ch* being turned into *k.*'
In the Shakespeare folio of 1623 the noun is always spelt
with *ch* and the verb with *k;* the verb rimes with *brake*
and *sake.* The noun was thus sounded like the name of
the letter *h;* and Hart (*An Orthographie,* 1569, p. 35)
says expressly, 'We abuse the name of h, calling it ache,
which sounde serveth very well to expresse a headache,
or some bone ache.' Indeed, the identity in sound of the
noun and the name of the letter gave rise to one of the
stock puns of the time; see for instance Shakespeare
(Ado III, 4, 56); 'by my troth I am exceeding ill, hey
ho.—For a hauke, a horse, or a husband?—For the
letter that begins them all, H,' and a poem by Heywood:
'It is worst among letters in the crosse row, For if thou
find him other [= either] in thine elbow, In thine arme,
or leg . . . Where ever you find ache, thou shalt not
like him.'

   175. Numerous substantives and verbs have the
same consonants, but a difference in the vowels, due
either to gradation (ablaut) or to mutation (umlaut).
But here, too, the creative powers of language may be
observed. Where in old times there was only a noun *bit*
and a verb to *bite,* we have now in addition not only a
verb to *bit* (a horse, to put the bit into its mouth) as in

Carlyle's 'the accursed hag "dyspepsia" had got me bitted and bridled' and in Coleridge's witty remark (quoted in the NED.): 'It is not women and Frenchmen only that would rather have their tongues bitten than bitted'—but also a noun *bite* in various meanings, e.g. in 'his bite is as dangerous as the cobra's' (Kipling) and 'she took a bite out of the apple' (Anthony Hope). From the noun *seat* (see above, § 72) we have the new verb to *seat* (to place on a seat), while the verb to *sit* has given birth to the noun *sit* (cf. § 172). No longer content with the old *sale* as the substantive corresponding to *sell,* in slang we have the new noun *a* (fearful) *sell* (an imposition); cf. also the American substantive *tell* (according to their tell, see Farmer and Henley). As *knot* (n.) was to *knit* (v.), so was *coss* to *kiss,* but while of the former pair both forms have survived and have given rise to a new verb to *knot* and a new noun, a *knit* (he has a permanent knit of the brow, NED.), from the latter the *o*-form has disappeared, the noun being now formed from the verb: a *kiss*. We have the old *brood* (n.) and *breed* (v.) and the new *brood* (v.) and *breed* (n.); a new verb to *blood* exists by the side of the old to *bleed,* and a new noun *feed* by the side of the old *food*. It is obvious that the language has been enriched by acquiring all these newly formed words; but it should also be admitted that there has been a positive gain in ease and simplicity in all those cases where there was no occasion for turning the existing phonetic difference to account by creating new verbs or nouns in new significations, and where, accordingly, one of the phonetic forms has simply disappeared, as when the old verbs *sniwan, scrydan, swierman* have given way to the new *snows, shroud, swarm,* which are like the nouns, or when the noun *swat, swot* (he swette blodes swot, *Ancrene Riwle*)

has been discarded in favour of *sweat,* which has the
same vowel as the verb.

176. In some cases the place of the stress serves to
distinguish substantives from verbs, the former having
initial and the latter final stress. Thus some native words
with prefixes: ᶦ*forecast* sb., *fore*ᶦ*cast* vb., similarly *over-*
throw, underline. In the same way a great many
Romanic words are differentiated, the substantives (adjectives) having fore-stress, the corresponding verbs
end-stress: e.g. *absent, accent, conduct, frequent, object,*
present, rebel, record, subject, interdict. Words like
compliment, experiment have an obscure vowel [ə] in
the sb., but a full vowel [e] in the vb., even if the final
syllable has not full stress.

177. Among the other points of interest presented
by the formations occupying us here I may mention
the curious oscillation found in some instances between
noun and verb. *Smoke* is first a noun (the smoke from
the chimney), then a verb (the chimney smokes, he
smokes a pipe); then a new noun is formed from the
verb in the last sense (let us have a smoke). Similarly
gossip (a) noun: godfather, intimate friend, idle talker,
(b) verb: to talk idly, (c) new noun: idle talk; *dart* (a)
a weapon, (b) to throw (a dart), to move rapidly (like
a dart), (c) a sudden motion; *brush* (a) an instrument,
(b) to use that instrument, (c) the action of using it:
your hat wants a brush; *sail* (a) a piece of canvas, (b) to
sail, (c) a sailing excursion; *wire* (a) a metallic thread,
(b) to telegraph, (c) a telegram; so also *cable;* in vulgar
language a verb is formed to *jaw* and from that a second
noun a *jaw* ('what speech do you mean?' 'Why that
grand jaw that you sputtered forth just now about repu-
tation,' F. C. Philips). Sometimes the starting point is a
verb, e.g., *frame* (a) to form, (b) noun: a fabric, a

border for a picture, etc., (c) verb: to set in a frame; and sometimes an adjective, e.g. *faint* (a) weak, (b) to become weak, (c) a fainting fit.

178. To those who might see in the obliteration of the old distinctive marks of the different parts of speech a danger of ambiguity, I would answer that this danger is more imaginary than real. I open at random a modern novel and count on one page 34 nouns which can be used as infinitives without any change, and 38 verbs the forms of which can be used as nouns,[4] while only 22 nouns and 9 verbs cannot be thus used. As some of the ambiguous nouns and verbs occur more than once, and as the same page contains adverbs, prepositions, and conjunctions[5] which are identical with nouns (adjectives) or verbs, or both, the theoretical possibilities of mistakes arising from confusion of parts of speech would seem to be very numerous. And yet no one reading that page would feel the slightest hesitation about understanding every word correctly, as either the ending or the context shows at once whether a verb is meant or not. Even such an extreme case as this line, which is actually found in a modern song, 'Her eyes like angels watch them still,' is not obscure, although *her* might be both accusative and possessive, *eyes* both noun and verb, *like* adjective, conjunction, and verb, *watch* noun and verb, and *still* adjective, verb and adverb. A modern Englishman, realizing the great advantage his language possesses

[4] Answer, brother, reply, father, room, key, haste, gate, time, head, pavement, man, waste, truth, thunder, clap, storey, bed, book, night, face, point, shame, while, eye, top, hook, finger, bell, land, lamp, taper, shelf, church,—whisper, wait, return, go, keep, call, look, leave, reproach, do, pass, come, cry, open, sing, fall, hurry, reach, snatch, lie, regard, creep, lend, say, try, steal, hold, swell, wonder, interest, see, choke, shake, place, escape, ring, take, light. (I have not counted auxiliary verbs.)

[5] Back, down, still, out, home, except, like, while, straight.

in its power of making words serve in new functions,
might make Shakespeare's lines his own in a different
sense:

So all my best is dressing old words new,
spending againe what is already spent.[6]

179. Word-composition plays a very important
part in English. Compounds are either fixed or free, i.e.
such that when the need arises any speaker can form
new compounds after the pattern of already existing
combinations. The former tend to be felt as independent
units, isolated from the component parts in sound and
(or) in meaning. *Daisy* was originally *dayes eye,* but no
one nowadays connects the word with either *day* or *eye.*
Woman was originally *wīf + man;* a reminder of the
[i]-sound is kept in the plural *women; nostril,* OE. *nosu-
þyrel* (the latter part means 'hole'), *fifteen, Monday,
Christmas* show shortening of the first element as compared with *nose, five, moon, Christ.* Compare the treatment of the second element in the numerous place-names
in *-ton,* from *town,* and in *-mouth,* pronounced [-meþ].
Cupboard is pronounced [kʌbəd]. Sometimes there is re-
composition as a reaction against isolation: OE. *hūs +
wif* in course of time lost *w,* both vowels were shortened,
s was sounded [z], and *f* became *v* or was even lost; in
the derived meanings 'needle-case' and 'jade' we find the
forms *huzzif, huzzive,* and *huzzy.* But in the original
sense the word was constantly revived: *housewife.* With
free compounds we may have even long strings, like
*railway refreshment room, New Year Eve fancy dress
ball,* his *twopence a week pocket-money,* etc.

180. With regard to the logical relation of the
parts of a compound very few are of the same type as

[6] Sonnet 76.

tiptoe = tip of the toe. In the majority the first part determines the second: a *garden flower* is a kind of flower, but a *flower garden* a kind of garden. The relation of the two parts may be very different, and is left to be inferred from the meaning of each. Compare for instance *lifeboat* on the one hand with *life-insurance, life member, lifetime, life class* (class of painters drawing from life) and on the other hand *steamboat, pilot boat, iron boat,* etc. *Home letters* (from h.), *home voyage* (to), *home life* (at). Sometimes a compound means 'at the same time A and B': *servantman = man servant, queen-dowager, deaf-mute* = deaf and dumb.

181. A special type of compounds is exemplified in *pick-pocket* = 'one who picks pockets.' This type (verb + object) seems to have originated in Romanic languages, but has in modern times proved very fertile in English: *cut-purse, know-nothing, sawbones, break-water, stopgap, scare-crow,* etc. Such compounds are very often used as first parts of new compounds, in which case they may be considered adjectives: *break-neck* pace, a very *tell-tale* face, a *lack-lustre* eye, a *make-shift* dinner.[7]

182. While in the old type of fixed compounds the first part had strong and the second weak stress, the stress tends in free compounds, such as *gold coin, coat tail, lead pencil, headmaster,* to be more level, so that it often varies rhythmically according to the context. Each part of the compound is felt as independent of and of equal weight with the other. As an adjective before a substantive is now just as uninflected as a substantive forming the first part of a compound, the two combinations are also made syntactically equal. They are co-ordinated in 'her Christian and *family*

[7] MEG. II, 8, 6 and 14, 7.

name,' 'all national, *State, county,* and municipal offices,' 'a *Boston* young lady.' The prop-word *one* may
be used as in 'two *gold* watches and a *silver* one,' 'give
me a paper, one of the *Sunday* ones.' The likeness with
adjectives is made even more obvious when an adverb
is used as in 'from a too exclusively *London* standpoint,'
'in purely *Government* work,' 'in the most *matter-of-
fact* way.' From being often used as first parts of compounds some substantives have really become regular
adjectives and are recognized as such by everybody:
chief, choice, commonplace; they may even form adverbs: *choicely,* and substantives like *commonplaceness.*
Dainty, originally a substantive meaning a delicacy (Old
French *daintie* from L. *dignitatem*), and *bridal* (originally *brydealu* 'bride-ale') are now practically nothing
but adjectives: note in both their seemingly adjectival
endings.[8]

183. Having thus considered the modes of forming new words by adding something to existing words,
by adding to them nothing at all, and by composition,
we shall end this chapter by some remarks on the formation of new words by subtracting something from old
ones.[9] Such 'back-formations,' as they are very con-
veniently termed by Dr. Murray, owe their origin to
one part of a word being mistaken for some derivative
suffix (or, more rarely, prefix). The adverbs *sideling,
groveling* and *darkling* were originally formed by means
of the adverbial ending *-ling,* but in such phrases as
he walks sideling, he lies groveling, etc., they looked

[8] See MEG. II, ch. XI.

[9] Otto Jespersen, 'Om subtraktionsdannelser, særligt på dansk
og engelsk,' in *Festskrift til Vilh Thomsen* (Copenhagen, 1894).
I have treated a few classes of back-formations in *Engl. Studien*
70, p. 117 ff. On the subtraction of *s,* as if it were a plural sign,
see below, § 198.

exactly like participles in *-ing,* and the consequence
was that the new verbs to *sidle,* to *grovel,* and to *darkle*
were derived from them by the subtraction of *-ing.* The
Banting cure was named after one Mr. Banting; the
occasional verb to *bant* is, accordingly, a back-forma-
tion. The ending *-y* is often subtracted; from *greedy* is
thus formed the noun *greed* (about 1600), from *lazy*
and *cosy* the two verbs *laze* and *cose* (Kingsley), and
from *jeopardy* (French *jeu parti*) the verb *jeopard.* The
old adjective corresponding to *difficulty* was *difficile* as
in French, but about 1600 the adjective *difficult* (= the
noun minus *y*) makes its appearance. *Puppy* from
French *poupée* was thought to be formed by means of
the petting suffix *y,* and thus *pup* was created; similarly
I think that *cad* is from *caddy, caddie* = Fr. *cadet*
(a youngster) and *pet* from *petty* = Fr. *petit,* the
transition in meaning from 'little' to 'favourite' being
easily accounted for. Several verbs originate from nouns
in *-er* (*-ar, -or*), which were not originally 'agent
nouns'; *butcher* is the French *boucher,* derived from
bouc 'a buck, goat' with no corresponding verb, but in
English it has given rise to the rare verb to *butch* and to
the noun a *butch-knife.* Similarly *harbinger, rover,
pedlar, burglar, hawker,* and probably *beggar,* call into
existence the verbs to *harbinge* (Whitman), *rove,
peddle, burgle, hawk,* and *beg;* and the Latin words
editor, donator, vivisector, produce the un-Latin verbs
to *edit, donate* (American), *vivisect* (Meredith), etc.,
which look as if they came from Latin participles. Some
of these back-formations have been more successful
than others in being generally recognized in Standard
English.

184. It is not usual in Germanic languages to form
compounds with a verb as the second, and an object

or a predicative as the first, part. Hence, when we find
such verbs as to *housekeep* (Kipling, Merriman), the
explanation must be that *-er* has been subtracted from
the perfectly legitimate noun a *housekeeper* (or *-ing*
from *housekeeping*). The oldest examples I know of
this formation are to *backbite* (1300), to *partake*
(parttake, 16th c.) and to *soothsay* and *conycatch*
(Shakesp.); others are to *hutkeep,* common in Australia, *book-keep* (Shaw), to *dressmake,* to *matchmake*
(women will match-make, you know, A. Hope), to
thoughtread (Why don't they thoughtread each other?
H. G. Wells), to *typewrite* (I could typewrite if I had
a machine, id., also in B. Shaw's *Candida*), to *merrymake* (you merrymake together, Du Maurier). It will
be seen that most of these are nonce-words. The verbs
to *henpeck* and to *sunburn* are back-formations from
the participles *henpecked* and *sunburnt;* and Browning
even says '*moonstrike* him!' (*Pippa Passes*) for 'let him
be moonstruck.'

185. We have seen (§ 7 ff.) that monosyllabism
is one of the most characteristic features of modern
English, and this chapter has shown us some of the
morphological processes by which the original stock
of monosyllables has been in course of time considerably increased. It may not, therefore, be out of place
here briefly to give an account of some of the other
modes by which such short words have been developed.
Some are simply longer words which have been shortened by regular phonetic development (cf. *love,* § 163);
e.g. *eight* OE. *eahta, dear* OE. *deore, fowl* OE. *ugol,
hawk* OE. *hafoc, lord* OE. *hlaford, not* and *nought* OE.
nawiht, pence OE. *penigas, ant* OE. *æmette,* etc. *Miss*
before the names of unmarried ladies is a somewhat
irregular shortening of 'missis' (mistress); though found

here and there in the seventeenth century, *Miss* was not yet recognized in the middle of the eighteenth century (cf. Fielding's Mrs. Bridgit, Mrs. Honour, etc.).

186. This leads us to the numerous popular clippings of long foreign words, of which rarely the middle (as in *Tench* 'the House of *Detention*' and *teck* 'detective') or the end (as in *bus* 'omnibus,' *baccer, baccy* 'tobacco,' *phone,* 'telephone'), but more often the beginning only subsists. Some of these stump-words have never passed beyond slang, such as *sov* 'sovereign,' *pub* 'public-house,' *confab* 'confabulation,' *pop* 'popular concert,' *vet* 'veterinary surgeon,' *Jap* 'Japanese,' *guv* 'Governor,' *Mods* 'Moderations,' an Oxford examination, *matric* 'matriculation,' *prep* 'preparation,' and *impot* or *impo* 'imposition' in schoolboys' slang, *sup* 'supernumerary,' *props* 'properties' in theatrical slang, *perks* 'perquisites,' *comp* 'compositor,' *caps* 'capital letters,' etc., etc. Some are perhaps now in a fair way to become recognized in ordinary speech, such as *exam* 'examination,' and *bike* 'bicycle'; and some words have become so firmly established as to make the full words pass completely into oblivion, e.g. *cab* (cabriolet), *fad* (fadaise), *navvy* (navigator in the sense of canal-digger and later railway labourer) and *mob* (mobile vulgus).

187. A last group of English monosyllables comprises a certain number of words the etymology of which has hitherto baffled all the endeavours of philologists. At a certain moment such a word suddenly comes into the language, nobody knowing from where, so that we must feel really inclined to think of a creation *ex nihilo.* I am not particularly thinking of words denoting sounds or movements in a more or less onomatopoetic way, for their origin is psychologically easy to account for, but of such words as the following, some of which belong now to the most indispensable speech material: *bad*,[10] *big*,[11] *lad* and *lass*, all appearing towards the end of the thirteenth century; *fit* adjective and *fit* substantive, probably two mutually independent words, the adjective dating from 1440, the substantive in the now current sense from 1547; *dad* 'father,' *jump, crease* 'fold, wrinkle,' *gloat,* and *bet* from the sixteenth century; *job, fun* (and *pun*), *blight, chum* and *hump* from the seventeenth century; *fuss, jam* verb and substantive, and *hoax* from the eighteenth, and *slum, stunt* and *blurb* from the nineteenth and twentieth centuries. Anyone who has watched small children carefully must have noticed that they sometimes create some such words without any apparent reason; sometimes they stick to it only for a day or two as the name of some plaything, etc., and then forget it; but sometimes a funny sound takes lastingly their fancy and may even be adopted by their playmates or parents as a real word.[12] Without pretending that such is the origin of all the words just mentioned I yet venture to throw out the suggestion that some of them may be due to children's playful inventiveness— while others may have sprung from the corresponding linguistic playfulness of grown-up people which forms the fundamental essence of the phenomenon called *slang*.

[10] See Zupitza's attempt at an explanation in the NED., which does not account for the origin of *bæddel*.

[11] The best explanation is Björkman's, see *Scand. Loan Words,* p. 157 and 259; but even he does not claim to have solved the mystery completely.

[12] Cf. my book *Language*, p. 151 ff. On the general theory of slang see ib. 298 ff., and *Mankind, Nation and Individual,* p. 149 ff.

CHAPTER IX

Grammar

188. The preceding chapter has already brought us near to our present province or rather has crossed its boundary, for word-formation is rightly considered one of the main divisions of grammar. In the other divisions a survey of the historical development shows us the same general tendency as word-formation does (§ 164), the tendency, as we might call it, from chaos towards cosmos. Where the old language had a great many endings, most of them with very vague meanings and applications, Modern English has but few, and their sphere of signification is more definite. The number of irregularities and anomalies, so considerable in Old English, has been greatly reduced so that now the vast majority of words are inflected regularly. It has been objected that most of the old strong verbs are still strong, and that this means irregularity in the formation of the tenses: *shake, shook, shaken* is just as irregular as Old English *scacan, scoc, scacen*. But it must be remembered, first, that there is a complete disappearance of a great many of those details of inflexion which made every Old English paradigm much more complicated than its modern successor, such as distinctions of persons and numbers, and nearly all differences between the infinitive, the imperative, the indicative, and the subjunctive; secondly that the number of distinct vowels

has been reduced in many verbs; compare thus *beran,
birep bær, bæron, boren* with *bear, bears, bore, bore,
born; feohtan, fieht, feaht, fuhton, fohten* with *fight,
fights, fought, fought, fought; bindan, band, bunden* with
bind, bound, bound; berstan, bærst, burston, borsten
with *burst, burst, burst, burst;* and thirdly, that the consonant change found in many verbs (*ceas, curon, snap,
snidon, teah, tugon*) has been abolished altogether except in the single case of *was, were.* The greatest change
towards simplicity and regularity is seen in the adjectives, where one form now represents the eleven different
forms used by the contemporaries of Alfred. But it must
not be imagined that the development has in every
minute particular made for progress; nothing has been
gained, for instance, by the modern creation of *mine*
and *thine* as primary possessive pronouns by the side of
my and *thy.* It is only when we compare the entire
linguistic structure of some remote period with the structure in modern times that we observe that the gain in
clearness and simplicity has really been enormous.

189. This grammatical development and simplification has taken place not suddenly and from one
cause, but gradually and from a variety of causes, most
of these the same that have worked and are working
similar changes in other languages. It cannot be said that
'the chief impulse to such changes is due to progressive
thinking and advancing culture which made the traditional forms insufficient for the abundance of ideas in
their mutual relations' (Morsbach), for some of the
changes took place with greatest rapidity in centuries
when culture was at a low ebb. Chief among the general
causes of the decay of the Old English apparatus of
declensions and conjugations must be reckoned the
manifold incongruities of the system: if the same vowel

did not everywhere denote the same shade of meaning,
speakers would naturally tend to indulge in the universal
inclination to pronounce weak syllables indistinctly
(and the OE. flexional endings were all unstressed):
thus *a, i, u* of the endings were levelled in the one colourless vowel *e,* and this could even after some time be
dropped altogether in most cases. The same want of
system would also favour the analogical extension of
those endings which were clearest in their forms and in
their sphere of employment, thus in substantives the
s-forms both as genitives and as plurals.[1] But beside
this general cause we must in each separate case inquire
into those special causes that may have been at work,
and even such a seemingly small step as that by which
the old declension of *ye* (nominative) and *you* (accusative and dative) has given way to the modern use of
you in all cases, has been the result of the activity of
many moving forces. In the following sections I shall
select a few points of grammar which seem to me illus-
trative of the processes of change in general, and (as
regards some of them) of the progressive tendency I
have mentioned.

190. (I.) The *s*-ending in nouns: In Old English
the *genitive* was formed in *es* in most masculines and
neuters, but beside this a variety of other endings were
in use with the different stems, in *-e,* in *-re,* in *-an;*
some words had no separate ending in the genitive, and
some formed a mutation-genitive (*boc* 'book,' gen.

---

[1] This is the view I have held since 1891 and expressed more
or less explicitly in various publications; see now *Language,*
books III and IV, also *Chapters on English.* On the influence of
speech-mixture on the rapidity of movement see above (§ 79);
on the rapidity of change due to wars, pestilences, etc., in the
fourteenth and fifteenth centuries, see *Language,* p. 261.

bec). Besides, the genitive of the plural never ended in *-s* but in *-a* or *-ra* or *-na* (*-ena, -ana*). With regard to syntax, the genitive case filled a variety of functions, possessive, subjective, objective, partitive, definitive, descriptive, etc. It was used not only to connect two substantives, but also after a great number of verbs and adjectives (rejoice at, fear, long for, remember, fill, empty, weary, deprive of, etc.); it sometimes stood before and sometimes after the governing word. In short, the rules for the formation as well as for the employment of that case were complicated to a very high degree. But gradually a greater regularity and simplicity prevailed in accidence as well as in syntax; the *s*-genitive was extended to more and more nouns and to the plural as well as the singular number, and now it is the only genitive ending used in the language though in the plural it is in the great majority of cases hidden away behind the *s* used to denote the plural number (*kings'*, cf. *men's*). The position of the genitive now is always immediately before the governing word, and this in connexion with the regularity of the formation of the case has been instrumental in bringing about the modern group-genitive, where the *s* is tacked on to the end of a word-group, with no regard to the logic of the older grammar: *the King of England's power* (formerly 'the kinges power of England'), *the bride and bridegroom's return, somebody else's hat,* etc.[2]

191. As for the use of the genitive, it has been in various ways encroached upon by the combination with *of*. First, its use is now in ordinary prose almost restricted to personal beings, and even such phrases as 'society's hard-drilled soldiery' (Meredith), where *so-*

---

[2] See the detailed historical account of the group-genitive, *Chapters on English*, 1918, ch. III.

ciety is personified, are felt as poetical; still more so, of course, 'thou knowst not golds effect,' (Sh.) or 'setting out upon life's journey' (Stevenson). But in some set phrases the genitive is still established, e.g. out of *harm's* way; he is at his *wits'* (or *wit's*) end; so also in the stock quotation from Hamlet, in my *mind's* eye, etc. Then to indicate measure, etc.: at a *boat's* length from the ship, and especially time: an *hour's* walk, a good *night's* rest, *yesterday's* post; and this is even extended to such prepositional combinations as *today's* adventures, *to-morrow's* papers.

192. Secondly, the genitive (of names of persons) is now chiefly used possessively, though this word must be taken in a very wide sense, including such cases as 'Shelley's works,' 'Gainsborough's pictures,' 'Tom's enemies,' 'Tom's death,' etc. The subjective genitive, too, is in great vigour, for instance in 'the King's arrival,' 'the Duke's invitation,' 'the Duke's inviting him,' 'Mrs. Poyser's repulse of the squire' (G. Eliot). Still there is, in quite recent times, a tendency towards expressing the subject by means of the preposition *by,* just as in the passive voice, for instance in 'the accidental discovery by Miss Knag of some correspondence' (Dickens); 'the appropriation by a settled community of lands on the other side of an ocean' (Seeley), 'the massacre of Christians by Chinese.' 'Forster's Life of Dickens' is the same thing as 'Dickens's Life, by Forster.' The objective genitive was formerly much more common than now, the ambiguity of the genitive being probably the reason of its decline. Still, we find, for instance, 'his expulsion from power by the Tories' (Thackeray), 'What was thy pity's recompense?' (Byron). 'England's wrongs' generally means the wrongs done to England; thus also 'my cosens wrongs' in Shakespeare's R 2, II,

3, 141, but 'your foule wrongs' (in the same play, III, 1, 15) means the wrongs committed by you. In 'my sceptre's awe' (ib. I, 1, 118) we have an objective, but in 'thy free awe pays homage to us' (Hamlet IV, 3, 63) a subjective genitive. But on the whole such obscurity will occur less frequently in English than in other languages, where the genitive is more freely used.

193. Now, *of* has so far prevailed that there are very few cases where a genitive cannot be replaced by it, and it is even used to supplant a possessive pronoun in such stock phrases as 'not for the death of me' (cf. Chaucer's 'the blood of me,' LGW. 848). *Of* is required in a great many cases, such as 'I come here at the instance of your colleague, Dr. H. J. Henry Jekyll' (Stevenson), and it is often employed to avoid tacking on the *s* to too long a series of words, as in 'Will Wimble's is the case of many a younger brother of a great family' (Addison) or 'the wife of a clergyman of the Church of England' (Thackeray), where most Englishmen will resent the iteration of *of*'s less than they do the repeated *s*'s in Mrs. Browning's 'all the hoofs of King Saul's father's asses' or in Pinero's 'He is my wife's first husband's only child's godfather.' Even long strings of prepositions are tolerated, as in 'on the occasion of the coming of age of one of the youngest sons of a wealthy member of Parliament,' or 'Swift's visit to London in 1707 had for its object the obtaining for the Irish Church of the surrender by the Crown of the First-Fruits and Twentieths' (Aitken) or 'that sublime conception of the Holy Father of a spiritual kingdom on earth under the sovereignty of the Vicar of Jesus Christ himself' (Hall Caine). I suppose that very few readers of the original books have found anything heavy or cumbersome in these passages, even if they may here, where their attention is drawn to the grammatical construction.

194. Speaking of the genitive, we ought also to mention the curious use in phrases like 'a friend of my brother's.' This began in the fourteenth century with such instances as 'an officere of the prefectes' (Chaucer G 368), where *officers* might be supplied (= one of the prefect's officers) and 'if that any neighebor of mine (= any of my neighbours) Wol nat in chirche to my wyf enclyne' (id. B 3091). In the course of a few centuries, the construction became more and more frequent, so that it has now long been one of the fixtures of the English language. A partitive sense is still conceivable in such phrases as 'an olde religious unckle of mine' (Sh. As III, 3, 362) = one of my uncles, though it will be seen that it is impossible to analyse it as being equal to 'one of my old religious uncles.' But it is not at all certain that *of* here from the first was partitive;[3] it is rather to be classed with the appositional use in *the three of us* = 'the three who are we'; *the City of Rome* = 'the City which is Rome.' The construction is used chiefly to avoid the juxtaposition of two pronouns, 'this hat of mine, that ring of yours' being preferred to 'this my hat, that your ring,' or of a pronoun and a genitive, as in 'any ring of Jane's,' where 'any Jane's ring' or 'Jane's any ring' would be impossible; compare also 'I make it a rule of mine,' 'this is no fault of Frank's,' etc. In all such cases the construction was found so convenient that it is no wonder that it should soon be used extensively where no partitive sense is logically possible, as in 'nor shall [we] ever see That face of hers againe' (Shakespeare, Lear I, 1, 267), 'that flattering tongue of yours' (As IV, 1, 188), 'Time hath not yet so dried

[3] See *Mod. Engl. Grammar*, III, p. 15 ff.

this bloud of mine' (Ado IV, 1, 195), 'If I had such a tyre, this face of mine Were full as lovely as is this of hers' (Gent. IV, 4, 190), 'this uneasy heart of ours' (Wordsworth), 'that poor old mother of his,' etc. When we now say 'he has a house of his own,' no one could think of this as meaning 'he has one of his own houses.'

195. In the *nominative plural* the Old English declensions present the same motley spectacle as the genitive singular. Most masculines have the ending *as,* but some have *e* (Engle, etc.), some *a* (suna, etc.) and a great many *an* (guman, etc.); some nouns have no ending at all, and most of these change the vowel of the kernel (fet, etc.), while a few have the plural exactly like the singular (hettend). Feminine words formed their plural in *a* (giefa), in *e* (bene), in *an* (tungan) or without any ending (sweostor; with mutation bec). Neuters had either no ending (word) or else *u* (hofu) or *an* (eagan). From the oldest period the ending *as* (later *es, s*) has been continually gaining ground, first among those masculines that belonged to other declensional classes, later on also in the other genders. The *an*-ending, which was common to a very great number of substantives from the very beginning, also showed great powers of expansion and at one time seemed as likely as (*e*)*s* to become the universal plural ending. But finally (*e*)*s* carried the day, probably because it was the most distinctive ending, and possibly under Scandinavian influence (§ 79). In the beginning of the modern period *eyen, shoon,* and *hosen, housen, peasen* still existed, but they were doomed to destruction, and now *oxen* is the only real plural in *n* surviving, for *children* as well as the biblical *kine* and *brethren* are too irregular to count as plurals made by the addition of *n*. The mutation plural has survived in some words whose signification causes the plural to occur more frequently than, or at least as frequently as, the singular: *geese, teeth, feet, mice, lice, men* and *women*. In all other words the analogy of the plurals in *s* was too strong for the old form to be preserved.

196. Instead of the ending *-ses* we often find a single *s;* in some cases this may be the continued use of the French plural form without any ending (*cas* sg. and pl.), as in *sense* (their sense are shut, Sh.), *corpse* (pl. Sh.), etc. In Coriolanus III, 1, 118, *voyce voyces* occur, both of them to be read as one syllable: 'Why shall the people give One that speakes thus, their voyce? —Ile give my reasons, More worthier than their voyces. They know the corne.' But when Shakespeare uses *princesse* and *balance* as plurals (Tp. I, 2, 173; Merch. IV, 1, 255), the forms admit of no other explanation than that of haplology (pronouncing the same sound once instead of twice). Thus also in the genitive case: 'his mistresse eye-brow' (As. II, 7, 149), 'your Highness' pleasure,' etc. Now it is more usual to give the full form *mistress's*, etc., yet in *Pears' soap* the juxtaposition of three *s*'s is avoided by means of the apostrophized form. The genitive of the plural is now always haplologized: 'the Poets' Corner,' except in some dialects: 'other folks's children' (George Eliot), 'the bairns's clease' (Murray, *Dial. of Scotl.,* 164). Wallis (1653) expressly states that the gen. pl. in *the Lord's House* (by him written *Lord's*) stands instead of *the Lords's House* (duo *s* in unum coincidunt). A phenomenon of the same order is the omission of the genitive sign before a word beginning with *s,* now chiefly before *sake:* for fashion sake, etc.

197. Sometimes an *s* belonging to the stem of the word is taken by the popular instinct to be a plural

ending.[4] Thus in *alms* (ME. *almesse, elmesse,* pl.
almesses; OE. *ælmesse* from Gr. *eleemosune*); it is significant that the word is very often found in connexions
where it is impossible from the context to discover
whether a singular or a plural is intended (ask alms,
give alms, etc.). In the Authorized Version the word
occurs eleven times, but eight of these are ambiguous,
two are clearly singular (asked an almes, gave much
almes) and one is probably plural (Thy praiers and
thine almes are come up). Nowadays the association between the *s* of the *alms* and the plural ending has become so firm that *an alms* is said and written very rarely
indeed, though it is found in Tennyson's *Enoch Arden.*
Riches is another case in point; Chaucer still lays the
stress on the second syllable (*richésse* as in French) and
uses the plural *richesses;* but as subsequently the final
e disappeared, and as the word occurred very often in
such a way that the context does not show its number
('Thou bearst thy heavie riches but a journie,' Sh. Meas.
III, 1, 27), thus in fourteen out of the twenty-four places
where Shakespeare uses it, it is no wonder that the form
was generally conceived as a plural, thus 'riches are a
power' (Ruskin). The singular use (the riches of the
ship is come on shore, Sh. Oth. II, 1, 83, too much
riches, R 2, III, 4, 60) is now wholly obsolete.

198. A further step is taken in those words that
lose the *s* originally belonging to their stem, because it
is mistakenly apprehended as the sign of plural.[5] Latin
pisum became in OE. *pise,* in ME. *pese,* pl. *pesen;*
Butler (1633) still gives *peas* as sg. and *peasen* as pl.,
but he adds, 'the singular is most used for the plural:
as . . . a peck of peas; though the Londoners seem to

[4] Cf. *Mod. Engl. Grammar,* II, ch. V.
[5] Cf. the other back-formations mentioned above (§ 183).

make it a regular plural, calling a *peas* a *pea.*' In compounds like *peaseblossom, peaseporridge* and *peasesoup* (Swift, Lamb) the old form was preserved long after *pea* had become the recognized singular. Similarly *a cherry* was evolved from a form in *s* (French *cerise*), *a riddle* from *riddles;* an *eaves* (OE. *efes,* cf. Got. *ubizwa,* ON. *ups*) is often made *an eave,* and vulgarly *a pony shay* is said for *chaise;* compare also Bret Harte's 'heathen *Chinee*' and the parallel forms *a Portuguee, a Maltee.* An interesting case in point is *Yankee,* if H. Logeman's ingenious explanation is to be accepted. The term was originally applied to the inhabitants of the Dutch colonies in North America (New Amsterdam, now New York, etc.). Now *Jan Kees* is a nickname still applied in Flanders to people from Holland proper. *Jan* of course is the common Dutch name corresponding to English John, and *Kees* may be either the usual pet form of the name Cornelis, another Christian name typical of the Dutch, or else a dialectal variation of *kaas* 'cheese' in allusion to that typically Dutch product, or—what is most probable—a combination of both. *Jankees* in English became *Yankees,* where the *s* was taken as the plural ending and eventually disappeared, and *Yankee* became the designation of any inhabitant of New England and even sometimes of the whole of the United States.

199. We have a different class of back-formations in those cases in which the *s* that is subtracted is really the plural ending, while one part of the word is retained which is logically consistent with the plural idea only. It is easily conceivable that most people ignorant of the fact that the first syllable of *cinque-ports* means 'five,' have no hesitation in speaking of Hastings as a *cinque-port;* but it is more difficult to see how the signification

of the numeral in *ninepins* should be forgotten, and yet
sometimes each of the 'pins' used in that play is called
a ninepin, and Gosse writes 'the author sets up his four
ninepins.'

200. In some words the *s* of the plural has become
fixed, as if it belonged to the singular, thus in *means.* As
is shown by the pun in Shakespeare's *Romeo,* 'no sudden meane of death, though nere so meane' the old
form was still understood in his time, but the modern
form too is used by him (*by that meanes,* Merch.; *a
means,* Wint.). Similarly: *too much pains, an honour-
able amends, a shambles, an innings,* etc., sometimes
a scissors, a tweezers, a barracks, a golf links, etc., where
the logical idea of a single action or thing has proved
stronger than the original grammar.

201. It is not, however, till a new plural has been
formed on such a form that the transformation from
plural to singular has been completed. This phenomenon, which might be termed plural raised to the second
power, will naturally occur with greater facility when
the original singular is not in use or when the manner of
forming the plural is no longer perspicuous. Thus OE.
broc formed its plural *brec* (cf. *gos, ges,* goose, geese),
but *broc* became *obsolete,* and *brec, breech* was free to
become a singular and to form a new plural *breeches.*
Similarly *invoices, quinces, bodices,* and a few others
have a double plural ending; but then the unusual sound
of the first ending (voiceless *s,* where the ordinary ending is voiced, as in *joys, sins*) facilitated the forgetting of
the original function of the *s* (written *-ce*). *Bodice* is
really nothing but a by-form of *bodies.* The old pronunciation of *bellows* and *gallows* had also a voiceless *s,*
which helps to explain the vulgar plurals *bellowses* and
gallowses. But in the occasional plural *mewses* (from *a*

mews, orig. *a mue*) the new ending has been added in spite of the first *s* being voiced. These plurals raised to the second power, to which must be added *sixpences, threepences,* etc., are particularly interesting because there really are cases where the want is felt of expressing the plural of something which is in itself plural, either formally or logically; cf. *many (pairs of) scissors.* Generally one plural ending only is used,[6] but occasionally the logically correct double ending is resorted to, especially among uneducated people; Thackeray makes his flunkey write: 'there was 8 sets of chamberses' (*Yellowplush Papers,* p. 39), and a London schoolboy[7] once wrote: 'cats have clawses' (one cat has claws!) and again 'cats have 9 liveses' (each cat has nine lives!). Dr. Murray[8] mentions a double plural sometimes formed in Scotch dialect from such words as *schuin* (one person's shoes), *feit* 'feet' and *kye* 'cows,' *schuins* meaning more than one pair of shoes, and he ingeniously suggests that this may illustrate such plurals as *children, brethren, kine;* the original plurals were *childer, brether, ky* (still preserved in the northern dialect), which may have 'come to be used collectively for the offspring or members of a single family, the herd of a single owner, so that a second plural inflection became necessary to express the *brethren* and *children* of many families, the *ky-en* of many owners . . . In modern English we restrict *brothers,* which replaces *brether,* to those of one family, using *brethren* for those who call each other *brother,* though of different families.'

[6] 'Then ensued one of the most lively ten minutes that I can remember' (Conan Doyle), plural of 'a lively ten minutes.'

[7] *Very Original English,* by Barker (London, 1889), p. 71.

[8] *Dialect of the Southern Counties of Scotland* (London, 1873), p. 161.

202. Most of the words that make their plural like the singular are old neuters, the *s*-ending belonging originally to masculines only and having only gradually been extended to the other two genders; thus, *swine, deer, sheep*. In some cases a difference sprang up between the singular in speaking of the mass and an individual plural (in *-s*), as seen most clearly in Shakespeare's 'Shee hath more *haire* then wit, and more faults then *hairs*' (Gent. III, 1, 362) and Milton's 'which thou from Heaven Feigndst at thy birth was giv'n thee in thy *hair*, Where strength can least abide, though all thy *hairs* Were bristles' (Sams. Ag., 1136). This difference was transferred to some old masculines, like *fish, fowl;* and a great many names of particular fishes and birds, especially those generally hunted and used for food, are now often unchanged in the plural (*snipe, plover, trout, salmon,* etc.), though with a great deal of vacillation. It is also noticeable that *much fruit = many fruits* and *much coal = many coals*. When we say 'four *hundred* men,' but '*hundreds* of men,' 'two *dozen* collars,' but '*dozens* of collars' and similarly with *couple, pair, score,* and some other words, we have an approach to the rule prevailing in many languages, e.g. Magyar, where the plural ending is not added after a numeral, because that suffices in itself to show that a plural is intended.[9]

203. (II) Disappearance of the old *word-gender*.[10] In Old English, as in all the old cognate languages, each substantive, no matter whether it referred to animate beings or things or abstract notions, belonged to one or other of the three gender-classes. Thus masculine

---

[9] Cf. *Mod. Engl. Gr.*, II, ch. III., Unchanged plurals, and ch. V., Mass-words.

[10] On the relation between gender and sex, see *Philosophy of Grammar,* ch. XVII.

pronouns and endings were found with names of a great many things which had nothing to do with male sex (e.g. *horn, ende* 'end,' *ebba* 'ebb,' *dæg* 'day') and similarly feminine pronouns and endings with many words without any relation to female sex (e.g. *sorh* 'sorrow,' *glof* 'glove,' *plume* 'plum,' *pipe*). Anyone acquainted with the intricacies of the same system (or want of system) in German will feel how much English has gained in clearness and simplicity by giving up these distinctions and applying *he* only to male, and *she* only to female, living beings. The distinction between animate and inanimate now is much more accentuated than it used to be, and this has led to some other changes, of which the two most important are the creation (about 1600) of the form *its* (before that time *his* was neuter as well as masculine) and the restriction of the relative pronoun *which* to things: its old use alike for persons and things is seen in 'Our father *which* art in Heaven.'

204. (III) *Numerals.* While the cardinal numerals show very little change during the whole life of the language, except what is a consequence of ordinary phonetic development,[11] the ordinals have been much more changed so that their formation is now completely regular, with the exception of the first three. *First* has ousted the old *forma* (corresponding to Latin *primus*), and the French *second* has been called in to relieve *other* of one of its significations, so that a useful distinction has been created between the definite and the indefinite numeral. As for the numbers from 4 upwards, the regularization has affected both the stem and the ending

---

[11] Note that in Old and Middle English the cardinals had an *e-* when used absolutely (*fif* men; they were *five*), and that it is this form that has prevailed. If the old conjoint form had survived, *five* and *twelve* would have ended in *f*, and *seven, nine* and *eleven* would have had no *-n*.

of the numeral. In Old English the *n* had disappeared from *seofoða, nigoða* and *teoða* (*feowerteoða,* etc.), but now it has been analogically reintroduced: *seventh, ninth, tenth* (*fourteenth,* etc.), the only survival of the older forms being *tithe,* which is now a substantive differentiated from the numeral, as seen particularly clearly in the phrase 'a tenth part of the tithe' (Auth. Version, Num. 18, 26). In *twelfth* and *fifth* we have the insignificant anomaly of *f* (which in the former is often mute) instead of *v,* and the consonant-group in the latter has shortened the vowel, but elsewhere there is complete correspondence between each cardinal and its ordinal. As for the ending, it used according to a well-known phonetic rule to be *-ta* (later *-te, -t*) after voiceless open consonants, thus *fifta, fift, sixta, sixt, twelfta, twelft;* and these are still the only forms in Shakespeare (*Henry the Fift,* etc.)[12] and Milton. The regular forms in *th* evidently were used in writing before they became prevalent in speaking, for Schade in 1765 laid down the rule that *th* was to be pronounced *t* in *twelfth* and *fifth. Eighth,* which would be more adequately written *eightth,* is also a modern form; the old editions of Shakespeare have *eight.* The formation in *-th,* which is now beautifully regular, has also been extended in recent times to a few substantives: *the hundredth, thousandth, millionth,* and *dozenth.*

205. (IV). The *pronominal system* has been reinforced by some new applications of old material. *Who* and *which,* originally interrogative and indefinite pronouns, are now used also as relatives. *Self* has entered

[12] *Twelfth Night* is in the folio of 1623 called *Twelfe Night* and similarly we have *twelfe day,* where the middle consonant of a difficult group has been discarded, just as in *the thousand part* (As IV. 1, 46).

into the compounds *myself, himself,* etc., and has developed a plural, *ourselves, themselves,* which was new in the beginning of the sixteenth century. With regard to the use of these *self*-forms, it may be remarked that their frequency first increased and then in certain cases decreased again: *he dressed him* became *he dressed himself,* and this is now giving way to *he dressed. One* has come to serve several purposes; as an indefinite pronoun (in 'one never can tell') it dates from the fifteenth century, and as a prop-word ('a little one,' 'the little ones') the modern usage goes no further back than to the sixteenth century.

206. (V). The history of the forms in *ing* is certainly one of the most interesting examples of the growth from a very small beginning of something very important in the economy of the language. The *ing,* as I shall for shortness call the form with that ending, began as a pure substantive,[13] restricted as to the number of words from which it might be formed and restricted as to its syntactical functions. It seems to have been originally possible to form it only from nouns, cf. modern words like *schooling, shirting, stabling;* as some of the nouns from which ings were derived had corresponding weak verbs, the ings came to be looked upon as derived from these verbs, and new ings were made from other weak verbs. (Also from French verbs, cf. above § 106.) But it was a long time before ings were made from strong verbs; a few occur in the very last decades of the Old English period, but most of them did not creep into existence till the twelfth or thirteenth century or even later, and it is not, perhaps, till the beginning of the fifteenth century that the formation had taken such a firm root in the language that an ing could be formed unhesitatingly

[13] The Old English ending was *ung* as well as *ing.*

from any verb whatever (apart from the auxiliaries *can,
may, shall, must,* etc., which have no ings).

207. With regard to its syntactical use the old ing
was a substantive and was restricted to the functions it
shared with all other substantives. While keeping all its
substantival qualities, it has since gradually acquired
most of the functions belonging to a verb. It was, and is,
inflected like a substantive; now the genitive case is rare
and scarcely occurs outside of such phrases as 'reading
for reading's sake'; but the plural is common: his com-
ings and goings; feelings, drawings, leavings, weddings,
etc. Like any other substantive it can have the definite
or indefinite article and an adjective before it: a beginning, the beginning, a good beginning, etc., so also a
genitive: Tom's savings. It can enter into a compound
noun either as the first or as the second part: a walking-
stick; sight-seeing. The ing can be used in a sentence in
every position occupied by an ordinary substantive. It is
the subject and the predicative nominative in 'com-
plimenting is lying,' the object in 'I hate lying'; it is governed by an adjective in 'worth knowing,' and governed
by a preposition in 'before answering,' etc. But we shall
now see how several of the peculiar functions of verbs
are extended to the ing. The coalescence in form of the
verbal substantive and of the present participle is, of
course, one of the chief factors of this development.

208. When the ing was a pure substantive the
object of the action it indicated could be expressed in
one of three ways: it might be put in the genitive case
('sio feding þara sceapa,' the feeding of the sheep, Alfred), or it might form the second part of a compound
(blood-letting) or—the usual construction in Middle
English—it might be added after *of* (in magnifying of
his name, Chaucer). The first of these constructions has

died out; the last is in our days especially frequent after
the article (since the telling of those little fibs, Thackeray). But from the fourteenth century we find a grow-
ing tendency to treat the ing like a form of the verb, and
accordingly, to put the object in the accusative case.
Chaucer's words, 'in getinge of your richesses and in
usinge hem' (B 2813) show both constructions in juxtaposition; so also 'Thou art so fat-witted with drinking
of olde sacke, and unbuttoning thee after supper' (Henry
IV A, 1, 2, 2). Chaucer's 'In liftinge up his hevy
dronken cors' (H 67) shows a double deviation from
the old substantival construction, for an ordinary substantive cannot in this way be *followed by an adverb,*
and in the old language the adverb was joined to the
ing in a different way (up-lifting, in-coming, down-
going). In course of time it became more and more
usual to join any kind of adverb to the ing, e.g. 'a man
shal not wyth *ones* [once] over redying fynde the ryght
understandyng' (Caxton), 'he proposed our *immediately*
drinking a bottle together' (Fielding), 'nothing distin-
guishes great men from inferior men more than their
always, whether in life or in art, knowing the ways
things are going' (Ruskin).

209. A substantive does not admit of any indication of *time; his movement* may correspond in meaning
to 'he moves (is moving),' 'he moved (was moving),' or
'he will move.' Similarly the ing had originally, and to a
great extent still has, no reference to time: 'on account
of his coming' may be equal to 'because he comes' or
'because he came' or 'he will come,' according to the
connexion in which it occurs. 'I intend seeing the king'
refers to the future. 'I remember seeing the king' to the
past, or rather the ing as such implies neither of these
tenses. But since the end of the sixteenth century the ing

has still further approximated to the character of a verb by developing a composite perfect. Shakespeare, who uses the new tense in a few places, e.g. Gent. I, 3, 16 ('To let him spend his time no more at home; Which would be great impeachment to his age, In *having knowne* no travaile in his youth') does not always use it where it would be used now; for in 'Give order to my servants that they take No note at all of our *being* absent hence' *being* corresponds in meaning to *having been,* as shown by the context (Merch. of Ven. V, 120). Like other nouns the ing was also at first incapable of expressing the verbal distinction between *the active* and *the passive voice.* The simple ing is still often neutral in this respect, and in some connexions assumes a passive meaning, as in 'it wants mending,' 'the story lost much in the telling.' This is extremely frequent in old authors, e.g. 'Use everie man after his desart, and who should scape whipping' (Hamlet II, 2, 554), 'Shall we . . . excuse his throwing into the water?' (Wiv. III, 3, 206 = his being, or having been, thrown), 'An instrument of this your calling backe' (Oth. IV, 2, 45). But about 1600 a new form came into existence, as the old one would often appear ambiguous, and it was felt convenient to be able to distinguish between 'foxes enjoy hunting' and 'foxes enjoy being hunted.' The new passive is rare in Shakespeare ('I spoke . . . of being taken by the insolent foe,' *Oth.* I, 3, 136), but has now for a long time been firmly established in the language.

210. Still another step must be mentioned in this long development of a form at first purely substantival into one partly substantival and partly verbal in function. The *subject* of the ing, like that of any verbal noun (for instance *Cæsar's* conquests, *Pope's* imitations of Horace), is for the most part put in the genitive case—nearly

always when it is a personal pronoun (in spite of *his*
saying so), and generally when it indicates a person (in
spite of *John's* saying so). But a variety of circumstances
led to the use in many instances of the common case
before the ing.[14] Here I must content myself with quoting
a few instances of the new construction: 'When we talk
of this man or that woman being no longer the same
person' (Thackeray), 'besides the fact of those three
being there, the drawbridge is kept up' (A. Hope),
'When I think of this being the last time of seeing you'
(Miss Austen), 'the possibility of such an effect being
wrought by such a cause' (Dickens), 'he insisted upon
the Chamber carrying out his policy' (Lecky), 'I have
not the least objection in life to a rogue being hung'
(Thackeray; here evidently no participle), 'no man ever
heard of opium leading into delirium tremens' (De
Quincey), 'the suffering arises simply from people not
understanding this truism' (Ruskin). These examples
will show that the construction is especially useful in
those cases where for some reason or other it is impossible to use the genitive case, but that it is also
found where no such reason could be adduced. Let me
sum up by saying that when an Englishman now says,
'There is some probability of the place having never
been inspected by the police,' he deviates in four points
from the constructions of the ing that would have been
possible to one of his ancestors six hundred years ago;
place is in the crude form, not in the genitive; the adverb; the perfect; and the passive. Thanks to these extensions the ing has clearly become a most valuable

---

[14] See *Society for Pure English,* Tract XXV (1926), p. 147 ff.
(against H. W. Fowler's view of 'Fused Participles'). Van der
Gaaf, in *Engl. Studies,* X, (1928) is probably wrong in attribut-
ing the construction to imitation of Old French.

means of expressing tersely and neatly relations that
must else have been indicated by clumsy dependent
clauses.

211. (VI). We proceed to the *verbal ending -s* (*he
loves*, etc.). In Old English *-th* (þ) was used in the
ending of the third person singular and in all persons
in the plural of the present indicative, but the vowel
before it varied, so that we have for instance:

infinitive	*3rd sg.*	*pl.*
sprecan	spricþ	sprecaþ
bindan	bindeþ, bint	bindaþ
nerian	nereþ	neriaþ
lufian	lufaþ	lufiaþ

But in the Northumbrian dialect of the tenth century
s was substituted for þ (singular *bindes*, plural *bindas*),
and as all unstressed vowels were soon after levelled, the
two forms became identical (*bindes*). As in the same
dialect the second person singular too ended in *s* (as
against the *-st* of the South), all persons sounded alike
except the first singular. But the development was not to
stop there. In Old English a difference is made in the
plural, according as the verb precedes *we* or *ge* ('ye')
or not (*binde we, binde ge*, but *we bindaþ, ge bindaþ*).
This is the germ of the more radical difference now
carried through consistently in the Scotch dialect, where
the *s* is only added when the verb is not accompanied by
its proper pronoun—but in that case it is used in all
persons. Murray gives the following sentences among
others:[15]

aa *cum* fyrst—yt's mey at *cums* fyrst.

wey *gang* theare—huz tweae quheyles *gangs* theare,

---

[15] *Dial. of the Southern Counties of Scotland*, 1873, p. 212,
where quotations from the earlier literature are also given.

they *cum* an' *teake* them—the burds *cums* an' *pæcks*
them. (I come first; it is I that come first; we go there;
we two sometimes go there; they come and take them;
the birds come and pick them.)

In the other parts of the country the development
was different. In the Midland dialect the *-en* of the subjunctive and of the preterit was transferred to the present
of the indicative, so that we have the following forms
in the standard language:

14*th century*	16*th century*
I falle	I fall
he falleth	he fall(e)th
we fallen (falle)	we fall

This is the only dialect in which the third person
singular is kept clearly distinct from the other persons.

In the South of England, finally, the *th* was preserved in the plural, and was even extended to the first
person singular. Old people in the hilly parts of Somer-
setshire and Devonshire still say not only [i wɔ·kþ] 'he
walks,' but also [ðei zeþ, ai zeþ] 'they say, I say.' In
most cases, however, *do* is used, which is made [də]
without any *th* through the whole singular as well as
plural.[16]

212. But the northern *s*'s wandered southward.
Three solitary examples are found in Chaucer for the
sake of the rime.[17] A century later Caxton used the
th-ending (eth, ith, yth) exclusively, and this remained
the usual form in writing till the 16th century, when *s*

[16] Elworthy, *Grammar of the Dialect of West Somerset*, p.
191 ff.

[17] *Telles : elles* Duch. 73, Fame 426; *falles : halles* Duch.
257. In the Reves Tale the *s*-forms are used to characterize the
North of England dialect of the two students (*gas* for Chaucer's
ordinary *gooth*, etc.).

began to be used in poetry. In Marlowe *s* is by far
the commoner ending, except after hissing consonants
(passeth, opposeth, pitcheth, presageth, etc., *Tamburlaine* 68, 845, 1415, 1622). Spenser prefers *s* in poetry.
In the first four cantos of the *Faerie Queene* I have
counted 94 *s*'s as against 24 *th*'s (besides 8 *has,* 18 *hath,*
15 *does,* and 31 *doth*). But in his prose *th* predominates
even much more than *s* does in his poetry. In the introductory letter to Sir W. Raleigh there is only one *s*
(it needs), but many *th*'s; and in his book on 'the Present
State of Ireland' all the third persons singular end in *th,*
except a small number of phrases (*me seems,* several
times, but *it seemeth; what boots it; how comes it,* and
perhaps a few more) that seem to be characteristic of
a more colloquial tone than the rest of the book. Shakespeare's practice is not easy to ascertain. In a great many
passages the folio of 1623 has *th* where the earlier
quartos have *s*. In the prose parts of his dramas *s* prevails,[18] and the rule may be laid down that *th* belongs
more to the solemn or dignified speeches than to everyday talk, although this is by no means carried through
everywhere. In Macbeth I, 7, 29 ff., Lady Macbeth is
more matter-of-fact than her husband (Lady: He *has*
almost supt . . . Macbeth: *Hath* he ask'd for me?
Lady: Know you not he *ha's*. Macbeth: . . . He *hath*
honour'd me of late . . .), but when his more solemn
mood seizes her, she too puts on the buskin (Was the
hope drunke, Wherein you drest your selfe? *Hath* it
slept since?). Where Mercutio mocks Romeo's love-sickness (II, 1, 15), he has the line: He *heareth* not, he

---

[18] Franz, *Shakespeare-Grammatik,* 3rd ed., p. 151: In Much
Ado (Q 1600) *th* is not found at all in the prose parts and only
twice in the poetical parts; the Merry Wives, which is chiefly in
prose, has only one *th*.

stirreth not, he *moveth* not, but in his famous description of Queen Mab (I, 4, 53 ff.) he has 18 verbs in *s* and only two in *th, hath* and *driveth,* of which the latter is used for the sake of the metre.

213. Contemporary prose, at any rate in its higher forms, has generally *th;* the *s*-ending is not at all found in the Authorized Version of 1611, nor in Bacon's *Atlantis* (though in his Essays there are some *s*'s). The conclusion with regard to Elizabethan usage as a whole seems to be that the form in *s* was a colloquialism and as such was allowed in poetry and especially in the drama. This *s* must, however, be considered a licence wherever it occurs in the higher literature of that period. But in the first half of the seventeenth century *s* must have been the ending universally used in ordinary conversation, and we have evidence that it was even usual to read *s* where the book had *th,* for Richard Hodges (1643) gives in his list of words pronounced alike though spelt differently among others *boughs boweth bowze; clause claweth claws; courses courseth corpses; choose cheweth,*[19] and in 1649 he says 'howsoever wee write them thus, leadeth it, maketh it, noteth it, we say lead's it, make's it, note's it.' The only exception seems to have been *hath* and *doth,* where the frequency of occurrence protected the old forms from being modified analogically,[20] so that they were prevalent till about the middle of the eighteenth century. Milton, with the exceptions just mentioned, always writes *s* in his prose as well as in his poetry, and so does Pope. No difference was then felt to be necessary between even the most elevated poetry and ordinary conversation in that respect. But it is well worth noting that Swift, in the Introduction to his

[19] See Ellis, *Early English Pronunciation,* IV, 1018.
[20] This applies, partially at least, to *saith* as well.

Polite Conversation, where he affects a quasi-scientific tone, writes *hath* and *doth,* while in the conversations themselves *has* and *does* are the forms constantly used.[21]

214. At church, however, people went on hearing the *th*-forms, although even there the *s*'s began to creep in.[22] And it must certainly be ascribed to influence from biblical language that the *th*-forms again began to be used by poets towards the end of the eighteenth century; at first apparently this was done rather sparingly, but nineteenth century poets employ *th* to a greater extent. This revival of the old form affords the advantage from the poet's point of view of adding at discretion a syllable, as in Wordsworth's

In gratitude to God, Who *feeds* our hearts
For His own service; *knoweth, loveth* us (Prelude 13, 276)

or in Byron's

Whate'er she *loveth,* so she *loves* thee not,
What can it profit thee? (Heaven and Earth, I, sc. 2.)

Sometimes the *th*-form comes more handy for the rime (as when *saith* rimes with *death*), and sometimes the following sound may have induced a poet to prefer one or the other ending, as in

[21] In the *Journal to Stella,* all verbs have *s,* except *hath,* which is, however, less frequent than *has.* Further details on *th* and *s* in E. Holmqvist, *History of the Engl. Pres. Inflections* (Heidelberg, 1922) and H. C. Wyld, *A History of Mod. Colloquial English* (2nd ed., London, 1936), p. 332 ff. Wyld may be right in thinking that the extremely common auxiliary *is* contributed to the popularity of the *s*-ending.

[22] See the Spectator, No. 147 (Morley's ed., p. 217), 'a set of readers [of prayers at church] who affect, forsooth, a certain gentleman-like familiarity of tone, and mend the language as they go on, crying instead of pardoneth and absolveth, pardons and absolves.'

. . . Coleridge *hath the* sway,
And Wordsworth *has supporters,* two or three,[23]

but in a great many cases individual fancy only decides
which form is chosen. In prose, too, the *th*-form begins
to make its reappearance in the nineteenth century, not
only in biblical quotations, etc., but often with the sole
view of imparting a more solemn tone to the style, as in
Thackeray's 'Not always *doth* the writer know whither
the divine Muse *leadeth* him.'

215. The nineteenth century has even gone so far
as to create a double-form in one verb, making a distinction between *doth* [pronounced dʌþ] as an auxiliary
verb and *doeth* [pronounced du·iþ] as an independent
one. The early printers used the two forms indiscriminately, or rather preferred *doth* where *doeth* would make
the line appear too closely packed, and *doeth* where
there was room enough. Thus in the Authorized Version
of 1611 we find 'a henne *doeth* gather her brood under
her wings' (Luke XIII, 34), and 'he that *doth* the will
of my father' (Matth. VII, 21), where recent use would
have reversed the order of the forms, but in 'whosoever
heareth these sayings of mine, and *doeth* them' (Matth.
VII, 24), the old printer happens to be in accordance
with the rule of our own days. When the *th*-form was
really living, *doeth* was certainly always pronounced in
one syllable (thus in Shakespeare). I give a few examples of the modern differentiation.[24] J. R. Lowell
writes (*My Love, Poems,* 1849, I, 129 = Poetical
Works in one volume, p. 6) 'She *doeth* little kindnesses
. . . Her life *doth* rightly harmonize . . . And yet *doth*

[23] *Don Juan* XI., 69.

[24] Which has not been noticed in N.E.D., though it mentions
the corresponding differences between *dost* and *doest* as 'in late
use.'

ever flow aright.' Rider Haggard has both forms in the
same sentence (*She*, 199), 'Man *doeth* this and *doeth*
that, but he knows not to what ends his sense *doth*
prompt him'; cf. also Tennyson's *The Captain:* 'He that
only rules by terror, *Doeth* grievous wrong.'

216. To sum up. If the *s* of the third person singular comes from the North, this is true of the outer form
only; the 'inner form,' to use the expression of some
philologists, is the Midland one, that is to say, *s* is used
in those cases only where the Midland dialects had *th*,
and is not extended according to the northern rules. In
vulgar English, *s* is used in the first person singular: *I
wishes; says I*, etc., as in *Rehearsal* (1671): 'I makes
'em both speak fresh' (Arber's reprint, p. 53). But it
will be seen that this is in direct opposition to the northern usage where the *s* is never found by the side of the
personal pronoun.

217. (VII). A notable feature of the history of the
English language is the building up of a rich system of
tenses[25] on the basis of the few possessed by Old English, where the present was also a sort of vague future,
and where the simple preterit was often employed as a
kind of pluperfect, especially when supported by *ær*,
'ere, before.' The use of *have* and *had* as an auxiliary
for the perfect and pluperfect began in the Old English
period, but it was then chiefly found with transitive
verbs, and the real perfect-signification had scarcely
yet been completely evolved from the original meaning
of the connexion: *ic hæbbe þone fisc gefangenne* meant
at first 'I *have* the fish (as) caught' (note the accusative

---

[25] See my *Modern Engl. Gr.*, vol. IV., especially chs. 12–14
(Expanded tenses) and 15–21 (will, shall, would, should),
Philosophy of Grammar, chs. 19 and 20, *Essentials of Engl.
Gr.*, chs. 23–25.

ending in the participle). By and by a distinction was
made between 'I had mended the table' and 'I had the
table mended,' 'he had left nothing' and 'he had nothing
left.' In Middle English *have* came to be used extensively
in the perfect of intransitive verbs as well as transitive;
I have been does not seem to occur earlier than 1200.
With such verbs as *go* and *come, I am* was usual in the
perfect for several centuries, where now *I have gone* and
I have come (*returned*, etc.) are the ordinary expressions. The verbs *will* and *shall* have in many contexts
come to be auxiliaries serving to express pure futurity,
the original meaning of volition and obligation being
more or less effaced; but owing partly to the fact that to
express the three distinct ideas of obligation, volition,
and simple futurity we have only those two verbs as
against German *sollen, wollen* and *werden,* the actual
rules for the employment of the two verbs are somewhat complicated, and where strict grammarians require
shall (I shall, shall you; he thinks that he shall die,
he = shifted first person), the verb *will* (and the shortened form 'll) is now more and more used, even in the
South of England. In Scotland, Ireland and North
America, *will* has long been almost exclusively used as
auxiliary. The present rules may be stated roughly thus:
To indicate pure, colourless future *will* is used everywhere, except in those cases in which it might be misunderstood as implying actual will. Often the unambiguous *is going to* is used, and in many cases the simple
present suffices: *I start to-morrow if it is fine.* To express
obligation or necessity we have the unambiguous expressions *must, has to,* and to express volition *want,
intend, mean, choose* are often preferred where *will* was
formerly used. The expanded tenses *I am reading, I was
reading, I have been reading, I shall be reading,* were

not fully developed even in Shakespeare's time; the distinction between the simple and the expanded tenses is now a wonderful means of expressing temporal and emotional nuances.[26] The passive construction (*the house is being built*) is an innovation dating from the very end of the eighteenth century.[27] Before that time the phrase was *the house is building,* i.e., *a-building* 'is in construction,' and the new phrase had to fight its way against much violent opposition in the nineteenth century before it was universally recognized as good English. Macaulay used it inadvertently a few times in letters in his youth, but avoided it in his books. A still more recent innovation is the use of *is being* before an adjective: After all, he was being sensible (Wells), i.e. was at that particular moment sensible. While the number of tenses has increased, the number of moods has tended to diminish, the subjunctive having now very little vital power left. Most of its forms have become indistinguishable from those of the indicative, but the loss is not a serious one, for the thought is just as clearly expressed in 'if he died,' where *died* may be either indicative or subjunctive, as in 'if he were dead,' where the verb has a distinctively subjunctive form.

218. It will be seen that the development of new tenses sketched in the preceding section greatly increased the number of sentences formed after the same pattern that we had already in the case of some small verbs, chief of which were *can, may, must.* First we have a small, in itself insignificant verb and afterwards the really important verb either in the infinitive (*can see,*

[26] The latest and best treatment of the expanded forms is F. Mossé, *Histoire de la Forme Périphrastique être + participe présent* II (Paris, 1938).

[27] The alleged earlier examples are shown by Mossé, p. 149, to be wrong.

will see, could see, etc.) or in some participle (*is seeing,
has seen, was seeing, had seen*). The number of sentences belonging to this type was enormously increased
by the gradual development of the periphrastic *do.*[28]
This verb was in OE. and early ME. used as a pro-verb
to avoid the repetition of a verb just used, and as a
causative, e.g. 'to do me live or deye' (Chaucer). In
the latter sense it disappeared and was replaced by
make. In ME. it came to be used more and more as an
auxiliary and may as such be placed by the side of the
other lesser verbs, as in 'Though this good man can not
see it: other men can see it, and haue sene it, and daily
do see it' (Sir T. More). At first it was used indiscriminately without any definite grammatical purpose. In
some poets such as Lydgate, in the beginning of the
fifteenth century, it served chiefly to fill up the line and
to make it possible to place the infinitive at the end as
a convenient rime-word. Sometimes it serves to make
the tense clear in those verbs that are alike in the present
and preterit: we do set, did set. Cf. also 'the holy
spyryte dyd and dothe remayne and shall remayne'
(J. Fisher, ab. 1535). The culmination was reached in
the sixteenth century, when it might almost seem as if
all full verbs were 'stripped of all those elements which
to most grammarians constitute the very essence of a
verb, namely, the marks of person, number, tense, and
mood' (*Progress in Lang.* 124), leaving them to lesser
verbs placed before them.

219. But then a reaction set in and gradually restricted the use of *do* to those cases that are well known
from grammars of Present English, and in which it serves

[28] The latest and fullest treatment is V. Engblom, *On the
Origin and Early Development of the Auxiliary do* (Lund,
1938), with bibliography and criticism of other writers.

a definite grammatical purpose. It is used (1) for the
sake of emphasis, especially in contrast: 'Shelley, when
he did laugh, laughed heartily'; thus in earnest requests:
'Do tell me,' even with *be:* 'Do be quiet!' (2) in negative
sentences with *not.* Here it ends a long development.
The earliest negative adverb is *ne,* placed before the
verb, OE. *ic ne secge.* But frequently this was strengthened by the addition of *noht* (from *nawiht, nowiht,*
meaning 'nothing') after the verb; *noht* became *not;* and
the typical ME. form thus was *I ne seye not.* Here *ne*
was pronounced with so little stress that it was apt to
be dropped altogether and the fifteenth century form
was *I say not.* This survived for some centuries in *I
know not* and a few other now obsolete combinations,
as well as with all the formerly mentioned lesser verbs.
By means of *do* that word-order is obtained which in
most languages is thought the most felicitous, *not* being
placed before the really significant verb: *I do not say,*
just as *I cannot say,* etc. In this position, however, *not*
tends to be weakened, and so we get the colloquial forms
I don't say, can't say, etc. (3) In such questions as are
not introduced by a pronominal subject, which naturally
has to stand first, the use of *do* as well as of the other
lesser verbs effects a compromise between the ordinary
interrogative word-order (verb before the subject) and
the universal tendency to have the subject before the
verb (that is, the verb that really means something):
Did he come? just as *Must he come?*

220. Now the curious thing is that a similar construction of sentences is often made possible by means
of the verbal substantives mentioned in § 171. These are
placed after verbs of small intrinsic meaning, to which
are attached the marks of person and tense, of negation
and question, in such familiar phrases as have a look

(peep) at, have a wash, a shave, a try, have a care, take care, take a drive, a walk, a rest; give a glance, look, kick, push, hint; make (pay) a call, make a plunge, make use of, he made his bow to the hostess, etc.

221. (VIII). There are some important innovations in the syntax of the *infinitive*. In such a sentence as 'it is good for a man not to touch a woman,' the noun with *for* was originally in the closest connexion with the adjective: 'What is good for a man?' 'Not to touch a woman.' But by a natural shifting this came to be apprehended as 'it is good | for a man not to touch a woman,' so that *for a man* was felt to be the subject of the infinitive, and this manner of indicating the subject gradually came to be employed where the original construction is excluded. Thus in the beginning of a sentence: 'For us to levy power Proportionate to th'enemy, is all impossible' (Shakespeare), and after *than:* 'I don't know, what is worse than for such wicked strumpets to lay their sins at honest men's doors' (Fielding); further, 'What I like best, is for a nobleman to marry a miller's daughter. And what I like next best, is for a poor fellow to run away with a rich girl' (Thackeray), 'it is of great use to healthy women for them to cycle.'[29] Another recent innovation is the use of *to* as what might be called a pro-infinitive instead of the clumsy *to do so:* 'Will you play?' 'Yes, I intend to.' 'I am going to.' This is one among several indications that the linguistic instinct now takes *to* to belong to the preceding verb rather than to the infinitive, a fact which, together with other circumstances, serves to explain the phenomenon usually mistermed 'the split infinitive.'

[29] See my article in *Festschrift Viëtor* (Marburg, 1910), p. 85 ff., and *Philos. of Grammar* 118, where a Slavic parallel is mentioned.

This name is bad because we have many infinitives without *to,* as 'I made him go.' *To* therefore is no more an essential part of an infinitive than the definite article is an essential part of a nominative, and no one would think of calling 'the good man' a split nominative. Although examples of an adverb between *to* and the infinitive occur as early as the fourteenth century, they do not become very frequent till the latter half of the nineteenth century. In some cases they decidedly contribute to the clearness of the sentence by showing at once what word is qualified by the adverb. Thackeray's and Seeley's sentences 'she only wanted a pipe in her mouth *considerably* to resemble the late Field Marshal' and 'the poverty of the nation did not allow them *successfully* to compete with the other nations' are not very happily built up, for the reader at the first glance is inclined to connect the adverb with what precedes. The sentences would have been clearer if the authors had ventured to place *to* before the adverb, as Burns does in 'Who dar'd to nobly stem tyrannic pride,' and Carlyle in 'new Emissaries are trained, with new tactics, to, if possible, entrap him, and hoodwink and handcuff him.'

222. This rapid sketch of a certain number of grammatical changes, though necessarily giving only a fraction of the material on which it is based, has yet, I hope, been sufficiently full to show that such changes are continually going on and that it would be a gross error to suppose that any deviation from the established rules of grammar is necessarily a corruption. Those teachers who know least of the age, origin and development of the rules they follow, are generally the most apt to think that whatsoever is more than these cometh of evil, while he who has patiently studied the

history of the past and trained himself to hear the
linguistic grass grow in the present age will generally
be more inclined to see in the processes of human
speech a wise natural selection, through which while
nearly all innovations of questionable value disappear
pretty soon, the fittest survive and make human speech
ever more varied and flexible, and yet ever more easy
and convenient to the speakers. There is no reason to
suppose that this development has come to a stop with
the twentieth century: let us hope that in the future the
more and more almighty schoolmaster may not nip too
many beneficial changes in the bud.

CHAPTER X

Shakespeare and the Language of Poetry

223. In this chapter I shall endeavour to characterize the language of the greatest master of English poetry and make some observations in regard to his influence on the English language as well as in regard to poetic and archaic language generally. But it must be distinctly understood that I shall concern myself with *language* and not with literary *style*. It is true that the two things cannot be completely kept apart, but as far as possible I shall deal only with what are really philological as opposed to literary problems.

224. Shakespeare's vocabulary is often stated to be the richest ever employed by any single man. It has been calculated to comprise 21,000 words ('rough calculation, found in Mrs. Clark's Concordance . . . without counting inflected forms as distinct words,' Craik), or, according to others, 24,000 or 15,000. In order to appreciate what that means we must look a little at the various statements that have been given of the number of words used by other authors and by ordinary beings, educated and not educated. Unfortunately these statements are in many cases given and repeated without any indication of the manner in which they have been arrived at.[1] Milton's vocabulary is said to comprise

---

[1] Max Müller, *Wissenschaft der Sprache*, I, 360, and *Lectures on the Science of Language*, 6th ed., I, 309. Wood, *Journal of*

7,000 or 8,000 words, that of the Iliad and Odyssey taken together 9,000, that of the Old Testament 5,642, and that of the New Testament 4,800; A. S. Cook (in *The Nation,* Sept. 12, 1912) computes the vocabulary of the English Authorized Version at 6,568 words, or at 9,884, if inflected forms of nouns, pronouns, or verbs are included.

225. Max Müller says that a farm-labourer uses only 300 words, and Wood that 'the average man uses about five hundred words' (adding 'it is appalling to think how pitiably we have degenerated from the copiousness of our ancestors'), and the same statements are found in writings by Abel, Sütterlin and other philologists. But both figures are obviously wrong. One two-year-old girl had 489 and another 1,121 words (see Wundt), while Mrs. Winfield S. Hall's boy used in his seventeenth month 232 different words and, when six years old, 2,688 words, at least, for it is probable that the mother and her assistants who noted down every word they heard the child use, even so did not get hold of its whole vocabulary. Now, are we really to believe that the linguistic range of a grown-up man, however humble, is considerably smaller than that of a two-year-old child of educated parents or is only one-seventh of that of a six-year-old boy! Any one going through the

Germanic Philology, I, 294. Smedberg, *Svenska landsmålen,* XI, 9 (57), 1896. Marius Kristensen, *Aarbog for dansk kulturhistorie,* 1897. E. H. Babbitt, *Common Sense in Teaching Modern Languages* (New York, 1895), 11, and *Popular Science Monthly,* April 1907 (cf. E. A. Kirkpatrick, ibid., Febr. 1907). Sweet, *History of Language,* 1900, 139. Weise, *Unsere Muttersprache,* 1897, 205. Mrs. Winfield S. Hall, *Child Study,* Monthly, March 1897, and *Journal of Childhood and Adolescence,* January 1902. G. H. McKnight, *Modern English in the Making,* 1928, p. 186. W. Wartburg, *Evolution et Structure de la Langue Française,* 1934, p. 238. M. Nice in *American Speech,* 2, 1.

lists given by Mrs. Hall will feel quite certain that no
labourer contents himself with so scanty a vocabulary.
School-books for teaching foreign languages often include some 700 words in the first year's course; yet
on how few subjects of everyday occurrence are our
pupils able to converse after one year's teaching. Sweet
also contradicts the statement about 300 words, saying
'When we find a missionary in Tierra del Fuego com-
piling a dictionary of 30,000 words in the Yaagan
language—that is, a hundred times as many—we cannot give any credence to this statement, especially if
we consider the number of names of different parts of
a waggon or a plough, and all the words required in
connexion even with a single agricultural operation, together with names of birds, plants, and other natural
objects.' Smedberg, who has investigated the vocabulary
of Swedish peasants and who emphasizes its richness
in technical terms, arrives at the result that 26,000 is
probably too small a figure, and the Danish and French
dialectologists Kristensen and Duraffour completely
endorse this view. Professor E. S. Holden tested himself
by a reference to all the words in Webster's Dictionary,
and found that his own vocabulary comprised 33,456
words. And E. H. Babbitt writes: 'I tried to get at the
vocabulary of adults and made experiments, chiefly with
my students, to see how many English words each knew.
. . . My plan was to take a considerable number of
pages from the dictionary at random, count the number
of words on those pages which the subject of the experiment could define without any context, and work
out a proportion to get an approximation of the entire
number of words in the dictionary known. The results
were surprising for two reasons. In the size of the
vocabulary of such students the outside variations were

less than 20 per cent, and their vocabulary was much larger than I had expected to find. The majority reported a little below 60,000 words.' People who had never been to college, but, with an ordinary common school education, were regular readers of books and periodicals, according to the same writer reported generally from 25,000 to 35,000 words, though some went higher, even to 50,000.

226. These statements are easily reconciled with the ascription of 20,000 words to Shakespeare. For it must be remembered that in the case of each of us there is a great difference between the words *known* (especially those of which he has a reading knowledge) and the words actually *used* in conversation. And then, there must always be a great many words which a man will use readily in conversation, but which will never occur in his writings, simply because the subjects on which a man addresses the public are generally much less varied than those he has to talk about every day.[2] How many authors have occasion to use in their books even the most familiar names of garden tools or common dishes or kitchen implements? If Milton as a poet uses only 8,000 against Shakespeare's 20,000 words, this is a natural consequence of the narrower range of his subjects, and it is easy to prove that his vocabulary really contained many more than the 8,000 words found in a Concordance to his poetical works. We have only to take any page of his prose writings, and we shall meet with a great many words not in the Concordance.[3]

[2] Inversely, many authors will use some (learned or abstract) words in writing which they do not use in conversation; their number, however, is rarely great.

[3] Thus, on p. 30 of *Areopagitica,* I find the following 21 words, which are not in Bradshaw's Concordance: Churchman, competency, utterly, mercenary, pretender, ingenuous, evidently,

227. The greatness of Shakespeare's mind is therefore not shown by the fact that he was acquainted with 20,000 words, but by the fact that he wrote about so great a variety of subjects and touched upon so many human facts and relations that he needed this number of words in his writings.[4] His remarkable familiarity with technical expressions in many different spheres has often been noticed, but there are other facts with regard to his use of words that have not been remarked or not sufficiently remarked. His reticence about religious matters, which has given rise to the most divergent theories of his religious belief, is shown strikingly in the fact that such words as *Bible, Holy Ghost* and *Trinity* do not occur at all in his writings, while *Jesus* (Jesu), *Christ* and *Christmas* are found only in some of his earliest plays; *Saviour* occurs only once (in Hamlet), and *Creator* only in two of the dubious plays (H 6 C and Troilus).[5]

228. Of far greater importance is his use of language to individualize the characters in his plays. In this he shows a much finer and subtler art than some modern novelists, who make the same person continually use

---

tutor, examiner, scism, ferular, fescu, imprimatur, grammar, pedagogue, cursory, temporize, extemporize, licencer, commonwealth, foreiner. And p. 50 adds 18 more words to the list: writing, commons, valorous, rarify, enfranchise, founder, formall, slavish, oppressive, reinforce, abrogate, mercilesse, noble (n.), Danegelt, immunity, newnes, unsutableness, customary.

[4] I have amused myself with making up the following sentences of words not used by Shakespeare though found in the language of that time: In Shakespeare we find no *blunders*, although *decency* and *delicacy* had *disappeared; energy* and *enthusiasm* are not in *existence*, and we see no *elegant expressions* nor any *gleams* of *genius* etc.

[5] The act against profane language on the stage (see below, § 254) is not sufficient to explain this reticence.

the same stock phrase or phrases. Even where he resorts
to the same tricks as other authors he varies them more;
Mrs. Quickly and Dogberry do not misapply words from
the classical languages in the same way. The everyday
speech of the artisans in *A Midsummer Night's Dream*
is comic in a different manner from the diction they
use in their play within the play, which serves Shakespeare to ridicule some linguistic artifices employed in
good faith by many of his contemporaries (alliteration,
bombast). Shakespeare is not entirely exempt from the
fashionable affectation of his days known as Euphuism,[6]
but it must be noticed that he is superior to its worst
aberrations and he satirizes them, not only in *Love's
Labour's Lost*, but also in many other places. Euphuistic
expressions are generally put in the mouth of some
subordinate character who has nothing to do except to
announce some trifling incident, relate a little of the
circumstances that lead up to the action of the play,
deliver a message from a king, etc. It is not improbable
that the company possessed some actor who knew how
to make small parts funny by imitating fashionable
affectation, and we can imagine that it was he who
acted Osric in *Hamlet,* and by his vocabulary and appearance exposed himself to the scoffs of the Danish
prince, and the nameless gentleman in *Lear,* III, sc. 1,
and IV, sc. 3.[7] But the messenger from Antony in
Julius Cæsar (III, 1, 122) speaks in a totally different
strain and gives us a sort of foretaste of Antony's elo-

[6] The various kinds of affected court style have been carefully
distinguished by M. Basse. *Stijlaffectatie bij Shakespeare,* vooral
uit het oogpunt van het Euphuisme (Université de Gand, 1895).
Cf. also L. Morsbach, *Shakespeare und der Euphuismus,*
Gesellsch. d. Wiss (Göttingen, 1908), S. 600 ff.

[7] See my interpretation of the well-known crux in that scene,
1, 19 ff., in *Linguistica,* 1933, p. 430.

quence. And how different again—I am speaking here
of subordinate parts only—are the gardeners in *Richard
the Second* (III, sc. 4) with their characteristic application of botanical similes to politics and vice versa. And
thus one might go on, for no author has shown greater
skill in adapting language to character.

229. A modern reader, however, is sure to miss
many of the *nuances* that were felt instinctively by the
poet's contemporaries. A great many words have now
another value than they had then; in some cases it is
only a slightly different colouring, but in others the
diversity is greater, and only a close study of Elizabethan usage can bring out the exact value of each
word. A *bonnet* then meant a man's cap or hat; Lear
walks unbonneted. To *charm* always implied magic
power, to make invulnerable by witchcraft, to call forth
by spells, etc.; 'charming words' were magic words and
not simply delightful words as in our days. *Notorious*
might be used in a good sense as 'well-known'; *censure,*
too, was a colourless word ('And your name is great
In mouthes of wisest censure' Oth. II, 3, 193). The
same is true of *succeed* and *success,* which now imply
what Shakespeare several times calls 'good success,'
whereas he also knows 'bad success'; cf. 'the effects he
writes of succeede unhappily,' Lear I, 2, 157. *Companion* was often used in a bad sense, like *fellow* now,
and inversely *sheer,* which is now used with such words
as 'folly, nonsense,' had kept the original meaning of
'pure,' as in 'thou sheere, immaculate, and silver foun-
taine' (R 2, V, 3, 61). *Politician* seems always to imply
intriguing or scheming, and *remorse* generally means
pity or sympathy. *Accommodate* evidently did not belong to ordinary language, but was considered affected;
occupy and *activity* were at least half-vulgar, while on

the other hand *wag* (vb.) was then free from its present
trivial or ludicrous associations ('Untill my eielids will
no longer wag,' Hamlet V, 1, 290, see Dowden's note
to this passage). *Assassination* (only Macbeth I, 7, 2)
would then call up the memory of the 'Assasines, a company of most desperat and dangerous men among the
Mahometans' (Knolles, *Hist. Turks,* 1603) or 'That
bloudy sect of Sarazens, called Assassini, who, without
feare of torments, undertake . . . the murther of any
eminent Prince, impugning their irreligion' (Speed,
1611, quoted NED.).

230. Even adverbs might then have another colouring than their present signification. *Now-a-days* was
a vulgar word; it is used by no one in Shakespeare
except Bottom, the grave-digger in *Hamlet,* and a
fisherman in *Pericles.* The adverb *eke,* in the nineteenth
century a poetic word, seems to have been a comic
expression; it occurs only three times in Shakespeare
(twice in the *Merry Wives,* used by Pistol and the Host,
once by Flute in *Midsummer Night's Dream*); Milton
and Pope avoid the word. The synonym *also* is worth
noticing. Shakespeare uses it only 22 times, and nearly
always puts it in the mouth of vulgar or affected persons
(Dogberry twice in *Ado,* the Clown once in *Wint.,* the
Second Lord in *As* II, sc. 2, the Second Lord in *Tim.*
III, sc. 6, the affected Captain in *Tw.* I, sc. 2; the knight
in *Lear* I, 4, 66, may belong here too; further Pistol
twice in grandiloquent speeches, H 4 B II, 4, 171 and
V, 3, 145, and two of Shakespeare's Welshmen, Evans
three times, and Fluellen twice). It is used twice in
solemn and official speeches (H 5 I, 2, 77, where Canterbury expounds lex Salica, and IV, 6, 10), and it is,
therefore, highly characteristic that Falstaff uses the
word twice in his euphuistic impersonation of the king

(H 4 A II, 4, 440 and 459) and twice in similar speeches in the *Merry Wives* (V, 1, 24, and V, 5, 7).[8]

231. Shylock is one of Shakespeare's most interesting creations, even from the point of view of language. Although Sir Sidney Lee has shown that there were Jews in England in those times and that, consequently, Shakespeare need not have gone outside his own country in order to see models for Shylock, the number of Jews cannot have been sufficient for his hearers to be very familiar with the Jewish type, and no Anglo-Jewish dialect or mode of speech had developed which Shakespeare could put into Shylock's mouth and so make him at once recognizable for what he was. I have not, indeed, been able to discover a single trait in Shylock's language that can be called distinctly Jewish. And yet Shakespeare has succeeded in creating for Shylock a language different from that of anybody else. Shylock has his Old

[8] The only passages not accounted for above are Gent. III, 2, 25, where the metre is wrong, Hamlet V, 2, 402, where the folios have *always* instead of *also,* and Cæs. II, 1, 329.—Shakespeare's sparing use of *also* would in itself suffice to disprove the Baconian theory if any proof were needed beyond the evidence of history and of psychology. For in Bacon, *also*'s abound, and I have counted on four successive small pages of Moore Smith's edition of the *New Atlantis* 22 instances, exactly as many as are found in the whole of Shakespeare. *Might* and *mought* seem to be nearly equally frequent in Bacon, but *mought* is found only once in Shakespeare, in the third part of *Henry VI,* a play which many competent judges are inclined not to ascribe to Shakespeare at all. At any rate, this one instance in one of his earliest works weighs nothing as against the thousands of times *might* is found. Shakespeare uses *among* and *amongst* indiscriminately, Bacon nearly always uses *amongst.* Bacon frequently employs the conjunction *whereas,* which is not found at all in the undoubtedly genuine Shakespearian plays, etc.—Since this was first written, the subject has been investigated by N. Bøgholm (*Bacon og Shakespeare,* Copenhagen, 1906), who has succeeded in pointing out an astonishing number of discrepancies between the two authors.

Testament at his fingers' ends, he defends his own way
of making money breed by a reference to Jacob's thrift
in breeding parti-coloured lambs, he swears by Jacob's
staff and by our holy sabbath, and he calls Lancelot
'that foole of Hagars off-spring.'[9] We have an interesting bit of Jewish figurative language in 'my houses eares,
I meane my casements' (II, 5, 34). Shylock uses some
biblical words which do not occur elsewhere in Shakespeare: *synagogue, Nazarite* and *publican; pilled* in
'The skilful shepheard pil'd me certain wands' is a
reminiscence from Genesis XXX, 37. But more often
Shylock is characterized by being made to use words
or constructions a little different from the accepted use
of Shakespeare's time.[10] He dislikes the word *interest*
and prefers calling it *advantage* or *thrift* ('my well-
worne thrift, which he cals interrest,' I, 3, 52), and
instead of *usury* he says *usance*. Furness quotes *Wylson
On Usurye,* 1572, p. 32, 'usurie and double usurie, the
merchants termyng it *usance* and double usance, by a
more clenlie name'—this word thus ranks in the same
category as *dashed* or *d–d* for *damned:* instead of pronouncing an objectionable word in full one begins as
if one were about to pronounce it and then shunts off
on another track (see other examples below, § 244).
Shylock uses the plural *moneys,* which is very rare in
Shakespeare, he says an *equal* pound for 'exact,' *rheum*
(rume) for 'saliva,' *estimable* for 'valuable,' *fulsome* for
'rank' (the only instance of that signification discovered
by the editors of the NED.); he alone uses the words
eaneling and *misbeliever* and the rare verb to *bane.* His

[9] Contrast with this trait the fondness for classical allusions
found in Marlowe's *Barrabas.*

[10] He says *Abram,* but *Abraham* is the only form found in the
rest of Shakespeare's works.

syntax is peculiar: we *trifle* time; *rend out,* where Shakespeare has elsewhere only *rend;* I have no mind *of feasting* forth to-night (always *mind to*); *and so following,* where *and so forth* is the regular Shakespearian phrase. I have counted some forty such deviations from Shakespeare's ordinary language and cannot dismiss the thought that Shakespeare made Shylock's language peculiar on purpose, just as he makes Caliban, and the witches in *Macbeth,* use certain words and expressions used by none other of his characters in order to stamp them as beings out of the common sort.

232. Shakespeare's vocabulary was not the same in all periods of his life. I have counted between two and three hundred words which he used in his youth, but not later, while the number of words peculiar to his last period is much smaller. Sarrazin[11] mentions as characteristic of his first period a predilection for picturesque adjectives that appeal immediately to the outward senses (*bright, brittle, fragrant, pitchy, snow-white*), while his later plays are said to contain more adjectives of psychological importance. But even apart from the fact that some of the adjectives instanced are really found in later plays (*bright* in *Cæs., Ant., Oth., Cymb., Wint. T.,* etc.), this statement would account for only a small part of the divergencies. Probably no single explanation can account for them all, not even that of the natural buoyancy of youth and the comparative austerity of a later age. It is noteworthy that in some instances he ridicules in later plays words used quite seriously in earlier ones. Thus *beautify,* which is found in *Lucrece, Henry VI B, Titus Andr., Two Gentlemen,* and *Romeo,* is severely criticized by Polonius when he hears it in Hamlet's letter: 'That's an ill

[11] *Shakespeare-Jahrbuch,* XXXIII, 122.

phrase, a vilde [i.e. vile] phrase, beautified is a vilde phrase.' Similarly *cranny,* which Shakespeare used in *Lucrece* (twice) and in the *Comedy of Errors,* is not found in any play written later than *Midsummer Night's Dream,* where Shakespeare takes leave of the word by turning it to ridicule in the mouth of Bottom and in the artisans' comedy. The fate of *foeman, aggravate* and *homicide* is nearly the same. Perhaps some of the words avoided in later life were provincialisms (thus possibly *pebblestone, shore,* in the sense of 'bank of a river,' *wood* 'mad,' *forefather* 'ancestor,' the pronunciation of *marriage* and of *Henry* in three syllables). In the first period Shakespeare used *perverse* with the unusual signification 'cold, unfriendly, averse to love,' later he avoids the word altogether. In such instances he may have been criticized by his contemporaries (we know from the *Poetaster* how severe Ben Jonson was in these matters), and that may have made him avoid the objectionable words altogether.

233. One of the most characteristic features of Shakespeare's use of the English language is his boldness. His boldness of metaphor has often been pointed out in books of literary criticism, and the boldness of his sentence structure, especially in his last period, is so obvious that no instances need be adduced here. He does not always care for grammatical parallelism, witness such a sentence as 'A thought which, quarter'd, hath but one part *wisedom* And ever three parts *coward*' (Hamlet IV, 4, 42). He does not always place the words where they would seem properly to belong, as in 'we send, To know what *willing* ransome he will give' for 'what ransom he will willingly give' (Henry V III, 5, 63), 'dismiss me Thus with his *speechlesse* hand' (Cor. V, 1, 68), 'the *whole* eare of Denmarke Is by a forged processe of my death Rankly abus'd' (the ear of all Denmark, Hamlet I, 5, 36), 'lovers *absent* howres' (the hours when lovers are absent, Othello III, 4, 174), etc. He is not afraid of writing 'wanted lesse impudence' for 'had less impudence' or 'wanted impudence more' (Wint. III, 2, 57) and 'a beggar without lesse quality' (Cymb. I, 4, 23), nor of mixing his negatives as he does in many other passages.[12] Alex. Schmidt, who collects many instances of such negligence, rightly remarks: 'Had he taken the pains of revising and preparing his plays for the press, he would perhaps have corrected all the quoted passages. But he did not write them to be read and dwelt on by the eye, but to be heard by a sympathetic audience. And much that would blemish the language of a logician, may well become a dramatic poet or an orator.'[13] There is an excellent paper by C. Alphonso Smith in the *Englische Studien,* vol. XXX, on 'The Chief Difference between the First and Second Folios of Shakespeare,' in which he shows that 'the supreme syntactic value of Shakespeare's work as represented in the First Folio is that it shows us the English language unfettered by bookish impositions. Shakespeare's syntax was that of the speaker, not that of the essayist; for the drama represents the unstudied utterance of people under all kinds and degrees of emotion, ennui, pain, and passion. Its syntax, to be truly representative, must be familiar, conversational, spontaneous; not studied and formal.' But the Second Folio is of unique service and significance in its attempts to render more 'correct' and bookish the unfettered syntax of the First. The First Folio is to the Second as spoken lan-

---

[12] Besides using such double negatives as were regular in all the older periods of the language (*nor, never,* etc.).

[13] *Shakespeare-Lexicon,* p. 1420.

guage is to written language. The 'bad grammar' of the
First Folio (1623) may not *always* be due to Shakespeare himself, but at any rate we have in that edition
more of his own language than in the 'correctness' of
the Second Folio (1632).

234. Shakespeare's boldness with regard to language is less conspicuous, though no less real, in the
instances I shall now mention. In turning over the pages
of the New English Dictionary, where every pain has
been taken to ascertain the earliest occurrence of each
word and of each signification, one is struck by the
frequency with which Shakespeare's name is found af-
fixed to the earliest quotation for words or meanings.
In many cases this is no doubt due to the fact that
Shakespeare's vocabulary has been registered with
greater care in Concordances and in Al. Schmidt's
invaluable *Shakespeare-Lexicon* than that of any other
author, so that his words cannot escape notice, while
the same words may occur unnoticed in the pages of
many an earlier author. But anyhow Shakespeare uses
a great many words which were new in his times,
whether absolutely new or new only to the written language, while living colloquially on the lips of the people.
My list[14] includes the following words: *aslant* as a
preposition, *assassination* (see above), *barefaced,* the
plural *brothers* (found also in Layamon's *Brut,* but
seemingly not between that and Shakespeare's youth:
Gosson, Lyly, Sidney, Marlowe), *call* 'to pay a short
visit,' *courtship, dwindle, enthrone* (also in Lyly, earlier
enthronize), *eventful, excellent* in the current sense
'extremely good,' *fount* 'spring' (also in Kyd, Drayton),

---

[14] See now also G. Gordon, *Shakespeare's English* (Soc. for
Pure Engl. XXIV, 1928) and G. H. McKnight, *Modern English
in the Making* (New York, 1928), ch. X.

fretful, get intransitive with an adjective, 'become' (only in 'get clear'), *I have got* for 'I have,' *gust, hint, hurry* (also in Kyd), *indistinguishable, laughable, leap-frog, loggerhead* and *loggerheaded, lonely* (but Sidney has *loneliness* some years before Shakespeare began to write), *lower* verb, *perusal, primy*. Further the following verbs (formed from nouns that are found before Shakespeare's time): *bound, hand, jade,* and nouns (formed from already existing verbs): *control, dawn, dress, hatch, import, indent*. Among other words which were certainly or probably new when Shakespeare used them, may be mentioned *acceptance, gull* 'dupe,' *rely,* and *summit*. I shall give below (§ 238) a list of words and expressions the existence of which in the English language is due to Shakespeare. The words here given would probably have found their way into the language even had Shakespeare never written a line, though he may have accelerated the date of their acceptance. But at any rate they show that he was exempt from that narrowness which often makes authors shy of using new or colloquial words in the higher literary style. Let me add another remark apropos of a list of hard words needing an explanation which is found in Cockeram's *Dictionarie* (1623). Dr. Murray writes:[15] 'We are surprised to find among these hard words *abandon, obhorre, abrupt, absurd, action, activitie* and *actresse,* explained as "a woman doer," for the stage actress had not yet appeared.' Now, with the exception of the last one, all these words are found in Shakespeare's plays.

235. Closely connected with this trait in Shakespeare's language is the proximity of his poetical diction to his ordinary prose. He uses very few 'poetical' words

[15] *The Evolution of English Lexicography*, Romanes Lecture (Oxford and London, 1900), p. 29.

or forms. He does not rely for his highest flights on the
use of words and grammatical forms not used elsewhere,
but knows how to achieve the finest effects of imagination without stepping outside his ordinary vocabulary
and grammar. It must be remembered that when he uses
thou and *thee*, *'tis*, *e'en*, *ne'er*, *howe'er*, *mine eyes*, etc.,
or when he construes negative and interrogative verbs
without *do*, all these things, which are now parts of the
conventional language of poetry, were everyday col-
loquialisms in the Elizabethan period. It is true that
there are certain words and forms which he never uses
except in poetry, but their number is extremely small.
I do not know of any besides *host* 'army,' *vale*, *sire*,
and *morn*. As for the synonym *morrow*, apart from
its use in the sense of 'next day' and in the salutation
good morrow, which was then colloquial, it occurs only
four times, and only in rime. There are some verb forms
which occur in rime only, but the number of occasions
on which Shakespeare was thus led to deviate from his
usual grammar is very small: *begun* (past tense) eight
times, *flee* once (the usual present is *fly*), *gat* once (in
the probably spurious *Pericles*), *sain* for *said* once,
sang once, *shore* participle once, *strown* once (the usual
form is *strewed*), *swore* participle once—fifteen instances in all, to which must be added eleven instances
of the plural *eyen*. Rhythmical reasons seem to make
do more frequent in Shakespeare's verse than in his
prose,[16] and rhythm and rime sometimes make him place
a preposition after instead of before the noun (e.g. go
the fools among[17]). All these things are rare enough to

[16] W. Franz, *Shakespeare-Grammatik*, 2nd ed., 478, and
Nachtrag, p. 590.

[17] Franz, p. 427.

justify the statement that a peculiar poetical diction is
practically non-existent in Shakespeare.

236. In the Old English period the language of
poetry differed, as we have seen (cf. § 53), very considerably from the language of ordinary prose. The old
poetical language was completely forgotten a few centuries after the Norman Conquest, and a new one did
not develop in the Middle English period, though there
were certain conventional tricks used by many poets,
such as those ridiculed in Chaucer's *Sir Thopas*. Chaucer
himself had not two distinct forms of language, one for
verse and the other for prose, apart from those unavoidable smaller changes which rhythm and rime are
always apt to bring about. We have now seen that the
same is true of Shakespeare; but in the nineteenth century we find a great many words and forms of words
which are scarcely ever used outside of poetry. This,
then, is not a survival of an old state of things, but a
comparatively recent phenomenon, whose causes are
well worth investigating. At first it might be thought
that the regard for sonority and beauty of sound would
be the chief or one of the chief agents in the creation
of a special poetical dialect. But very often poetical
forms are, on the contrary, less euphonious than everyday forms; compare, for example, *break'st thou* with
do you break. Those who imagine that *gat* sounds better
than *got* will scarcely admit that *spat* or *gnat* sounds
better than *spot* or *not:* non-phonetic associations are
often more powerful than the mere sounds.

237. More frequently it is the desire to leave the
beaten track that leads to the preference of certain
words in poetry. Words that are too well known and
too often used do not call up such vivid images as words
less familiar. This is one of the reasons that impel poets

to use archaic words; they are 'new' just on account of
their being old, and yet they are not so utterly unknown
as to be unintelligible. Besides they will often call up
the memory of some old or venerable work in which
the reader has met with them before, and thus they at
once secure the reader's sympathy. If, then, the poetical
language of the nineteenth century contains a great many
archaisms, the question naturally presents itself, from
what author or authors do most of them proceed? And
many people who know the pre-eminent position of
Shakespeare in English literature will probably be surprised to hear that his is not the greatest influence on
English poetic diction.

238. Among words and phrases due to reminiscences of Shakespeare may be mentioned the following:
antre (Keats, Meredith), *atomy* in the sense 'atom, tiny
being,' *beetle* ('the dreadfull summit of the cliffe, That
beetles o'er his base into the sea'), it *beggars all description, broad-blown, charactery* (Keats, Browning), *coign
of vantage* (*coign* is another spelling of *coin* 'corner'),
cudgel one's brain(s), daff the world aside, *eager* 'cold'
('a nipping and an eager ayre'), *eld* (superstitious eld),
nine *farrow, fitful* ('Life's fitfull fever'), *forcible feeble,
a foregone conclusion, forgetive* (Falstaff: 'of uncertain
formation and meaning.' Commonly taken as a deriva-
tion of *forge* v., and hence used by writers of the nineteenth century for: 'apt at forging, inventive, creative.'
NED.), a *forthright* (rare), *gaingiving* (Coleridge),
gouts of blood, *gravel-blind, head and front* ('A Shake-
sperian phrase, orig. app. denoting "summit, height,
highest extent or pitch"; sometimes used by modern
writers in other senses.' NED.), *hoist with his own
petard, lush* (in the sense 'luxuriant in growth'), in my
mind's eye, the *pink* (of perfection, in Shakespeare

only, 'I am the very pinck of curtesie'; George Eliot has 'Her kitchen always looked the pink of cleanliness,' and Stevenson 'he had been the pink of good behaviour'), *silken dalliance, single blessedness, that way madness lies* ('Too kind! Insipidity lay that way,' Mrs. Humphrey Ward), *weird.* The last word is interesting; originally it is a noun and means 'destiny, fate'; the three *weird sisters* means the fate sisters or Norns. Shakespeare found this expression in Holinshed and used it in speaking of the witches in *Macbeth,* and only there. From that play it entered into the ordinary language, but without being properly understood. It is now used as an adjective and generally taken to mean 'mystic, mysterious, unearthly.' Another word that is often misunderstood is *bourne* from *Hamlet* (The undiscovered country, from whose borne No traveller returns); it means 'limit,' but Keats and others use it in the sense 'realm, domain' (In water, fiery realm, and airy bourne; quoted NED.). There are two things worth noting in this list. First, that it includes so many words of vague or indefinite meaning, which perhaps were not even clearly understood by the author himself. This explains the fact that some of them have apparently been used in modern times in a different sense from that intended by Shakespeare. Second, that the re-employment of these words nearly always dates from the nineteenth century and that the present currency of some of them is due just as much to Sir Walter Scott or Keats as to the original author. *To cudgel one's brains* is now more of a literary phrase than when Shakespeare put it in the mouth of the grave-digger (Hamlet V, 1, 63), evidently meaning it to be a rude or vulgar expression. Inversely, *single blessedness* is now generally used with an ironical or humorous tinge which it certainly had not in Shakespeare (Mids. I, 1, 78).

239. It must be noted also that none of the words thus traceable to Shakespeare belong now to what might be called the technical language of poetry. Modern archaizing poetry owes its vocabulary more to Edmund Spenser than to any other poet. Pope and his contemporaries made a very sparing use of archaisms, but when poets in the middle of the eighteenth century turned from his rationalistic and matter-of-fact poetry and were eager to take their romantic flight away from everyday realities, Spenser became the poet of their heart, and they adopted a great many of his words which had long been forgotten. Their success was so great that many words which they had to explain to their readers are now perfectly familiar to every educated man and woman. Gilbert West, in his work *On the Abuse of Traveling, in imitation of Spenser* (1739), had to explain in footnotes such words as *sooth, guise, hardiment, Elfin, prowess, wend, hight, dight, paramount, behests, caitiffs*.[18] William Thompson, in his *Hymn to May* (1740?), explains *certes* surely, certainly, *ne* nor, *erst* formerly, long ago, *undaz'd* undazzled, *sheen* brightness, shining, *been* are, *dispredden* spread, *meed* prize, *ne recks* nor is concerned, *affray* affright, *featly* nimbly, *defftly* finely, *glenne* a country borough (the real meaning is 'valley'; the wrong sense here given to it is due to E.K.'s notes to Spenser's *Shepherd's Calendar*), *eld* old age, *lusty-head* vigour, *algate* ever, *harrow* destroy, *carl* clown, *perdie* an old word for

---

[18] W. L. Phelps, *Beginnings of the Romantic Movement*, p. 63. Cf. also K. Reuning, *Das Altertümliche im Wortschatz der Spenser-Nachahmungen* (Strassburg, 1912). H. G. de Maar, *A History of Mod. Engl. Romanticism* (Oxford, 1924), ch. IV.

asserting anything, *livelood* liveliness, *albe* altho', *scant* scarcely, *bedight* adorned.

240. In later times, Coleridge, Scott, Keats, Tennyson, William Morris and Swinburne must be mentioned as those poets who have contributed most to the revival of old words. Coleridge in the first edition of the *Ancient Mariner* used so many archaisms in spelling, etc., that he had afterwards to reduce the number in order to make his poem more palatable to the reading public. Sometimes *pseudo*-antique formations have been introduced; *anigh,* for instance, which is frequent in Morris, is not an old word, and *idlesse* is a false formation after the legitimate old *noblesse* and *humblesse* (OFr. noblesse, humblesse). But on the whole, many good words have been recovered from oblivion, and some of them will doubtless find their way into the language of ordinary conversation, while others will continue their life in the regions of higher poetry and eloquence. On the other hand, many pages in the works of Shakespeare, of Shelley, and of Tennyson show us that it is possible for a poet to reach the highest flights of eloquent poetry without resorting to many of the conventionally poetical terms.

241. As for the technical *grammar* of modern poetry, the influence of Shakespeare is not very strong, in fact not so strong as that of the Authorized Version of the Bible. The revival of *th* in the third person singular was due to the Bible, as we have seen above (§ 205).[19] *Gat* is more frequent than *got* in the Bible, while Shakespeare's ordinary form is *got;* the solitary instance of *gat* (see § 235) only serves to confirm the

---

[19] When modern clergymen in reading the Bible pronounce *lovèd, dancèd,* etc., they are reproducing a language about two hundred years earlier than the Authorized Version.

rule.[20] The past tense of *cleave* 'to sever' in Shakespeare is *clove* or *cleft; clave* does not occur in his writings at all, but is the only biblical past of this verb. *Brake* is the only preterit of *break* found in the Bible; in Shakespeare *brake* is rarer than *broke;* Milton and Pope have only *broke*; Tennyson, Morris, and Swinburne prefer *brake*.

242. On the whole, however, modern poets do not take their grammar from any one old author or book, but are apt to use any deviation from the ordinary grammar they can lay hold of anywhere. And thus it has come to pass in the nineteenth century that while the languages of other civilized nations have the same grammar for poetry as for prose, although retaining here and there a few archaic forms of verbs, etc., in English a wide gulf separates the grammar of poetry from that of ordinary life. The pronoun for the second person is in prose *you* for both cases in both numbers, while in many works of poetry it is *thou* and *thee* for the singular, *ye* for the plural (with here and there a rare *you);* the poetical possessives *thy* and *thine* never occur in everyday speech. The usual distinction between *my* and *mine* does not always obtain in poetry, where it is thought

[20] *Gat* is the only form of this verb admitted by some modern poets, who avoid *get* and *got* altogether. Shakespeare uses the verb hundreds of times. In the Authorized Version *get* is pretty frequent, but *got* is avoided in the New Testament, while it is found seven times in the Old Testament (in five of these places the revisers of 1881 substituted other words: gathered, bought, come); *gat* is used 20 times, all of them in the O.T. (three of these were changed in 1881); *gotten* is found 23 times in the O.T., and twice in the N.T. (five of these, among them both the instances in the N.T., were changed in 1881). Milton makes a very sparing use of the verb (which he inflects *get, got, got*, never *gat* in the past or *gotten* in the participle); all the forms of the verb only occur 19 times in his poetical works, while, for instance, *give* occurs 168 times and *receive* 73 times. The verb is rare in Pope too. Why is this verb tabooed in this way?

refined to write *mine ears,* etc. For *they sat down* the poetical form is *they sate them down;* for *it's* poets write *'tis,* and for *whatever* either *whatso* or *whatsoever* (or *whate'er*), for *does not mend* they often write *mends not,* etc. Sometimes they gain the advantage of having at will one syllable more or less than common people: *taketh* for *takes, thou takest* for *you take, movèd* for *moved, o'er* for *over,* etc.; compare also *morn* for *morning.* But in other cases the only thing gained is the impression, produced by uncommon forms, that we are in a sphere different from or raised above ordinary realities. As a matter of course, this impression is weakened in proportion as the deviations become the common property of any rimer, when a reaction will probably set in in favour of more natural forms. The history of some of the poetical forms is rather curious: *howe'er, e'er, e'en* were at first vulgar or familiar forms, used in daily talk. Then poets began to spell these words in the abbreviated fashion whenever they wanted their readers to pronounce them in that way, while prose writers, unconcerned about the pronunciation given to their words, retained the full forms in spelling. The next step was that the short forms were branded as vulgar by schoolmasters with so great a success that they disappeared from ordinary conversation while they were still retained in poetry. And now they are distinctly poetic and as such above the reach of common mortals.

243. Among the elements of ordinary language, some can be traced back to individual authors. Besides those already mentioned I shall cite only a few. *Surround* originally meant to overflow (Fr. sur-onder, Lat. superundare); but according to Skeat, both the modern signification, which implies an erroneous reference to *round,* and the currency of the word are due to Milton.

The soft impeachment is one of Mrs. Malaprop's expressions (in Sheridan's *Rivals,* act V, sc. 3). *Henchman* was made generally known by Scott, and *to croon* by Burns. Burke originated the expression *the Great Unwashed.* A certain number of proper names in works of literature have been popular enough to pass into ordinary language as appellatives,[21] as for instance *pander* or *pandar* from Chaucer's *Troilus and Criseyde, Abigail* 'a servant-girl' from Beaumont and Fletcher's *Scornful Lady, Mrs. Grundy* as a personification of middle-class ideas of propriety from Morton's *Speed the Plough, Paul Pry* 'a meddlesome busybody' from Poole's comedy of that name, *Sarah Gamp* 'sick nurse of the old-fashioned type' and 'big umbrella' from Dickens's *Martin Chuzzlewit, Pecksniff* 'hypocrite' from the same novel, *Sherlock Holmes* 'acute detective' from Conan Doyle's stories.

244. Ordinary language sometimes makes use of the same instruments as poetry. Above (§ 56) we have seen a number of alliterative formulas; here I shall give some instances of riming locutions: *highways* and *byways, town* and *gown*, it will neither *make* nor *break* me (cf. the alliterative *make . . . mar*), *fairly* and *squarely, toiling* and *moiling*, as *snug* as a *bug* in a *rug* (Kipling), *rough* and *gruff*, 'I mean to take that girl—*snatch* or *catch*' (Meredith), *moans* and *groans*.[22] Compare also such popular words as *handy-dandy, hanky-panky, namby-pamby, hurly-burly, hurdy-gurdy, hugger-mug-*

---

[21] Aronstein, *Englische Studien*, XXV, p. 245 ff., Josef Reinius, *On Transferred Appellations of Human Beings* (Göteborg, 1903), p. 44 ff.

[22] As Old English has *mænan* 'moan,' the modern verb may have derived its vowel from the frequent collocation with *groan*, OE. *granian*. *Square* may owe one of its significations to the collocation with *fair*.

ger, hocus pocus, hoity toity or *highty tighty, higgledy-piggledy* or *higglety-pigglety, hickery-pickery. Hotchpot* (from French *hocher* 'shake together' and *pot*) was made *hotch-potch* for the sake of the rime; then the final *tch* was changed into *dge* (cf. *knowledge* from *knowl-eche*): *hotchpodge,* and the rime was re-established: *hodge-podge.*

245. Rhythm undoubtedly plays a great part in ordinary language, apart from poetry and artistic (or artificial) prose. It may not always be easy to demonstrate this; but in combinations of a monosyllable and a disyllable by means of *and* the short word is in many set phrases placed first in order to make the rhythm into the regular ¹aa ¹aa instead of ¹aaa ¹a (¹ before the *a* denotes the strongly stressed syllable). Thus we say 'bread and butter,' not 'butter and bread'; further: bread and water, milk and water, cup and saucer, wind and weather, head and shoulders, by fits and snatches, from top to bottom, rough and ready, rough and tumble, free and easy, dark and dreary, high and mighty, up and doing.[23] It is probable that rhythm has also played a great part in determining the order of words in other fixed groups of greater complexity.[24]

[23] Compare also such titles of books as Songs and Poems, Men and Women, Past and Present, French and English, Night and Morning. In some instances, rhythm is obviously not the only reason for the order, but in all I think it has been at least a concurrent cause. F. N. Scott, in *Modern Language Notes,* 1913, has collected a number of combinations in which this rhythmical rule is not observed, but in many of these the word-order is obviously determined by other causes.

[24] P. Fijn van Draat, *Rhythm in English Prose* (Heidelberg, 1910), has many interesting observations on the influence of rhythm, though I would not subscribe to all his conclusions. Much of what he has written on the subject in later papers in the *Anglia* also appears to me very doubtful.

CHAPTER XI

Conclusion

246. In the preceding chapters we have considered the early vicissitudes of the English language, the various foreign influences brought from time to time to bear on it, its inner growth, lexical and grammatical, and the linguistic tendencies of its poets. It now remains to look at a few things which have contributed towards shaping the language, but which could find no convenient place in any of the preceding chapters, and then to say something about the spread and probable future of the language.[1]

247. Aristocratic and democratic tendencies in a nation often show themselves in its speech; indeed, we have already regarded the adoption of French and Latin words from that point of view. It is often said, on the Continent at least, that the typical Englishman's self-assertion is shown by the fact that his is the only language in which the pronoun of the first person singular is written with a capital letter, while in some other languages it is the second person that is honoured by this distinction, especially the pronoun of courtesy (German *Sie,* often also *Du,* Danish *De* and in former times, *Du,* Italian *Ella, Lei,* Spanish *V.* or *Vd.,* Finnish *Te*). Weise

---

[1] On some recent tendencies in English, I may refer to Stuart Robertson, *The Development of Modern English,* 1934, besides the works mentioned above (§ 161).

goes so far as to say that 'the Englishman, who as the ruler of the seas looks down in contempt on the rest of Europe, writes in his language nothing but the beloved *I* with a big letter.'[2] But this is little short of calumny. If self-assertion had been the real cause, why should not *me* also be written *Me*? The reason for writing *I* is a much more innocent one, namely, the orthographic habit in the middle ages of using a 'long i' (that is, j or I) whenever the letter was isolated or formed the last letter of a group; the numeral 'one' was written j or I (and three, iij, etc.), just as much as the pronoun. Thus no sociological inference can be drawn from this peculiarity.

248. On the other hand, the habit of addressing a single person by means of a plural pronoun was decidedly in its origin an outcome of an aristocratic tendency towards class-distinction. The habit originated with the Roman Emperors, who desired to be addressed as beings worth more than a single ordinary man; and French courtesy in the middle ages propagated it throughout Europe. In England as elsewhere this plural pronoun (*you, ye*) was long confined to respectful address. Superior persons or strangers were addressed as *you; thou* thus becoming the mark either of the inferiority of the person spoken to, or of familiarity or even intimacy or affection between the two interlocutors. English is the only language that has got rid of this useless distinction. The Quakers (the Society of Friends) objected to the habit as obscuring the equality of all human beings; they therefore *thou*'d (or rather *thee*'d) everybody. But the same democratic levelling that they wanted to effect in this way was achieved a century and a half later in society at large, though in a roundabout manner, when the pronoun *you* was gradually extended to

[2] *Charakteristik der lateinischen Sprache*, 1889, p. 21.

lower classes and thus lost more and more of its previous character of deference. *Thou* then for some time was reserved for religious and literary use as well as for foul abuse, until finally the latter use was discontinued also and *you* became the only form used in ordinary conversation.

249. Apart from the not very significant survival of *thou,* English has thus attained the only manner of address worthy of a nation that respects the elementary rights of each individual. People who express regret at not having a pronoun of endearment and who insist how pretty it is in other languages when, for instance, two lovers pass from *vous* to the more familiar *tu,* should consider that no foreign language has really a pronoun exclusively for the most intimate relations. Where the two forms of address do survive, *thou* is very often, most often perhaps, used without real affection, nay very frequently in contempt or frank abuse. Besides, it is often painful to have to choose between the two forms, as people may be offended, sometimes by the too familiar, and sometimes by the too distant mode. Some of the unpleasant feeling of Helmer towards Krogstad in Ibsen's *Dukkehjem* (*A Doll's House* or *Nora*) must be lost to an English audience because occasioned by the latter using an old schoolfellow's privilege of *thou*-ing Helmer. In some languages the pronoun of respect often is a cause of ambiguity, in German and Danish by the identity in form of *Sie* (*De*) with the plural of the third person, in Italian and Portuguese by the identity with the singular (feminine) of the third person. When all the artificialities of the modes of address in different nations are taken into account—the *Lei, Ella, voi* and *tu* of the Italians, the *vossa mercê* ('your grace,' to shopkeepers) and *você* (shortened form of the same,

to people of a lower grade) of the Portuguese (who in
addressing equals or superiors use the third person singular of the verb without any pronoun or noun), the *gij,
jij, je* and *U* of the Dutch, not to mention the eternal
use of titles as pronouns in German and, still more, in
Swedish ('What does Mr. Doctor want?' 'The gracious
Miss is probably aware,' etc.)—the English may be
justly proud of having avoided all such mannerisms and
ridiculous extravagances, though the simple Old English way of using *thou* in addressing one person and *ye*
in addressing more than one would have been still better.

250. Religion has had no small influence on the
English language. The Bible has been studied and
quoted in England more than in any other Christian
country and a great many Biblical phrases have passed
into the ordinary language as household words. The
style of the Authorized Version has been greatly admired by many of the best judges of English style, who
—with some exaggeration—recommend an early familiarity with and a constant study of the English Bible
(and of that great imitator of Biblical simplicity and
earnestness, John Bunyan) as the best training in the
English language.[3] Tennyson found that parts of *The
Book of the Revelation* were finer in English than in

---

[3] See the long series of quotations given in Albert S. Cook's
little book, *The Bible and English Prose Style* (Boston, 1892).
On the other hand, Fitzedward Hall says, 'To Dr. Newman, and
to the myriads who think as he does about our English Bible,
one would be allowed to whisper, that the poor "Turks" of the
Prayer Book talk exactly in their own fashion, and for reasons
strictly analogous to theirs, about the purity of diction, and
what not, of "the Blessed Koran." . . . Ever since the Reformation, the ruling language of English religion has been, with
rare exception, an affair either of studied antiquarianism or of
nauseous pedantry. Simplicity, and little more, was aimed at,
originally; and it sufficed for times of real earnestness. But the

Greek, and he said that 'the Bible ought to be read, were
it only for the sake of the grand English in which it is
written, an education in itself.'[4] The rhythmical character of the Authorized Version is seen, for instance, in
the well-known passage (Job III, 17), 'There the wicked
cease from troubling: and there the wearie be at rest,'
which Tennyson was able to use as the last line of his
May Queen with scarcely any alteration: 'And the
wicked cease from troubling, and the weary are at rest.'

251. C. Stoffel has collected quite a number of
scriptural phrases and allusions used in Modern English[5] such as 'Tell it not in Gath,' 'the powers that be,'
'olive branches' (children), 'strain at (*or* out) a gnat,'
'to spoil the Egyptians,' 'he may run that readeth it,'
'take up his parable,' 'wash one's hands of' something, 'a
still small voice,' 'thy speech bewrayeth thee.' Some
which Stoffel does not mention may find their place here.
The modern word a *helpmate* is a corruption of the two
words in Gen. II, 18: 'I will make him an *helpe meet*
for him' (*meet* 'suitable'); the slang word a *rib* 'a wife'
is from Genesis, too, and so is the expression 'the lesser
lights.' 'A howling wilderness' is from Deuteron. XXXII,
10. 'My heart was still hot within me; then spake I with
my tongue' (used, for instance in Charlotte Brontë's
The Professor, p. 161) is from Psalms XXXIX, 3, and
'many inventions' from Ecclesiastes VII, 29. From the
New Testament may be mentioned 'to kill the fatted

---

very quaintness of phrase which King James countersigned has
attained to be canonized, till a *hath*, or a *thou*, delivered with
conventional unction, now well nigh inspires a sensation of
solemnity in its hearer, and a persuasion of the sanctanimity of
its utterer.' (*Modern English*, p. 16–17.)

[4] *Life and Letters*, II, 41 and 71.

[5] *Studies in English, Written and Spoken*, 1894, p. 125.

calf,'[6] 'whited sepulchres,' 'of the earth, earthy,' and 'to comprehend with all saints, what is the breadth, and length, and depth and height.' But people now begin to complain that scriptural allusions are to a great extent lost to the younger generation.

252. The scriptural 'holy of holies,' which contains a Hebrew manner of expressing the superlative,[7] has given rise to a great many similar phrases in English, such as 'in my heart of hearts' (Shakespeare, Hamlet III, 2, 78; Wordsworth, *Prelude* XIV, 281), 'the place of all places' (Miss Austen, *Mansfield P.* 71), 'I remember you a buck of bucks' (Thackeray, *Newcomes,* 100), 'every lad has a friend of friends, a crony of cronies, whom he cherishes in his heart of hearts' (ib. 148), 'the evil of evils in our present politics' (Lecky, *Democr. and Lib.* I, 21), 'the woman is a horror of horrors' (H. James, *Two Magics,* 60), 'that mystery of mysteries, the beginning of things' (Sully, *Study of Childhood,* 71), 'she is a modern of the moderns' (Mrs. H. Ward, *Eleanor,* 265), 'love like yours is the pearl of pearls, and he who wins it is prince of princes' (Hall Caine, *Christian,* 443), 'chemistry had been the study of studies for T. Sandys' (Barrie, *Tommy and Grizel,* 6). Compare also 'I am sorrowful to my tail's tail' (Kipling, *Sec. Jungle B.,* 160).

253. Some scriptural proper names have often been used as appellatives, such as *Jezebel* and *Rahab;* when a driver is called a *jehu* in slang, the allusion is to 2 Kings IX, 20, where Jehu's furious driving is mentioned. There is an American slang expression 'to give a person *jessie'* meaning 'to beat him soundly' which is

---

[6] While the phrase *prodigal son* is not found in the text of the Bible, it occurs in the heading of the chapter (Luke XV).

[7] Cf. I Timothy VI, 15, 'the King of kings, and Lord of lords.'

not explained in the dictionaries (quotations may be found in Bartlett and in Farmer and Henley). Is it not in allusion to the *rod* mentioned in Isaiah II, 1? ('There shall come forth a rod out of the stem of Jesse.') The NED. has the spelling *jesse* with the meaning 'a genealogical tree representing the genealogy of Christ . . . a decoration for a wall, window, vestment, etc., or in the form of a large branched candlestick.'

254. The influence of Puritans, though not strong enough to proscribe such words as *Christmas,* for which they wanted to substitute *Christtide* in order to avoid the Catholic *mass,* was yet strong enough to modify the custom of swearing. In Catholic times all sorts of fantastic oaths were fashionable:

Hir othes been so grete and so dampnable,
That it is grisly for to here hem swere;
Our blissed lordes body they to-tere;
Hem thoughte Jewes rente him noght ynough.[8]

This practice was continued after the Reformation, and all sorts of alterations were made in the name of *God* in order to soften down the oaths: *gog, cocke, gosse, gosh, gom, Gough, Gad,* etc. Similarly instead of (the) *Lord* people would say something like *Law, Lawks, Losh,* etc. Sometimes only the first sound was left out ('Odd's lifelings,' Shakespeare, Tw. V, 187), more often only the genitive ending survived: 'Sblood (God's blood), 'snails, 'slight, 'slid, 'zounds (God's wounds). The final sound of the nominative is kept in *'drot it* (God rot it), which was later made *drat it* (or with a playful corruption *rabbit it*). Many of these disguised oaths were extremely popular, and some survive to this day. *Good-*

---

[8] Chaucer C. T., C. 472 ff., also see Skeat's note to this passage, *Chaucer's Works,* V, p. 275.

ness gracious me, which defies all grammatical analysis, is one among numerous compromises between the inclination to swear and the fear of swearing; note also Rosalind's words: 'By my troth, and in good earnest, and so God mend mee, and by all pretty oathes that are not dangerous.' (As IV, 1, 192.)

255. The Puritans caused a law to be enacted in 1606 by which profane language was prohibited on the stage (3 James I, chap. 21), and consequently words like *'zounds* were changed or omitted in Shakespearian plays, as we see from a comparison of the folio of 1623 and the earlier quartos; *Heaven* or *Jove* was substituted for *God,* and *'fore me* (*afore me*) or *trust me* for (*a*)*fore God;* 'God give thee the spirit of persuasion' (H 4 A I, 2, 170) was changed into 'Maist thou have the spirit of perswasion,' etc. But in ordinary life people went on swearing, and from the comedies of the Restoration period a rich harvest may be reaped of all sorts of curious oaths. By little and little, however, the Puritan spirit conquered, and the English came to swear less than other European nations. Even the usual terms for oaths—'profane language' and 'expletives'—point to a greater purity in this respect. Instead of *My God,* an Englishwoman will often say *Dear me!* or *Oh my!* or *Good gracious!* Note also euphemisms like 'deuce' for devil and 'the other place' or 'a very uncomfortable place' for hell.[9] Among words that used to be tabooed in England one finds a great number which in other countries would be considered quite innocent, and the English have shown a really astonishing inventiveness in 'apologies' for strong words of every kind. *Damn* was considered extremely objectionable, and even such a mild substitute for it as *confound* was scarcely allowed

[9] Compare also 'I will see you *further.*'

in polite society.[10] In Bernard Shaw's *Candida,* Morell is provoked into exclaiming 'Confound your impudence!' whereupon his vulgar father-in-law retorts, 'Is that becomin' language for a clorgyman?' and Morell replies, 'No, sir, it is not becoming language for a clergyman. I should have said damn your impudence: that's what St. Paul or any honest priest would have said to you.' Other substitutes for *damned* are *hanged, somethinged* (much rarer)[11] and a few that originate in the manner in which the objectional word is — *not* printed: *dashed* (a — or 'dash' being put instead of it), *blanked* or *blanky* (from the same manner), *deed* (from the abbreviation d—d; sometimes the verb is printed *to D*). *Darned* is perhaps nothing but a purely phonetical development of *damned,* which is not without analogies, while *danged,* which occurs in Tennyson, is a curious blending of *damned* and *hanged.*[12] Thus we have here a whole family of words with an initial *d,* allowing the speaker to begin as if he were going to say the prohibited word, and then to turn off into more innocent channels.[13] The same is the case with the *bl-*words. *Blessed* by a process which is found in other similar cases[14] came to mean the opposite of the original meaning, and became a synonym of cursed; *blamed* had the same sig-

---

[10] In the original sense it has often to be accompanied by *together* to avoid misunderstanding.

[11] Cf. the similar use of *something* in 'Where the something are you coming to?' (Pett Ridge, *Lost Property,* 167.)

[12] 'I'm doomed!' Corp muttered to himself, pronouncing it in another way. (Barrie, *Tommy and Grizel,* p. 122.) This shows another way of disguising the word *in print.*

[13] Cf. also the expression: 'Kingsley's struggles with the fourth letter of the alphabet' (a little swearing was thought no blemish in your muscular Christian), *Life of Leslie Stephen,* 138.

[14] Cf. *silly,* French *benêt,* etc.

nification.[15] Instead of these strong expressions people
began to use other adjectives, shunting off after pronouncing *bl-* into some innocent word like *bloody,* which
soon became a great favourite with the vulgar and therefore a horror to ears polite, or *blooming,* which had the
same unhappy fate in the latter half of the nineteenth
century. Few authors would now venture to term their
heroines 'blooming young girls' as George Eliot does
repeatedly in *Middlemarch.* Similarly Shakespeare's expression 'the bloody book of law' is completely spoilt to
modern readers, and lexicographers now have to render
Old English *blodig* and the corresponding words in foreign languages by 'bleeding,' 'blood-stained,' 'sangui-
nary' or 'ensanguined'; but even *sanguinary* is often
made a substitute for 'bloody' in reporting vulgar speech.

256. This is the usual destiny of euphemisms; in
order to avoid the real name of what is thought indecent
or improper people use some innocent word. But when
that becomes habitual in this sense it becomes just as
objectionable as the word it has ousted and now is re-
jected in its turn. *Privy* is the regular English development of French *privé;* but when it came to be used as a
noun for 'a privy place' and in the phrase 'the privy
parts,' it had to pe supplanted in the original sense by
private, except in 'Privy Council,' 'Privy Seal' and 'Privy
Purse,' where its official dignity kept it alive. The plural
parts was an ordinary expression for 'talents, mental
ability,' until the use of the word in veiled language
made it impossible.[16]

---

[15] There exists also a word *blarned,* a blending of *blamed* and
damned (darned). Cf. also *I swan, I swow,* and other similar
ways of saying *I swear.*

[16] Cf. from America 'He-biddy—a male fowl. A product of
prudery and squeamishness.' Farmer, *Americanisms,* p. 293.
Cf. also Storm, *Engl. Philologie,* p. 887 (roosterswain).

257. The twentieth century, and especially the time after the Great War, has put a stop to many of the linguistic prohibitions that flourished in the Victorian era. People are not now so afraid of saying *damn* and *bloody* as their ancestors were, and many sexual things are now spoken of quite openly. The present generation shake their heads at the prudery of Boston ladies who would speak of the *limbs* of a piano or their own *benders* instead of *legs*.[17] Many absurd names (inexpressibles, inexplicables, indescribables, unmentionables, unwhisperables, my mustn't mention-'em, etc.) were used to avoid the simple word *trousers*, at which no one takes offence nowadays. According to F. T. Elworthy[18] even Somerset peasants thought such names as *bull, stallion, boar, cock, ram* indelicate. All this now belongs to ancient history.

258. This volume has in so far been one-sided as it has dealt chiefly with Standard English, and has left out of account nearly everything that is not generally accepted as such, apart from here and there a nonce-formation or a bold expression which is not recognized as good English though interesting as showing the possibilities of the language and perhaps in some cases deserving popularity just as well as many things that nobody finds fault with. I have had no space in this little volume for the question how one form of English came to be taken as standard in preference to dialects,[19] nor for chapters on provincialisms, cockneyisms and vulgarisms, on

[17] Cf. Opie Read, *A Kentucky Colonel*, p. 11. 'He was so delicate of expression that he always said limb when he meant leg.'

[18] *Transactions of the Philological Society*, 1898.

[19] See now *Mankind, Nation and Individual* (Oslo, 1925), ch. III and IV, where the development of common languages in general is discussed.

American and Colonial English, on slang[20] and cant,[21] on Pidgin-English and other exotic forms of English,[22] etc. I have also deliberately omitted all the problems connected with that pseudo-historical and anti-educational abomination, the English spelling.[23] At present I shall conclude with a few remarks on what might be called the Expansion of English.

259. Only two or three centuries ago, English was spoken by so few people that no one could dream of its ever becoming a world language. In 1582 Richard Mulcaster wrote, 'The English tongue is of small reach, stretching no further than this island of ours, nay not there over all.' 'In one of Florio's Anglo-Italian dialogues, an Italian in England, asked to give his opinion of the language, replied it was worthless beyond Dover. Ancillon regretted that the English authors chose to write in English as no one abroad could read them. Even such as learned English by necessity speedily forgot it. As late as 1718, Le Clerc deplored the small number of scholars on the Continent able to read English.'[24] Compare what Portia replies to Nerissa's question about Fauconbridge, the young baron of England (Merch. I, 2, 72): 'You know I say nothing to him, for hee understands not me, nor I him: he hath neither Latine, French, nor Italian, and you will come into the Court

[20] Ibid. ch. VIII.

[21] Ibid. ch. X.

[22] Cf. *Language,* ch. XII, on Beach-la-Mar and Pidgin.

[23] An historical account of the English sound-system and English spelling may be found in my *Modern English Grammar* I (Heidelberg, Carl Winter, 1909). A later, but unfortunately only half-finished treatment is Karl Luick, *Historische Grammatik der englischen Sprache* (Leipzig, 1914–1929).

[24] Ch. Bastide, *Huguenot Thought in England,* Journal of Comparative Literature I (1903), p. 45.

and sweare that I have a poore pennie-worth in the English. Hee is a proper man's picture, but alas, who can converse with a dumbe show?' In 1714 Veneroni published an Imperial Dictionary of the four chief languages of Europe, that is, Italian, French, German and Latin.[25] Nowadays, no one would overlook English in making even the shortest possible list of the chief languages, because in political, social and literary importance it is second to none, and because it is the mothertongue of a greater number of human beings than any of its competitors.

260. It would be unreasonable to suppose, as is sometimes done, that the cause of the enormous propagation of the English language is to be sought in its intrinsic merits. When two languages compete, the victory does not fall to the most perfect language as such. Nor is it *always* the nation whose culture is superior that makes the nation of inferior culture adopt its language. It sometimes happens in a district of mixed nationalities that the population which is intellectually superior give up their own language because they can learn their neighbours' tongue while these are too dull to learn anything but their own. Thus a great many social problems are involved in the general question of rivalry of languages, and it would be an interesting but difficult task to examine in detail all the different reasons that have in so many regions of the world determined the victory of English over other languages, European and non-European. Political ascendancy would probably be found in most cases to have been the most powerful influence.

[25] Das kayserliche Spruch- und Wörterbuch, darinnen die 4 europäischen Hauptsprachen, als nemlich: das Italiänische, das Frantzösische, das Teutsche und das Lateinische erklärt werden.

261. However that may be, the fact remains that no other European language has spread over such vast regions during the last few centuries, as shown by the following figures, which represent the number of millions of people speaking each of the languages enumerated:[26]

Year	English	German	Russian	French	Spanish	Italian
1500	4(5)	10	3	10(12)	8½	9½
1600	6	10	3	14	8½	9½
1700	8½	10	3(15)	20	8½	9½(11)
1800	20(40)	30(33)	25(31)	27(31)	26	14(15)
1900	116(123)	75(80)	70(85)	45(52)	44(58)	34(54)
1926	170	80	80	45	65	41

The latest figures that have come to hand are those in H. L. Mencken, *The American Language*, 4th ed., 1936, p. 592: 'First, let us list those to whom English is their native tongue. They run to about 112,000,000 in the continental United States, to 42,000,000 in the United Kingdom, to 6,000,000 in Canada, 6,000,000 in Australia, 3,000,000 in Ireland, 2,000,000 in South Africa, and probably 3,000,000 in the remaining British colonies and in the possessions of the United States. All these figures are very conservative, but they foot up to 174,000,000. Now add the people who, though born to some other language, live in English-speaking communities and speak English themselves in their daily business, and whose children are being brought up to it —say 13,000,000 for the United States, 1,000,000 for Canada, 1,000,000 for the United Kingdom and Ireland, and 1,000,000 for the rest of the world—and you have a grand total of 191,000,000.' Mencken gives the figures for Spanish as 100, for Russian as 80, and for

[26] The numbers given are necessarily approximate only, especially for the older periods. Where my authorities disagree, I have given the lowest and in parenthesis the highest figure. The figures for 1926 are from L. Tesnière's *Appendice* to A. Meillet's *Les Langues dans l'Europe Nouvelle* (Paris, 1928).

German as 85 millions, and adds: 'Thus English is far ahead of any competitor. Moreover, it promises to increase its lead hereafter, for no other language is spreading so fast or into such remote areas . . . Altogether, it is probable that English is now spoken as a second language by at least 20,000,000 persons throughout the world—very often, to be sure, badly, but nevertheless understandably.'

Whatever a remote future may have in store, one need not be a great prophet to predict that in the near future the number of English-speaking people will increase considerably. It must be a source of gratification to mankind that the tongue spoken by two of the greatest powers of the world is so noble, so rich, so pliant, so expressive, and so interesting as the language whose growth and structure I have been here endeavouring to characterize.

Phonetic Symbols

ˈ stands before the stressed syllable.

· indicates length of the preceding vowel.

[a·]	as in *a*lms.	[ʌ]	as in h*u*t.
[ai]	as in *i*ce.	[u·]	as in French ép*ou*se.
[au]	as in h*ou*se.	[uw]	as in wh*o;* practically
[æ]	as in h*a*t.		= [u·].
[ei]	as in h*a*te.	[y]	as in French v*u.*
[ə]	as in *a*bout, colo*ur.*	[þ]	as in *th*in.
[i·]	as in French d*i*se.	[ð]	as in *th*is.
[ij]	as in h*ea*t; practically	[s]	as in *s*eal.
	= [i·].	[z]	as in *z*eal.
[ou]	as in s*o.*	[ʃ]	as in *sh*in; [tʃ] as in
[ɔ]	as in h*o*t.		*ch*in.
[ɔ·]	as in h*a*ll.	[ʒ]	as in vi*s*ion; [dʒ] as
			in *g*in.

See my *Modern English Grammar* I (1909).

Abbreviations

OHG. = Old High German.
NED. = A New English Dictionary, by Murray, Bradley, Craigie, and Onions.

The titles of Shakespeare's plays are abbreviated as in Al. Schmidt's *Shakespeare-Lexicon*, thus Ado = *Much Ado about Nothing*, Gent. = *The Two Gentlemen of Verona*, H4A = *First Part of Henry the Fourth*, Hml. = *Hamlet*, R2 = *Richard the Second*, Tp. = *Tempest*, Tw. = *Twelfth Night*, Wiv. = *The Merry Wives of Windsor*, etc. Acts, scenes and lines as in the Globe edition.

Index

References are to sections, not to pages.
Only the more important words used as examples are included.

References are to the number of the sections.